# A
# CLOUD
# OF
# WITNESSES

# HERMAN HOEKSEMA

# A
# CLOUD
# OF
# WITNESSES

*Sermons on Selected Passages from the
Epistle to the **Hebrews***

Edited by Marco Barone

REFORMED
FREE PUBLISHING
ASSOCIATION
Jenison, Michigan

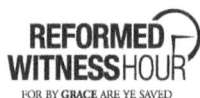

# CONTENTS

### Part Three:
## THE RACE THAT IS SET BEFORE US

# INTRODUCTION

More than seven decades ago, Herman Hoeksema mounted the pulpit of First Protestant Reformed Church of Grand Rapids, Michigan, and announced to the worshipers gathered there that he was beginning a new series of sermons. According to sermon notes taken by Martin Swart (1891–1977),[1] Hoeksema said:

> As I make a beginning with this tonight, I do so with fear and trembling because the epistle to the Hebrews is one of the most difficult parts of Scripture…Often I have been on the verge of preaching a series on this epistle, but the fear has always kept me from it, that I would not be able to treat the epistle as a whole in such a way…to make it understandable to you.[2]

These humble words were only the beginning of a lengthy series of sermons, many *Standard Bearer* devotionals, many Reformed Witness Hour messages, and even a spiral-bound book transcribed from sermons on the eleventh chapter of Hebrews[3]—very important material for Reformed Bible studies.

This present publication offers a taste of Hoeksema's work on Hebrews. Through it, readers will develop a bit of insight into Hoeksema's thoughts on Hebrews, particularly as those thoughts came to hearers on the Reformed Witness Hour.

Let us, too, reflect on Hebrews for a moment.

---

1   On Martin Swart, see David J. Engelsma's short biography in Herman Hoeksema, *Righteous by Faith Alone: A Devotional Commentary on Romans*, ed. David J. Engelsma (Grandville, MI: Reformed Free Publishing Association, 2002), xxiii–xxiv.

2   Herman Hoeksema, "The Word of God Spoken Through Christ," sermon on Hebrews 1:3–4, transcribed by Martin Swart, book 63. From the archives of Jerome Julien.

3   These transcripts were titled *A Cloud of Witnesses*, printed July 1975 by Nanning Klaver, second edition in spiralbound format, self-published.

When was Hebrews written? Conservative scholars date it between AD 50 and AD 95. About AD 95, Clement of Rome quoted from it in his letter to the Corinthian church.[4] The content of Hebrews seems to refer to the Temple being in use, as it was in AD 70. If the Temple were in ruins, the references to it would probably be in the past tense (Heb. 8:4; 13:10). Some, therefore, suggest that the letter was written before AD 70.

Although the biblical book of Hebrews is entitled in the King James Version: "The Epistle of Paul to the Hebrews," this is not its title in the Greek New Testament. There, it is named simply: "To the Hebrews," with no reference to Paul; nor is it called an epistle. As one writer points out, Hebrews "begins like an essay, proceeds like a sermon, and ends as a letter."[5]

Many students of Scripture say that Hebrews was not written as a general letter to the churches, but rather as a letter written to Jewish Christians, who had neither heard nor seen Jesus, but had heard about him from a believer (Heb. 2:3). The first readers, perhaps because of weakness or the severity of the trials they were experiencing for their faith, were beginning to question the uniqueness of Christ and, thus, were tempted to return to the Old Testament Levitical system. Thus, the author, not anonymous to them (5:11–12; 6:9, 10; 10:32–34; and chapter 13), warned these struggling believers not to crucify "to themselves the Son of God afresh, and put him to shame" (6:6). Whatever the audience, the inspired writer directs the reader's eye of faith to Jesus Christ, who is greater than the angels, as a revealer, a greater mediator than Moses, a greater provider of rest than Joshua, and a greater high priest than Aaron. Therefore, they are to trust in him (10:22), the fulfillment of the Old Testament.

How beautifully John Calvin summarizes all of this in the opening pages of his commentary:

4 Clement of Rome, "First Epistle to the Corinthians," chapters 17 and 36, in *Ante-Nicene Fathers*, eds. Alexander Roberts and James Donaldson, vol. 1 (Peabody, MA: Hendrickson, 1995), 10–11, 14–15.
5 Thomas Rees, "Hebrews, Epistle to the," in *The International Standard Bible Encyclopedia*, vol. 2 (Chicago, IL: Howard Severance, 1915), 1355.

There is, indeed, no book in the holy Scriptures which speaks so clearly of the priesthood of Christ, which so highly exalts the virtue and dignity of that only true sacrifice which he offered by his death, which so abundantly deals with the use of ceremonies as well as of their abrogation, and, in a word, so fully explains that Christ is the end of the law.[6]

In the later chapters of Hebrews, the writer demonstrates that the Old Testament people lived out of faith, regardless of how filled with blessings or trials their lives were. After this, in chapter 13, the writer gives some personal comments for the Lord's people: not only for those who received this letter, but also for the church today.

There is one question still before us: Who was used of God to write this marvelous and precious book? Many traditionally attribute it to Paul. Yet, even though the fourth article of the Belgic Confession says that it is the work of Paul, in reality no one knows. In the early church, there was no definite assurance about the author. In fact, many well-known leaders were suggested as authors. Since the time of Jerome and Augustine in the fourth and fifth centuries, it has been generally attributed to Paul. However, Calvin wrote:

I can adduce no reason to show that Paul was its author...The manner of teaching and the style sufficiently show that Paul was not the author; and the writer himself confesses in the second chapter that he was one of the disciples of the apostles, which is wholly different from the way in which Paul spoke of himself.[7]

Despite questions that remain, the message of this New Testament book is firm and the comfort is sure. The author's sole point with the book, made by using numerous quotes from the Old Testament, was to show that Christ is the fulfillment of the Old Testament. What God teaches us in these words will bring any student of the Bible to thank the Lord for his precious word and glorious truth.

---

6 John Calvin, *Hebrews and 1 and 2 Peter*, trans. William B. Johnston, eds. David W. Torrance and Thomas F. Torrance, Calvin's Commentaries (Grand Rapids, MI: Eerdmans, 1963), 1.

7 Calvin, *Hebrews and 1 and 2 Peter*, 1.

Hoeksema's schedule in his congregation and denomination was very busy, so busy that many younger ministers of today would shrink back in utter fear. Yet, he would say that he would die if he could not preach, and preach he did. As we spend time with these messages given by Hoeksema, may we grow in our Lord and in his grace. May our hearts and minds be directed to our wonderful Savior.

—REV. JEROME JULIEN,
emeritus minister in the United Reformed Churches
in North America

# EDITOR'S FOREWORD

M y gratitude, first, to the triune God; second, to the board and
relevant committee of the Reformed Free Publishing Association (RFPA) for allowing me to be the editor of this volume; and,
third, to a man named Nanning Klaver.[1] Of a collection of sermons by
Herman Hoeksema (1886–1965) that Klaver self-published in 1975
under the title of "A Cloud of Witnesses," Klaver says:

> "A Cloud of Witnesses" is a series of sermons which were preached
> by the late Rev. Herman Hoeksema in the years 1954–1956 and
> recorded at that time. The sermons have been transcribed from
> the tapes by Mr. Nanning Klaver. They have been left as Rev.
> Hoeksema delivered them, with a minimum of editing. May the
> Lord use this effort to bring the witness of the saints of old before
> our conscience in these days of indifference.[2]

Klaver's labor planted, so to speak, the first seed of a general interest in the Hebrews sermons by Hoeksema. That interest later led the
RFPA to consider the possibility of republishing Klaver's transcripts.
Around the same time the transcripts were under evaluation, I was
exploring the archives of the Reformed Witness Hour (RWH)[3] while
working on something else.[4] In those archives, I came across Hoeksema's radio sermons, not only on Hebrews 11, but also on other
passages of that same epistle. I collected all the sermons by Hoeksema
on Hebrews that I was able to find, and I brought the whole to the

---

1  I was not able to find more information about him.
2  In Herman Hoeksema, *A Cloud of Witnesses*, printed July 1975 by Nanning
   Klaver, second edition in spiralbound format, self-published.
3  A Protestant Reformed radio program founded in October 1941 and still active
   today.
4  Herman Hoeksema, *I Believe: Sermons on the Apostles' Creed*, ed. Marco Barone
   (Jenison, MI: Reformed Free Publishing Association, 2023).

attention of the RFPA. The result of those endeavors is the book the reader is holding now.

*A Cloud of Witnesses: Sermons on Selected Passages from the Epistle to the Hebrews* consists of radio sermons delivered by Hoeksema through the RWH over a number of years.[5] Besides treating more passages from Hebrews than Klaver's transcripts, the RWH's transcripts made for better reading material than Klaver's. For these reasons, a decision was made to prefer the RWH's transcripts over Klaver's.

*A Cloud of Witnesses* is divided into three parts. The first part, titled "Jesus, Our Forerunner," focuses on the person and work of the Lord Jesus Christ, which person and work serve as the proper foundation for a study of the lives of God's witnesses mentioned in the eleventh chapter of Hebrews. The second part, titled "A Cloud of Witnesses," expounds the lives of those witnesses of old. The chapters of the third part, titled "The Race That Is Set before Us," are practical exhortations to follow such witnesses' examples and, on the basis of Christ's perfect work, to believe in him and follow him, bearing his cross and reproach, the only way to communion with the triune God and to final, everlasting glory. As a whole, by combining doctrine and practice, *A Cloud of Witnesses* is both a powerful exposition of the glory of Christ *and* (on that basis) a call to a life of active faith and conscious discipleship. As Hoeksema himself says:

God and Christ, heaven and perfection, the kingdom of glory that is to be established in the end, the crown after which we are striving, they are all invisible. They all belong to the world of unseen things. Self we deny for Christ, this world for the world to come, the seen for the unseen. So is the race. So we must run. But this is possible only by faith. For faith is the evidence of things unseen. By faith we know that this world of unseen things, though it may not be perceptible by our natural eye, nevertheless is not a product of the imagination but is actually existing, is very real indeed, and that as we strive for it we do not pursue a phantom but tangible reality, tangible, however, only by faith.

# EDITOR'S FOREWORD

And therefore, faith is indispensable. For by faith we keep our eye fixed on the goal set before us. And inspired by the beauty and the glory of the crown, we gladly deny ourselves and sacrifice the world of visible things if necessary for the attainment of the crown.[6]

Finally, a few words about the editorial work done on this book. Any editing and copyediting has been done with full respect to both the wording and the meaning of the original transcripts of Hoeksema's sermons. Only the following changes have been made throughout:

1. Obvious typos and grammatical mistakes have been corrected;
2. Scripture references and references to other works have been added where Hoeksema does not provide them;
3. A few explanatory footnotes have been added (all footnotes are mine);
4. Occasional phrases related to the timeframe in which Hoeksema's sermons were delivered have been omitted (for example, "in the present sermon," "Today we take the subject of our radio sermon," "In my radio sermons this season," and similar). These have been omitted, first, because these phrases prevent an easier reading of the text; and, second, they neither add to nor take anything away from the author's messages.

Besides these minor changes, Hoeksema's sermons have been presented here essentially unchanged from how they appear in the original transcripts. May this book bless and encourage God's people as they look to Jesus, the author and finisher of our faith (Heb. 12:12), and as they strive to go outside the camp, bearing Christ's reproach (Heb. 13:13).

—MARCO BARONE

---

6 Chapter 36, "Running With Patience," page 309.

# BROADCAST TIMELINE

The Great Salvation — March 18, 1962

The Divine Necessity of Jesus' Suffering — March 25, 1962

The Tyrant of Death is Destroyed — March 24, 1946

Like Unto His Brethren — April 8, 1962

Coming to the Throne of Grace — March 3, 1957

Christ Learning Obedience — April 15, 1962

Hope, the Anchor of Our Soul — February 24, 1957

Christ Our High Priest — January 5, 1964

After the Order of Melchizedek — January 12, 1964

The Power to Purge Our Conscience — March 31, 1946

Faith, the Secret of the Christian's Life (1) — December 1, 1957

Faith, the Secret of the Christian's Life (2) — December 8, 1957

Abel's More Excellent Sacrifice (1) — December 15, 1957

Abel's More Excellent Sacrifice (2) — December 29, 1957

Enoch, the Lonely Witness, Translated by Faith (1) — January 5, 1958

Enoch, the Lonely Witness, Translated by Faith (2) — January 12, 1958

Noah by Faith Building the Ark (1) — January 19, 1958

Noah by Faith Building the Ark (2) — January 26, 1958

Abraham's Blind Obedience by Faith (1) — February 2, 1958

Abraham's Blind Obedience by Faith (2) — February 9, 1958

Sarah's Faith, the Medium of Her Strength (1) — February 16, 1958

Sarah's Faith, the Medium of Her Strength (2) — February 23, 1958

Abraham's Sacrifice of Isaac (1) — March 2, 1958

# A CLOUD OF WITNESSES

*Part One*

# JESUS, OUR FORERUNNER

# Chapter 1

# THE GREAT SALVATION

5. For unto the angels hath he not put in subjection the world to come, whereof we speak.
6. But one in a certain place testified, saying, What is man, that thou art mindful of him? or the son of man, that thou visitest him?
7. Thou madest him a little lower than the angels; thou crownedst him with glory and honour, and didst set him over the works of thy hands:
8. Thou hast put all things in subjection under his feet. For in that he put all in subjection under him, he left nothing that is not put under him. But now we see not yet all things put under him.
9. But we see Jesus, who was made a little lower than the angels for the suffering of death, crowned with glory and honour; that he by the grace of God should taste death for every man.

—*Hebrews 2:5-9*

It is customary in Reformed churches to call special attention to the suffering of Christ in the Lenten season. And this custom we will also follow.[1] And we will do so on the basis of the text found in Hebrews 2:5-9. You will readily understand that it is not our purpose to interpret this entire section of the epistle to the Hebrews. That would be impossible. But we will call special attention to the great salvation that God through Jesus Christ has wrought, and which implies that Christ, and through him his people, is crowned with glory and honor, and that all things are subject under him.

---

1  This speech was delivered on March 18, 1962.

In verse 5 the text speaks of the world that is to come. We are probably all acquainted with the fact that in Scripture the word *world* has different meanings. There is, first of all, the word *cosmos*, which refers to creation as an organic whole. There is another word that really means "age" and refers to the world from the viewpoint of time. And finally, there is the word that is used in the words of our text, which we may literally translate "economy"[2] and which refers to the management, the household arrangement, the set-up of the various creatures in their different positions. This is the meaning of the word here. It means the set-up of the world that is to come. There is a new set-up, a new management, of the internal affairs of the world that is different from any set-up that ever was. It is different from the present set-up, in which, after sin came into the world, it became the stage for the antithesis between sin and grace. But it is also different from the original set-up or arrangement of creation. For before sin entered into the world, Adam had dominion and was king of the earthly creation.

Now the text speaks of the world that is to come. We readily understand that this phrase refers to the world after the *parousia*, after the second coming of Christ, the world that will be ushered in by the second coming. And the phrase "to come" expresses two different ideas. In the first place, it emphasizes the certainty of that coming world. And the certainty of that coming rests on the basis that it is not at all dependent on man: God will cause that new world to come in our Lord Jesus Christ. The second idea that is expressed in this phrase is that it is always near, it is always about to come. This idea is emphasized in all Scripture.

Now we may for a moment ask and answer the question: What are the characteristic features of that new world that is to come? Then it is evident that the text emphasizes that in that new world man will

---

2   The Greek word for "world" used in Hebrews 2:5 is οἰκουμένην (*oikoumenēn*), from οἰκουμένη (*oikoumenē*), which refers to the world or the whole earth, and it can hardly be translated as "economy." Hoeksema is perhaps confusing *oikoumenē* (the world, the whole earth) with οἰκονομία (*oikonomia*, that is, administration, dispensation, or, as Hoeksema says, economy); the two terms are cognate (that is, they have the same linguistic derivation). However, this little confusion does not essentially affect Hoeksema's exposition. (My gratitude to Martyn McGeown for his help with the Greek.)

have dominion. He will have dominion over all things, over heaven and earth. For in that new economy heaven and earth will be united into one. In other words, in that new world all creatures, rational and irrational, and all the powers of that world shall serve man and obey him. They will obey him not by main force, but according to and by the will of God. In that new world man will be crowned king. He will be clothed with power and authority, so that all creatures shall willingly serve him and submit themselves unto him.

Now the author proves this idea from the Old Testament, particularly from Psalm 8:

6. But one in a certain place testified, saying, What is man, that thou art mindful of him? or the son of man, that thou visitest him?
7. Thou madest him a little lower than the angels; thou crownedst him with glory and honour, and didst set him over the works of thy hands:
8. Thou hast put all things in subjection under his feet. (Heb. 2:6–8; see Ps. 8:4–6)

Now apparently this psalm appears to speak of man's dominion in the present world. And his glory is exactly that he is a little lower than the angels. Nevertheless, the author of this epistle to the Hebrews emphasizes the expression "all things" in such a way that he may draw and does draw the conclusion that this phrase is all-inclusive. It is true indeed, according to the text, that man originally was made a little lower than the angels. Nevertheless, he is destined to be set over all the works of God's hand. And, according to the author, the psalm ultimately refers to the world that is to come.

Now the question may be asked: Can we already see something of that glorious world that is to come? In answer, we may say, first of all, that in the present world this set-up, this new economy, is not visible. This is due to the fact, in the first place, that man was made a little lower than the angels. The angels are heavenly beings, while man is of the earth, earthy. The angels evidently have dominion over heavenly things, over the heavenly world, while man's dominion was limited to earthly things, to the things that are below.

Second, we must not forget that man fell into sin and that he has lost most of his original power. He has no more the right to have dominion over all things in the earth. Only a small remnant remains of this glorious dominion. Oh, even in his present state in the world and by the remnants of his original power he still does mighty things. Nevertheless, the fact remains that in his state of righteousness man had unspeakably much more power and dominion over all things than he now has by the remnants of that power. Nor, we may emphasize, is that original power restored by grace in Christ Jesus our Lord. And therefore, the author speaks of the world that is to come. Then, and then only, will that dominion over all things be realized.

But can we see nothing at all of that glorious world that is to come? Oh, to be sure, we do. For according to verse 9 of the words of my text the author says: "But we see Jesus, who was made a little lower than the angels for the suffering of death, crowned with glory and honour." We see Jesus. But how do we see him? Certainly not with our physical eye; but we do see him by faith, which is the evidence of things unseen (Heb. 11:1). Moreover, by faith we see Jesus as he is revealed in the gospel, as he died on the accursed tree, as he was raised from the dead, and as he ascended into heaven and is now seated at the right hand of God, crowned with glory and honor. He, the Son of God, the Lord of heaven and earth, was made a little lower than the angels. He was made such, not as the punctuation of the text would have it, by the suffering of death. But he was made such by his incarnation. Through that incarnation he became like unto his brethren. He came in the likeness of sinful flesh, even though without sin itself. And it is through his suffering and on the basis of his suffering that he is now crowned with glory and honor.

Now, according to all Scripture, our Lord Jesus Christ has all power in heaven and on earth. Angels and principalities and powers are all subject under him. According to the author, the exaltation of our Lord Jesus Christ is the fulfillment of Psalm 8. Centrally, the text means to say, the glory and dominion of man over all things and the fact that all things are in subjection under his feet is realized in this exaltation of Christ. The glory of Christ is the pattern; and all the elect will share in that new world in the glory of their Lord. It was for the elect that he merited this glory. And not only this, but through the Spirit who was given unto him in his exaltation, he has also the power to impart this glory unto them. The new economy will be that of a royal priesthood, with Christ as the eternal high priest–king.

Now the question arises and must be answered: How, in what way, did Christ attain to this glory? How, in what way, did he merit that glory, not only for himself, but also for those whom the Father had given unto him? And how, in what way, did he obtain the power to impart his glory unto all his people?

This question may be answered negatively, that this glory cannot be merited or attained by the sinner as such; and positively, we may say that the right to this glory must certainly be based on righteousness. The sinner as such certainly has no right whatever to share in the glory of Christ. He has no right to this favor of God. Besides, one who is so honored must certainly employ all his glory and power in God's service and to his glory only. He may not and he must not glorify himself. He must be king-servant. If the sinner could possibly have this power and glory, he undoubtedly would employ it to the destruction of all things. And therefore, I say once more, the glorious gift of this dominion must certainly be based upon righteousness. And when I speak of righteousness, I do not refer only to legal righteousness, but also, and emphatically, to moral, spiritual, ethical righteousness, and that, too, in the highest possible sense of the word. This means, of course, that a man who is righteous in that sense wills the will of God, and that, moreover, he can never fall into sin again, as did the first man, Adam.

This basis of righteousness is realized in the death and resurrection of our Lord Jesus Christ. That is the reason why the text speaks of Christ's suffering and death, and moreover of the fact that Christ should taste death for every man. I have already called attention to the fact that the punctuation of the text is not quite correct. In other words, we should not read "who was made a little lower than the angels for the suffering of death," but rather that "for the suffering of death [he was] crowned with glory and honor." Moreover, the text emphasizes that Christ not only died, or that he merely suffered death, but that he tasted death. And we may undoubtedly say that he tasted death throughout his whole life and not only on the accursed tree. His death must be an atoning death. It must be a death that forevermore blots out the sins of all whom the Father has given unto him. Moreover, he must not only atone for the sins of his people, but he must obtain for them perfect and eternal righteousness, in order that they may share in his power and dominion and glory. And for that reason, he must not only die, but he must taste death.

This implies that he died by his own will. No one could possibly take his life away from him. Even though the enemies—Judas, the Pharisees, the Sanhedrin, Pilate, and the soldiers who crucified him—were guilty, the fact remains that no one could ever have nailed him to the accursed tree, and no one could ever have inflicted unto him the suffering of death, but by his own will. He willed to die. And the motive of that will to die was principally the love of God and the love of his own elect. His suffering and death was therefore an act of his own. He hanged on the accursed tree only as long as he was conscious of the fact that he tasted death in the love of God and in the love of his own. Not one moment longer did Christ remain on the cross. He descended into the depth of hell and completely tasted death, until he could cry out: "It is finished!" And when he had said this, he gave up the ghost (John 19:30).

Now the text says that Christ suffered and died and that he tasted death for every man. That this cannot mean every individual of the whole human race is evident from all Scripture. Grace is neither common nor general; and the same is true of the atonement of Christ. Hence, we must interpret the text as meaning every man who is destined to inherit this great salvation. Or, if you please, he tasted death for those whom the Father had given him. That is why the Lord could say to the unbelieving Pharisees and Jews:

26. But ye believe not, because ye are not of my sheep, as I said unto you.
27. My sheep hear my voice, and I know them, and they follow me:
28. And I give unto them eternal life; and they shall never perish, neither shall any man pluck them out of my hand.

29. My Father, which gave them me, is greater than all; and no man is able to pluck them out of my Father's hand" (John 10:26–29)

Moreover, the text says that Christ tasted death for every man by the grace of God. By that grace we were chosen in Christ from before the foundation of the world. By that grace God sent his only begotten Son into the world. By that grace God sent him into death. And by that grace he causes the death of Christ to be efficacious unto all whom the Father has given unto him.

Hence, the conclusion is that we must see Jesus. We must not see him in man. We must not see him in any conferences of man. But we must see him as the central realization of the better world that is to come. We must see him as the author and finisher of the great salvation that is in the economy of that new world in which all things shall be under the dominion of man, that is, of those who are in Christ Jesus forevermore. And in that new economy man, in Christ, shall surely have dominion over all things, but in order that he may serve and glorify God in all eternity.

*Chapter 2*

# THE DIVINE NECESSITY OF JESUS' SUFFERING

For it became him, for whom are all things, and by whom are all things, in bringing many sons unto glory, to make the captain of their salvation perfect through sufferings.

*—Hebrews 2:10*

The weeks preceding Easter are generally devoted by the church to a special contemplation of the suffering of our Lord Jesus Christ. Certainly, that is a good custom, and, if followed not out of habit, but with believing and humble hearts, not without its fruit for the children of God. The cross remains the nearest source, the deepest source always being the love of God manifested in that cross. From that cross all our salvation springs. We love to sing:

> There is a green hill far away,
> Without a city wall,
> Where the dear Lord was crucified,
> Who died to save us all.[1]

Hence, for this reason we will adhere to this good custom of the church and concentrate our attention on the suffering and death of our blessed Savior.[2]

Now the passion of Jesus is, of course, many-sided and may be considered from many a point of view. Let us follow him on the *via dolorosa*, the way of suffering and grief, from the viewpoint of the truth expressed in the words of our text: the Captain of our salvation

---

1   "There Is a Green Hill Far Away," by Cecil Frances Alexander (1848).
2   This speech was delivered on March 25, 1962.

was made perfect through suffering. This is emphasized in the words of our text, Hebrews 2:10.

First of all, then, we wish to call your attention to the Captain of our salvation, as he occurs in the words of our text. We understand, of course, that when the text speaks of the Captain of our salvation, it means something different from merely referring to our Captain. He certainly is also our Captain in a general sense of the word. That is, he leads us and rules over us. We obey him. He is our Lord. And as such, he is our Captain. But here the text does not merely refer to Christ as our Captain, but to him as the Captain of our salvation. Therefore, we must first of all ask and answer the question: What is implied in our salvation?

In answer to this question we remark, first of all, that salvation is deliverance from the greatest evil. Thus we have learned to describe salvation already when we were children. And, in general, there is no reason to depart from this definition or to change it. Salvation, surely, is deliverance from the greatest evil and being made partakers of the highest good. But we must nevertheless ask and answer the question: What is the greatest evil? And the answer is: it is our sin and our guilt, our natural corruption. Through our sin we, who were created after the image of God, in true righteousness and holiness and knowledge of God, are now separated from him. We are no longer by nature children who are the objects of the love of God, but we are children of wrath. In the power of sin and death we lie, from which we are unable to deliver ourselves.

And what is the highest good? It is, according to the meaning of our text, the heavenly glory, the final goal of heavenly perfection, the goal of eternal life and bliss. Let us remember this. Salvation does not bring us back to paradise, as we have often expressed, but makes us partakers of an altogether new and different life, partakers of heavenly glory, heirs of the unspeakably glorious inheritance that God has in store for those who fear him and who are his own elect children from before the foundation of the world.

Now Christ in the words of our text is called the Captain of our salvation. The general meaning will now be plain. He is the one who heads the host of those whom the Father gave him; and he is the one, as the Captain of our salvation, who leads the children of God to glory. He is the one who superintends all that is necessary for their salvation and actually leads the people of God into the heavenly rest. He is the one who actually brings the children of God, who are Christ's brethren, to the heavenly rest.

Hence, he is the one, as Captain of our salvation, who delivers those whom the Father has given him from the greatest evil. He is the one who breaks the bonds of sin and guilt and corruption. He is the one who delivers them from the dominion of death, from the dominion of the devil, and from the eternal suffering and agony in hell. He is the one who makes them partakers of the highest good. He is the one who bestows upon them the blessing of the new life, imparting unto them his own blessed life, the life of the resurrection, and that, too, through the Spirit whom God has given him. He is the one who clothes them with garments of righteousness, with which they can appear before God. He is the one, as Captain of our salvation, who sanctifies and purifies them and prepares them for the heavenly glory. He is the one also who prepares heaven for them and all that belongs to the eternal glory in the kingdom of perfection. He is also the one who guards and defends them and fights for them against the enemies who would always do them harm. In short, Jesus, as the Captain of their salvation, makes them partakers of salvation, of the salvation that God has in store for all his children.

Now the text says that this Captain of our salvation is made perfect through suffering. Who is the one who makes him perfect? The answer is: God! God willed to lead many sons unto glory. Let us notice that this is the real basis of the text. The text brings us undoubtedly to God's eternal counsel. He has many sons, according to the text. He has many sons in distinction from his only begotten Son. And the question is: How did God get these sons? The answer is: God chose them from all eternity. He adopted them even in his counsel as his beloved children. He decreed even in his eternal counsel to lead those sons to glory, to eternal, heavenly bliss, to the highest exaltation possible, to make them like unto the image of his Son.

To do so, he appointed them a captain. He appointed his own Son to be their head, not only in a legal, or juridical, sense, but also in the organic sense of the word. He appointed his Son to be the head of his people, in order that he should take care of all the affairs concerning their salvation and do all that was necessary unto their salvation. And God it was, also, who made this Captain of their salvation perfect. Perfect, you understand, not in the spiritual, ethical sense of the word: for Christ had no sin, and he was perfect from the very beginning of his conception and birth. But he made him perfect in the sense that he was clothed with authority and power to save the sons of God, to quicken them and sanctify them and glorify them.

Now the text says that this Captain of our salvation was made perfect through suffering. To the perfecting of this Captain of our salvation belongs all that Christ ever became and did. The Son of God became flesh and assumed the likeness of our sinful nature, though without sin, in order that he might be the Captain of our salvation. In the divine nature he could never be the Captain of our salvation. But God sent him into our flesh. In our flesh the Son came under the law, in order to be the Captain of our salvation. The Son suffered and shed his lifeblood and died, in order to be the Captain of our salvation. The Son of God in our flesh arose and was filled with a new life for that same purpose. The Son ascended into heaven and was clothed with power and glory in order to be able to accomplish his work as the Captain of our salvation. The Son received the Spirit and himself became the quickening Spirit, having all power in heaven and on earth, for the same purpose. Not until all this was finished is the Captain of our salvation perfected.

But the text calls our attention especially to the element of suffering. He was made perfect through suffering. This calls attention to all the manifold suffering of our Savior, suffering in body and soul and spirit, sufferings from man and sufferings from God, sufferings even from his own who did not receive him and from the world that did not know him. From the manger of Bethlehem to the cross of Calvary, the Captain of our salvation suffered. It calls attention to this suffering as the way through which the Captain of our salvation passed in order to be perfected as our Captain.

And oh, what a terrible way of suffering he walked. What reproach and humiliation and shame was his, as long as he was in the world, and especially when he approached the cross of Calvary. What pains and sorrows he endured! What buffetings and beatings and stripes he bore! And, above all, what death and hell he suffered as the Captain of our salvation! The text calls attention to this suffering from the viewpoint that God led him through it all. After all, this wicked world—Judas, the Jews, the Sanhedrin, Pilate and the cruel Roman sword, the devil and all his host—were indeed the wicked hands by which the Lord, our Savior and Redeemer, was crucified. But behind it all stood the Father, leading his Son through his awful suffering, in order to make him perfect as the Captain of our salvation.

But notice that the text emphasizes that this suffering of the Captain of our salvation was necessary, divinely necessary. The text says, "It became him," that is, it became God. Not, you understand, as if anything could ever be imposed upon the Most High from without! He is God alone, and he executes all his good pleasure. But it is a necessity that follows from God's own nature. That is why the author designates God as the one through whom and to whom are all things. He is the author of all things and here especially the author of the salvation of his children. It is his work, and not the work of man. Hence, all things are also unto him. They must ultimately be to his glory. And in order to be to his glory, they must display his virtues, even through the suffering of his Son. To God, then, it was becoming. It was in harmony with his divine nature and his divine being. It would be to his glory and praise, if he would lead the children to glory, that he would make the Captain of their salvation perfect through suffering. There was no other way.

Perhaps you ask the question: Why is this becoming to God? And the answer is, first, because the Lord God is holy and righteous. They are the virtues of his being. These he can never deny, without denying himself. And therefore, if he is to lead the children to glory, it must be in harmony with these virtues of righteousness and holiness that he does so. And, second, do not forget that we are guilty. We are in sin and corruption. We are by nature children of wrath. We have forfeited every blessing of God. And we have deserved eternal condemnation.

Hence, if we are to be led unto glory, that glory must be merited, and the righteousness and justice of God must be satisfied. If the

Captain of our salvation is to be empowered to make us partakers of glory eternal, it must be through suffering and for the satisfaction of God's righteousness. Sin must be punished. Punishment is the payment of the penalty of sin, as only that payment of the penalty for sin could satisfy the justice of God. And that is why the suffering of Christ was absolutely necessary. He stood in our stead. All our sins and iniquities were heaped upon him. For us he bore the wrath of God. And all the vials of the wrath of God were poured over him alone. Hence, look at the Captain of your salvation on the cross. And from the cross turn to the open grave and look upward to the glorified Captain of our salvation. Salvation is in no other. But in Christ Jesus, the Captain of our salvation, that salvation is sure and perfect, so that we may look unto eternal glory.

*Chapter 3*

# THE TYRANT OF DEATH
# IS DESTROYED

14. Forasmuch then as the children are partakers of flesh and
    blood, he also himself likewise took part of the same; that
    through death he might destroy him that had the power of
    death, that is, the devil;
15. And deliver them who through fear of death were all their
    lifetime subject to bondage.

*—Hebrews 2:14–15*

The word of the cross is the power of God unto salvation. And
when we hear that word, as a word of God unto us, so that we
experience its saving power in our souls, we are liberated from the
slavery of sin, from the dominion of the devil, and from the fear of
the bondage of death. The truth of this is taught throughout Scripture,
and expressed in many different ways; most directly and concisely,
perhaps, in Hebrews 2:14–15. This is a very rich passage of Holy Writ.
Let us look at it a moment in the light of its context.

God, so we learn from this chapter, purposes to lead many sons
unto glory. Unto this end, he appointed over them a captain, the Captain of their salvation, his own and only begotten Son, Jesus Christ
our Lord. His task now is to lead the children whom the Father gave
him to the eternal glory ordained for them. Those children, however,
are partakers of flesh and blood, that is, they exist, together with all
mankind, in the human nature. Through that human nature, by partaking of it, the children are in the sphere and bondage of death. They
are in death's fortress, hopelessly imprisoned. And in that fortress the
devil reigns. He is lord, and the children whom God wants to lead to
eternal glory are under the dominion and subject to the slavery of the

devil. Christ, therefore, must lead them all the way out of that mighty and dark forest of death into the glory if eternal life. To do this he himself becomes partaker of flesh and blood, overcomes the devil, and liberates the children the Father has given him. He does this through death. This, therefore, is the power of the cross: it liberates us from the dominion of him that has the power of death, that is, the devil.

The passage raises several questions, which we should briefly try to answer. What is this power of death in which we are hold by nature? What does it mean that the devil has this power? How did he obtain it? What does it mean that Christ destroyed him? In what way did he do this? And how are we thereby delivered from that power and from the fear of death?

In answer to the question, what is the power of death in which we are held by being partakers of the human nature, we must not think primarily of what we usually call death. According to philosophy, we live as long as we are in our present flesh and blood, and we die when we leave it. As long as we are in this world, can move about, see and hear and talk, eat and drink, and do our work, we live; but presently, when we breathe our last, are put into the coffin, and buried, we are dead. But according to Scripture, the matter is quite different. True, physical death, the death of our body, is a phase of death. But it's not its real essence, nor do we begin to die when we lie on the deathbed. On the contrary, we are dead exactly because we partake of flesh and blood. We are born in death. Death is the punishment of sin. And together with the while human race, we are subject to this punishment under the just wrath of God.

Death is the opposite of life. And life for man is not that he can move about, eat and drink and be merry; but that he enjoys the fellowship of God's friendship, his favor and lovingkindness, and that, in order to enjoy this communion with his God, he stands in the light of true knowledge of God, perfect righteousness, and the pure holiness of being consecrated to God with his whole being. To know the true God in love, to will his will, to love him with all our heart and mind and soul and strength, and to dwell in his house, where we may taste his goodness—that is life for man, God's image-bearer. The opposite is death. Death is to be forsaken of God in his wrath, to be conscious of his presence as a consuming fire, to dwell in the darkness of the lie, of enmity against God, of corruption and iniquity; and thus, to suffer the holy and cursing anger of the Most High. Such is death. Now, in this death, we all are born.

Once, in the state of rectitude in paradise, we lived. For in his image God had created us. We had true knowledge of God. We were righteous, capable of doing the will of God. And we were perfectly holy, consecrated to God with our whole being from the sanctuary of the heart. Thus, we came forth from the hand of our Creator. And, endowed with these excellent gifts, we lived. We were friend-servants of the Most High. He walked with us and talked with us; we tasted that the Lord is good, and delighted in his fellowship.

But we sinned. We violated the commandment of life, rejected the word of God, and preferred the word of the devil. Thus, we became guilty, worthy of God's wrath, and of the punishment of sin, which is death. And that punishment was inflicted upon us at once. In Adam, our representative and father of the whole human race, we all became guilty, and all mankind entered into the state of death. Hence, all that are born in the flesh and blood, that is, in the human nature, are in the realm of death and under its dominion. Physically, they are subject to corruption, and their existence in this world is nothing but a continual death.[1] Spiritually, they are in the bondage of sin, darkened in their understanding (Eph. 4:18), perverse of will, polluted in all their desires, exiles from the fellowship and favor of God, "children of wrath" (Eph. 2:3).

And thus, they are filled with the fear of death throughout their whole life here on earth. All fear is principally fear of death. Take death and its dominion away, and there is no room for fear. And this fear is, first of all, an apprehension of the just anger of God, and of the fact that death is the penalty for sin. And, secondly, it is the expectation of the wrath and death to come. For there is no way out for man. He

---

1   A reference to the Form for the Administration of Baptism, in *The Psalter with Doctrinal Standards, Liturgy, Church Order, and added Chorale Section*, reprinted and revised edition of the 1912 United Presbyterian Psalter (Grand Rapids, MI: Wm. B. Eerdmans Publishing Co., 1927; rev. ed. 1995), 89.

proceeds from death to death. Daily he increases his guilt and damnableness, and in his deepest heart to know it. When he looks forward, no matter how proudly and vainly he may boast, he knows that death is waiting for him, and that the grave will swallow him up. And in his heart of hearts he also has the testimony that this is not the end, that after death must come the righteous judgment of God, that in that judgment he cannot stand and be justified, and that, therefore, he has nothing to hope for but eternal wrath and desolation in hell. This fear pursues him all his life, in all his earthly living, for he knows not when the hour of his execution may strike, it may be some years from now, but it may also be this very day.

Hence, by this fear of death he is held in bondage. Always it is with him. It pursues him in all his activities. Whether he is in his home or in his office, whether he seeks a few moments of respite in revelry and banqueting, or whether he attends to the funeral of his dear one or friend, always that fear of death pursues him. He tries to find a way out, but there is none. He struggles as long as possible to escape the clutches of this enemy, but he must give it up. He boasts that he is brave, and that he can stand it, but he knows that he is lying. Throughout their life, in all their living in the world, the children that partake of flesh and blood are held in bondage through the fear of death.

Now, the text tells us that the devil has the power of death. What may this mean? To be sure, it cannot convey the idea that the devil has the power to kill, for only God has that power. Nor can it mean that the devil has the power to judge or to execute the judgment of death, for also this is God's prerogative only. But I take it that the meaning is that in the realm of death, of the lie, of darkness and spiritual corruption, the devil has power to rule over us, so that we are his slaves and he is our lord. Willing slaves we are, to be sure, for in our death we love the darkness rather than the light, yet slaves withal. In the prison of death, in which we are as partakers of flesh and blood, we are nothing but slaves of the devil—in that prison, he is the rightful lord!

Is there, then, no way out?

There is, indeed! Christ is appointed to lead the children God gave him out of that prison of death, unto everlasting glory and life in God's heavenly tabernacle. And the text tells us that he, the Son of God himself, deliberately entered into our prison of death, and destroyed him that had the power of death, that is, the devil.

In order to clarify the meaning of this, permit me to put it all into the form of an extended metaphor. The figure is not quite true in every detail, but it will serve the purpose of bringing the meaning of the text clearly before our mind in a few words.

When man sinned against God, the Most High shut him up in the prison of death as his just punishment. And He gave the key to the devil. By this key, you understand, I do not mean the power to open the prison door and liberate prisoners, but the power to keep the prisoners within, and to rule over them. The devil is the prince of darkness. You must remember that in Adam all men fell, and that, therefore, also the children whom the Father had given to Christ were shut up in the prison of death.

Now, into that prison Christ entered. This is the meaning of the text when it declares that he also partook of flesh and blood. He was not born in that prison as all other men. He was under no condemnation of death personally. On the contrary, he was the Son of God. He came from above. But he assumed the flesh and blood of the children. Freely he took upon himself the human nature from the virgin Mary. And by doing so, he came under the law. Moreover, he came as the divinely appointed representative for his brethren. He took their sins upon himself. By assuming the likeness of sinful flesh, he entered into the realm of death. Thus, then, by partaking of the flesh and blood of the children, Christ, the Son of God, very really entered into the prison of death in which the devil had power and dominion.

Pursuing the metaphor, we say that, when the Son of God thus entered into the prison of death, he said to the devil: "I come to lead my brethren out of this prison into the glorious liberty of the children of God. I am going to take that key of death away from you, and destroy you as the one that has power over death. I am the Servant of Jehovah, appointed to put you to nought."

And the devil preferred to try a compromise with this Servant of Jehovah, of whom he was, indeed, afraid, and him he recognized as the one that was promised long ago, and that would crush his head. So he said unto the Christ: "All that are in this prison of death are my slaves by divine right. If you choose to be here, you must also be my servant. I can see that you are an able man, and I don't want any trouble between us. I will *give* you this key of death, and make you my superintendent, if you will only acknowledge my authority, and fall down in worship before me."

But the Lord answered: "Far be it from me, Satan, to worship thee. I came as the Servant of the living God, whom alone I worship. And from him, in the way of his righteousness, I expect to receive the right to destroy thy power, and to secure that key of death and of Hades. Thy power of death over my brethren is based on their sin and guilt. But I came to take their sins upon myself, and so to die for them, that their sins are for ever blotted out, and that they are clothed with eternal righteousness. And doing so, I will destroy thee in the way of God's righteousness, and deliver my brethren from this fortress of death!"

And this Christ did. He destroyed the devil. The meaning is not that Christ annihilated the devil, but that he put him to nought as the tyrant of death. He took the power of death away from him. And he accomplished this through death. For his death is the right to liberty for all his brethren. By his death on the cross, he obtained for all his brethren the right to deliver them from the prison of sin and the bondage of the fear of death. That death was his own free act of obedience to God. Oh, it is true, when this Servant of Jehovah in that prison of death refused to worship the devil, the forces of darkness set themselves against him, and released all their satanic fury against him. They took him, and condemned him, and spit upon him, and buffeted him, and scourged him, and put him to nought, and finally nailed him to the accursed tree. Yet, they were but instruments to open for him the way into death and hell, and voluntarily he descended into its dark and gloomy depth. Every drop of blood they drew, he shed willingly upon the altar of the love of God. Thus, his death was a sacrifice, the perfect sacrifice for sin. And as a sacrifice, it satisfied the justice of God against sin; not his own, for he had none, but against the sins of all his brethren. For them, he obtained eternal righteousness. And this righteousness is their right to be delivered from the prison of sin, the slavery of the devil, the power of death, and to be translated unto everlasting glory.

Through death, he destroyed him that had the power of death, that is, the devil.

This is the power of the cross!

But how are these brethren actually delivered from that prison of death, and from the bondage of sin and the devil? Does he, Christ, stand at their prison door, and invite them to come out, assuring them that he obtained for them the right of their salvation? God forbid!

If such were the situation, no one would ever be saved from the bondage of the fear of death. But Christ himself delivers them, so the text teaches us: "And deliver them who through fear of death were all their lifetime subject to bondage" (Heb. 2:15). Christ not only redeemed us, he also delivered us. He not only obtained the right of our liberation, he also set us free. He came into the prison of our death, and went through death into the glory of his resurrection. And he is exalted at the right hand of God with all power in heaven and on earth. He holds the keys of death and of hell. By his Spirit, this mighty Lord now enters into our prison, and leads us out. He opens wide the door; he breaks the shackles of sin that hold us in bondage of the will of the devil; he gives us a new heart, a new life, new light, new love, new knowledge and wisdom. He gives us the saving faith whereby we know him as our deliverer, put all our trust in him, and appropriate him and all the blessings of salvation in him.

And then he calls us out through the word of the cross, the word of reconciliation, of freedom, of deliverance from the slavery of sin. And we hear that word, the voice of Jesus calling: "Come unto me, and rest!" And we come to him, we find rest, we repent, and are forgiven. We experience the marvelous power of the word of the cross. No longer do we accomplish the will of the devil, but we have our delight in pleasing him, our new Lord. And no longer does the fear of death pursue us, for in his resurrection we see the way out into the glorious liberty of the children of God!

This is the power of the cross!

*Chapter 4*

# LIKE UNTO
# HIS BRETHREN

Wherefore in all things it behoved him to be made like unto his brethren, that he might be a merciful and faithful high priest in things pertaining to God, to make reconciliation for the sins of the people.

—*Hebrews 2:17*

I wrote in connection with verse 10 of Hebrews 2 on the fact that, first, God wanted to bring many sons unto glory; second, that those whom God wished to bring to everlasting glory are partakers of flesh and blood; and, third, that for that very reason Christ, who was to bring these sons unto glory, also partook of the same, that is, of flesh and blood. This is emphasized once more in verse 16 of the same chapter. The Jews were looking for a glorious Messiah. And the lowly Jesus, who partook of the flesh and blood of the children, was a stumbling block to them. Christ as they expected him had to appear with angelic glory. But in verse 16 of this chapter it is emphasized that he took not on him the nature of angels but that he took on him the seed of Abraham.

And then follow the words of our text (Heb. 2:17), on which we wish to meditate for a few moments in our present chapter. Speaking on this verse, we ask first of all: Unto whom was Christ to be made like? The text says: he was made like unto his brethren. Second, we ask the question: Why was he made like unto his brethren? Or, he was made like unto his brethren in order to be able to do what? This is expressed in the last part of our text, namely: "To make reconciliation for the sins of the people." And finally, we ask the question: He was made like unto his brethren in order to be what? Also this the text expresses in the words "that he might be a merciful and faithful high priest in things pertaining to God."

First of all, then, unto whom was Christ made like? And the answer is: he was made like unto his brethren. These brethren are the same as the sons of God who are mentioned in verse 10: "For it became him, for whom are all things, and by whom are all things, in bringing many sons unto glory, to make the captain of their salvation perfect through sufferings." God wanted, as we have said before, to bring many sons unto glory. That glory consisted chiefly, not in the fact that they would enter into a glorious heaven, although that is also true, but rather in the fact that they would be made like unto the image of his Son, the image of the only begotten of the Father. And in the same text that we quoted a moment ago, he is also called the Captain of their salvation. And this Captain of their salvation is not ashamed, according to verse 11, to call those whom this Captain must lead to glory his brethren.

These brethren, however, are also called "the seed of Abraham" in verse 16. Christ did not take upon himself "the nature of angels," but the seed of Abraham. We understand, of course, that this seed of Abraham certainly is, first, not the Jews as such, although this seed of Abraham was in the old dispensation of the Jews. That this is true is clearly expressed in the ninth chapter of Paul's epistle to the Romans, where we read in verse 6 and following:

6. Not as though the word of God hath taken none effect. For they are not all Israel, which are of Israel:
7. Neither, because they are the seed of Abraham, are they all children: but, In Isaac shall thy seed be called.
8. That is, They which are the children of the flesh, these are not the children of God: but the children of the promise are counted for the seed. (Rom. 9:6–8)

Hence, we may say that the brethren of whom the text speaks are not his carnal brethren, according to the flesh; but they are the spiritual seed of Abraham, both of the old and of the new dispensation. The line of the promise for a time indeed followed the line of the carnal seed of Abraham, although they were not all children of the promise. But the same line of the promise continued in the generations of believers of all nations in the new dispensation.

This is mentioned here also because it was indeed the flesh and blood of the seed of Abraham that he assumed. He assumed his human nature not from any other nation—not from the Romans, or the Assyrians, or the Egyptians, or any other nation—but only from the seed of Abraham. And when the text speaks of the brethren of our Lord Jesus Christ, it certainly means that he became like unto Abraham's seed even from an outward and carnal point of view. Nevertheless, not all the seed of Abraham are his brethren, but only those whom God chose from before the foundation of the world and whom he predestinated to be the sons whom he would lead to glory.

Now, the implication of this, according to all Scripture, is very plain. It means, first, that he assumed the human nature, that he became man. It means that the only begotten Son of God, who himself is essentially God, who is eternal, who is the Infinite One, who is in himself the immutable God, who is in himself the Lord of all, the Lord of heaven and earth, also became man. This is emphasized in the words of our text. He became in all things like unto his brethren: in all things, mind you. This does not refer to a mere outward similarity, but to a very real and essential likeness. He did not *look* like his brethren; he did not *look* like a man. He *became* man. He took upon himself the nature of his brethren, the nature of man, the human nature.

This means, too, that he did not take upon himself a general human nature, as some would have it. For this is not according to Scripture; and besides, this would mean nothing. We cannot conceive of a general human nature. But he took upon himself a very specific human nature. And although we do not have any painting of Jesus, and although all the paintings that exist in our day are mere inventions, yet the human nature of Jesus was so specific that, if it had been possible in that day to take a picture of him, Christ could certainly have been photographed.

On the other hand, although we do not believe in a so-called general human nature, we may nevertheless say that he took upon himself a *central* human nature. By this central human nature, I mean that he was of the seed of the woman that already was mentioned in the promise of Genesis 3:15. Moreover, as we know, he was of the seed of Abraham. He was of the tribe of Judah. He was of the family of David. He was of the seed of the woman as it culminated in the virgin Mary.

Second, we must understand that the incarnation of the Son of God did not mean that the Son of God changed into a man. But it means that the very person of the Son of God, who was eternally in the divine nature, in the fullness of time also entered into the human nature.

Third, we must also emphasize that when the text says that he became like unto his brethren in all things, it does not mean that he became two persons, the person of the Son of God and the person of the Son of Man. On the contrary, he remained one person. And he assumed his human nature in personal union with the divine nature. All these truths have been contested in the past but have always been maintained by the church. And it is very important that we also understand this and that we maintain the truth concerning the incarnation of the Son of God.

Moreover, when the text says that he became like unto his brethren in all things, it also means that he lived our life. He thought our thoughts; he had a human mind. He lived our emotional life. He experienced all our weaknesses, our joys and our sorrows, our hunger and thirst, and all the different experiences of our soul and body. Still more, he lived in our world, the world that was under sin and under the curse. And he lived in all the different relationships that are in the world—the home, the church, society, the state.

One more thing: he came in the likeness of sinful flesh, as is evident from all Scripture and as is also evident from Romans 8:3. This does not mean that by assuming the human nature he also became sinful, corrupt, or that he became personally guilty before God. The very contrary is true, of course. But he came in the *likeness* of sinful flesh. He was not immortal, but mortal. His human nature was not incorruptible as he assumed it from the virgin Mary, but corruptible. He was subject to all the suffering of this present time, to all the suffering of mankind. As the prophet Isaiah has it in chapter 53: "He hath no form nor comeliness; and when we shall see him, there is no beauty that we should desire him. He is despised and rejected of men; a man of sorrows, and acquainted with grief" (vv. 2–3). This, then, is the implication of the expression in the words of our text that he became like unto his brethren in all things.

Now the question is: Why did the Son of God become man? What must he do as the person of the Son of God in human nature? The text answers, first, that he must do the things pertaining to God; and second, that he must make reconciliation for the sins of the people. The necessity of the lowliness of Christ is emphasized in the words of our text. He could not possibly have appeared in the glory of the angels. Why? He was high priest. That Christ was the high priest is mentioned here for the first time in the epistle.

Now the high priest in the old dispensation was the chief servant of God in the temple, in the house of God. As such, he represented the people over whom he was high priest. And as high priest he had to accomplish the "things pertaining to God" (Heb. 2:17), as it is translated here in the King James Version. Literally, we can translate "the things which were toward God." And the things toward God implied all the things concerning the salvation of the people of God, concerning the salvation of the brethren of Jesus Christ our Lord.

As high priest, he must lead all the sons of God who are mentioned in verse 10 of this same chapter to everlasting glory. As high priest, he himself must build the house of God, the temple of God, not as it was made with hands, but the true, spiritual temple of God. That is, he must realize the eternal covenant of God, the most intimate communion of God with those whom he had chosen from before the foundation of the world. He must realize the eternal kingdom of heaven, in which God is supreme and in which Christ is the chief King-Servant forever and in whose reign the people of God will participate in all eternity. All these things, which must be realized in Christ Jesus our Lord, are things pertaining to God, or things toward God, or things that chiefly have respect unto God. For all these things must be a revelation of the eternal perfection of the Most High. That is the chief purpose of all things. And all these things the high priest, our Lord Jesus Christ, had to realize and accomplish all alone. And to do this, he must certainly become like unto his brethren in all things.

Again we ask: What must this high priest do, and why must he become like unto his brethren in order to accomplish what had to be done? The answer of the words of our text is in the very last part: he must make reconciliation for the sins of the people. Oh, he must do many more things. But this is basic. Unless he could accomplish the realization of the reconciliation of his people, he could never do anything else. And once more, to make reconciliation for the sins of his people, it was absolutely necessary that he became like unto his brethren in all things.

Reconciliation does not mean that God must be reconciled unto his people, but that his people must be reconciled to him. And in order to accomplish that reconciliation, the high priest must make propitiation for sin. He must expiate sin, so that the guilt of sin is absolutely removed and exists no more. Only in this way of satisfaction, only in the way therefore of taking all the sins of his people upon himself, and with those sins of his people upon his mighty shoulders, he must make a perfect act of obedience, of obedience, that is, under the wrath of God. He alone must suffer, as the Son of God in human nature, all the punishment of sin for all his brethren. It must be a positive act of obedience, of obedience in the love of God, even under the load of God's wrath. He must willingly bear all the punishment of sin for all whom the Father had given him. And willingly, in the love of God, he must lay down his life. And he must lay down his life, consciously suffer all the wrath of God, even unto the end. This is the meaning of the cross. On that cross hangs indeed the Son of God in human nature, who was made like unto his brethren in all things, in order that in human nature he could bear the punishment of sin.

But there is more. If we ask the question why Christ must be made like unto his brethren in all things, we must also emphasize that he must be this in order, as the text has it, to be the merciful and the faithful high priest. Oh, he must certainly be merciful. He must be the merciful high priest in order to be able and to be willing in the love of God to expiate the sins of his people and make reconciliation for them. Mercy, as you know, is only one aspect of love. Christ loves his brethren, and he has loved them even unto the death of the cross. Mercy is that aspect of love according to which we wish to make the object of our love as blessed as possible—blessed, in other words, in the highest sense of the word.

And this is surely true of the mercy of Christ. He was merciful because he loved them. He was merciful in order to lead his brethren unto everlasting life and glory. He means to lead his brethren, the sons of God, to everlasting glory in the highest possible sense of the word, which implies, of course, that he must deliver them from the guilt and from the corruption of sin, in order that they may be righteous before God, and in order that they may be able, even, to live in and enjoy this everlasting glory. Oh, how strong that mercy of our Lord Jesus Christ was, so strong that he could suffer the agonies of death and hell, and so strong that he could suffer these agonies while we were yet sinners, sinners who hated him and who hated God. Therefore, he had to become like unto his brethren.

One more thing we must mention, according to the text. We should read the text in this way, that he, that is, Christ, might be merciful so as to be faithful, so as to be the faithful high priest in things pertaining to God. Faithfulness is the virtue of remaining constant in a certain relationship and in certain conditions. Here it means that this servant of Jehovah, this high priest of the Lord, accomplishes his calling and discharges it, no matter what happens to him. This means that he was faithful without any defect in all his suffering and death. And again I say, how great is that faithfulness of our beloved Lord and Savior Jesus Christ. Faithful he was, even unto death, even unto the death of the cross, even unto his descension into hell. He was faithful, faithful to God and faithful unto the people whom God had given him. Faithful he was in the face of all opposition, of all contradiction. Faithful he was in order that he might obtain for all his brethren everlasting life and glory!

# Chapter 5

# COMING TO THE THRONE
# OF GRACE

15. For we have not an high priest which cannot be touched with the feeling of our infirmities; but was in all points tempted like as we are, yet without sin.
16. Let us therefore come boldly unto the throne of grace, that we may obtain mercy, and find grace to help in time of need.

—*Hebrews 4:15-16*

This indeed is a most important and also very beautiful exhortation. The exhortation is that we must come to the throne of grace, and also that we must come boldly, that is, with perfect confidence that we shall surely be received and accepted by him who sits on the throne of grace. The fact that the throne to which we must approach is a throne of grace is mentioned in order that we may be encouraged to come to that throne with boldness. But we are also encouraged to come to that throne by the knowledge that in the sanctuary where this throne of grace is established, we have a high priest who was in all points tempted as we are and who because of this can be touched with the feeling of our infirmities.

This particular exhortation to come boldly to the throne of grace occupies the last place in a series of admonitions and must be regarded as the only way in which these exhortations may be heeded. Unless we heed this present admonition, namely, that we come boldly to the throne of grace, all the preceding exhortations cannot possibly be fulfilled. In the preceding context the writer had expressed that there is a rest that remains for the people of God, the rest of God's everlasting covenant, the rest from sin and corruption and death and unto righteousness, light, and fellowship with God. Into that rest we

30

must constantly labor to enter, that is, we must walk in newness of life, we must labor to love the Lord our God with all our heart, with all our mind, with all our soul, and with all our strength, must crucify our old nature, and walk in a new and holy life.[1]

Moreover, the writer admonishes us to hold fast to our profession (Heb. 10:23). Our flesh is forevermore tempting us to depart from our profession. And besides, we live in a world that is evermore opposed to the profession of our faith, that Jesus is Lord and that he is our Lord forever and ever. We are exhorted to cling to that profession and to realize it in all our life and walk in the midst of the world. All this, you realize, we will never be able to accomplish in our own strength. Ever we are in need of mercy and grace to help in time of need. And this mercy and grace is to be obtained only at the throne of grace. Hence, the exhortation in the words of our text: "Let us therefore come boldly unto the throne of grace."

The expression "the throne of grace" is a most beautiful figure, and it conveys to our mind a most important concept. The words must not be interpreted as referring to the throne of Christ, as some would explain it. Neither must they be explained as simply meaning the throne on which grace reigns, as others would have it. But the words indicate the throne of God; and therefore they refer to God's absolute sovereignty, as that sovereignty is characterized and motivated by grace.

The throne of God is a symbolic expression referring to his absolute sovereignty. God is the Lord. He is the Creator of the heavens and of the earth, who called the things that are not as if they were, and who made all things according to his sovereign counsel and good pleasure. He is therefore also the sole proprietor of all things. "The earth is the LORD's, and the fullness thereof; the world, and they who dwell therein" (Ps. 24:1). His alone is the prerogative to do with them according to his sovereign good pleasure; and no one dares to say to him, "What doest thou?" Moreover, he is also the sole Lawgiver, who alone is above the law, and whose will is the sole criterion for every creature; the only judge, who executes his judgment in righteousness and

---

1    A reference to the Form for the Administration of Baptism, in *The Psalter*, 86.

equity. And he governs all things, upholding them by the word of his power and directing them, individually and as a whole, to the end he ordained and purposed in himself before the foundation of the world, so that no creature moves and nothing betides but by the will of this sovereign Lord. That is the meaning of God's throne. It simply refers to God in his glorious majesty, his undisputed sovereignty, his absolute authority and universal power, his holiness, righteousness, and truth.

Notice that according to the text this throne of the absolute Sovereign of heaven and earth is a throne of grace. What a glorious truth is expressed in this term. It signifies that in God authority and love, holiness and loving-kindness, righteousness and grace, justice and mercy, are united in perfect and most blessed harmony. Grace, as we know, has different meanings in Holy Writ, and we need not call attention to them all in this connection. Let it suffice to say that in the words of our text it refers to that attitude and disposition of favor in God that shines upon us, his people, through the face of Jesus Christ our Lord, his only begotten Son.

Christ is the revelation of the God of our salvation. In the face of Christ, who is God of God, Light of Light,[2] who is eternally in the bosom of the Father, who reached down to us as the arm of the Lord, who united himself with us, assumed our nature, our flesh and blood, tabernacled among us, laid down his life for us on Calvary, was raised on the third day and exalted above the heavens at the right hand of the Majesty on high—in him we behold the face of the Sovereign of heaven and earth, beaming upon us in everlasting grace. The Potentate of potentates is our Father in heaven; the sovereign Lord and creator of all things is our gracious redeemer. Such is the meaning of the expression "the throne of grace." It means that God purposed all things, that he created all things, that he governs all things, that he directs all things, that he judges all things, according as he is motivated by his grace over us in Jesus Christ our Lord. The Lord of all is our sovereign friend and our Father in heaven!

To that throne of grace we are exhorted in the words of our text to come boldly. The meaning is not merely that we come to that throne

---

2    A reference to the Nicene Creed. See also page 70.

of grace in prayer, at least, not if by prayer is meant an occasional approach to that throne of grace, in order then to return again and draw back into the night of our present existence, into the darkness and gloom and hopelessness of our present death. Of course, all our coming to that throne of grace is always an act of prayer. But certainly, the text does not simply refer to an occasional act of prayer. The meaning rather is that we must come to that throne in the sense of entering into his fellowship.

The text means to exhort us: let us approach to the God of our salvation with our whole being, with all our mind and heart and soul and strength, to worship and adore, to praise and to serve him who sits upon the throne. Let us come to him as the overflowing fount of all good, to drink from that fount to the satisfaction of our souls, to taste his marvelous mercy and grace, and to know that the Lord is good. Let us come, not to depart again, never to withdraw again into our own night, but to abide in his tabernacle all the days of our life, to behold the beauty of the Lord and to inquire in his temple.

Such a coming to the throne of grace implies, first, a profound consciousness and acknowledgment of our own emptiness, of our sin and death, of our need of grace and mercy. It also implies the spiritual apprehension of the fullness of God, of the riches of righteousness and life, of blessedness and glory, that are in him as he stands revealed to us in all the beauty of his grace in the face of Jesus Christ our Lord. It signifies also a deep longing for his fellowship, a thirsting after God, as the hart pants after the water brooks and after streams of living water. And finally, it means that with confidence of faith we appropriate all the spiritual blessings revealed unto us, promised us by the symbol of that throne of grace.

Hence, the writer exhorts us: "Let us therefore come *boldly*" (Heb. 4:16). Oh, the meaning is not that we come with a boldness that is devoid of holy fear. For the throne of grace is still a throne, and that, too, the throne of the most high Majesty in the heavens. Nor does it mean that we come with a certain carnal confidence that is based on our own worthiness. For God resists the proud, while he gives grace to the humble only (1 Peter 5:5–6; James 4:6–7). But the meaning is that we must come with a confidence that is inspired only by the sight of that throne of grace. It is the boldness of faith by which we must come. It is the confidence that for Christ's sake he who sits upon the throne will not cast us off but receive us even though all things testify against us. Such is the meaning of coming boldly to the throne of grace.

The purpose of that coming to the throne of grace is expressed in the words of our text: "That we may obtain mercy, and find grace to help in time of need" (v. 16).

Mercy and grace you will surely find when you come to the throne of our sovereign Redeemer.

Mercy and grace are closely related. Yet they may be distinguished and are also distinguished in the text. Mercy is God's will to bless, to bestow bliss upon us in his fellowship, to render us blessed even as he is blessed. It means that God is filled with holy, eternal longing to lead his children into the glory of his everlasting tabernacle. With a view to our present state of sin and death, it denotes that virtue in God, that disposition of the divine heart to us, according to which he longs to deliver us from the misery of our sin and lead us into the state of perfect righteousness, to raise us out of the deep darkness of our death and alienation from God to the glory of eternal life and to the heavenly fellowship of his everlasting tabernacle with men. Grace is the power by which all this is accomplished, the marvelous power whereby he redeems us, bestows upon us the forgiveness of sins and perfect righteousness, makes us partakers of the adoption of children, regenerates us, calls us out of darkness into his marvelous light, gives us faith and hope and confidence and love and all the riches of grace in Jesus Christ our Lord.

For this we must always come to the throne of grace. Constantly we must approach that throne. Always you are in need of mercy, and constantly you need grace to help. Mercy and grace are not gifts that are once bestowed upon you—say, in the moment of your regeneration—and that ever since you possess in yourselves, apart from the God of your salvation. They are, on the contrary, a constant stream that flows into your soul from its source, the throne of grace. They are rather to be compared to the golden glory of light that radiates from the sun and in whose brightness you may rejoice as you remain in the sphere of its radiation but which you cannot take with you into the darkness of a mountain cave. Not for a moment can you withdraw yourselves from the throne of grace without forfeiting the blessings of mercy and grace as far as your consciousness of them is concerned.

Hence, the time of need is now. It is an ever-present time. Mercy and grace you need today and tomorrow and forevermore. Besides, you need grace to help, to help in time of need that is now and constantly. Help you need, that you may daily enter into God's rest, that you may put off the old and put on the new man, that you may put on the whole armor of God, fight the good fight of faith, and be able to stand in the evil day. Help you need, to hold fast your profession, not to be tossed to and fro by every wind of doctrine, nor to be seduced by the pleasures and treasures of Egypt, nor to be intimidated by the fury of the powers of darkness. Your only help is in God's grace. Without him you can do nothing. Now, therefore, is the time of need. Now you must obtain grace. Hence, come, always come boldly, to the throne of grace, that you may obtain mercy and grace to help in time of need.

Are you afraid? Do you hesitate to come to the throne of grace with confidence? Oh, but there is no reason to hesitate. For as you approach that throne of grace, you are met in the sanctuary of God by a high priest who is over the whole house of God, who intercedes with him, who sits upon that throne of grace, and who is able to sympathize with all your infirmities. Those infirmities indeed are many; but he knows them all. They include all your present sufferings and death, suffering of soul and body, of mind and spirit. They are our trials and temptations in the world, our tribulations with which we suffer for Christ's sake as we hold fast the profession of our faith. They include our temptations from within through the sinfulness of our flesh, and our temptations from without through the seducing influence of the world. They include all our weaknesses and sins, our inclinations to stumble in the way. He, our merciful high priest, is acquainted with them all. And he intercedes for us with the Father and constantly prays for us.

He is acquainted with the weakness of our flesh. For he came in the likeness of our sinful flesh, though without sin. He knows all our sufferings and all our temptations. For he was tempted in all things, even as we are, though in all his temptations he never once stumbled.

He knows what it is to be utterly amazed at the justice and wrath of God against sin and at the presence of his holiness. For he bore it all upon the tree and entered into our death and hell. He knows by experience what it means to be tempted by the wicked machinations of evil men. For he endured all the contradictions of sinners against himself. Never is your path of suffering and temptation so deep, but you find there the imprint of his feet.

Come, then, boldly to the throne of grace, with your eye on that sympathizing high priest who is in the tabernacle of God and who always intercedes for you. Come boldly, for Christ, our sympathizing high priest, is there, and he has the right and the power to sympathize with your infirmities and to obtain mercy and grace to help in time of need. Fear not, but come boldly to the throne of grace. Pray without ceasing. Let your whole life be an approach to that marvelous throne, that you may obtain mercy and grace to help in time of need. And that grace and mercy you shall surely receive. You may come boldly, for your reception is assured!

*Chapter 6*

# CHRIST LEARNING OBEDIENCE

7. Who in the days of his flesh, when he had offered up prayers and supplications with strong crying and tears unto him that was able to save him from death, and was heard in that he feared;

8. Though he were a Son, yet learned he obedience by the things which he suffered.

*—Hebrews 5:7–8*

Christ is the Captain of our salvation. Thus we learned from Hebrews 2:10. Moreover, this Captain of our salvation, so it was expressed in that verse, was made perfect through sufferings. And this does not mean that Christ had to be made perfect in a moral, or ethical, or spiritual sense of the word. He had no sin whatsoever. But the meaning is that through his sufferings Christ was made fit, was prepared, to be the Captain of our salvation. He was clothed with authority and power to save us from sin and death and to make us partakers of heavenly glory. And this was done through suffering, that is, in the way of suffering, the way in which the Father led him. The same idea is fundamentally expressed in the words of our text (Heb. 5:7–8).

Let us, first of all, note, as our whole text strongly expresses it, that Jesus feared, feared because of the way he had to travel in his suffering. We should never forget this element in the suffering of Jesus. We are very apt to forget this. Jesus, so we reason, was the Son of God. And therefore, although he certainly suffered all the agonies of soul and body and spirit, he did not for a moment fear, he was not for a moment afraid to travel the way of his suffering. In a way, according to this opinion, although he bore a very heavy load of suffering, yet we reason, because he was the Son of God, he could easily bear it and he could certainly not have been afraid to travel the way.

But that is not the impression at all that the words of our text leave us. It tells us that he "offered up prayers and supplications with strong crying and tears unto him that was able to save him" (v. 7). And so it is. We must never forget that he bore our sufferings in his earthly frame, weak and corruptible. As the text has it, in the days of his flesh he offered up prayers and supplications. And in his earthly nature he was certainly afraid of the suffering he anticipated. He abhorred it with his entire earthly being. He abhorred his suffering undoubtedly even more so than we are able to do in our sinful nature. The very thought of his suffering made our Lord Jesus Christ tremble with fear. His entire frame was shaken.

And thus it is very emphatically expressed in the words of our text, which tell us what he did when he feared to go ahead on the way. First of all, the text tells us that he offered up prayers. He sent his petitions to the throne of grace, expressing what was in his heart concerning his suffering through which he had to pass step by step. Moreover, the text tells us that he offered up supplications. This is, of course, essentially the same as prayers. Only it is more strongly expressed. He pleaded! He took hold of God and said: "I will not let thee go until thou bless me."[1] Moreover, he prayed in such a way that great trouble was expressed in his prayers. He prayed with strong cryings, like a man who is in great trouble of soul and body. Loud crying was expressed; and that loud crying was pressed from his very heart. It was an expression of urgent need: "Help me, Father, before I succumb under the load of my sufferings." Moreover, according to the author in the words of our text, he expressed this prayer and supplication with tears, expressive of great sorrow of heart, of fear and agony.

He prayed to him, according to our text, "who was able to save him from death" (v. 7). This designation of God tells us also for what he prayed. He prayed for salvation from death. And this may mean either of two things. First of all, it may mean that he prayed that God would not allow that death would take hold of him. But it also denotes

---

1    A paraphrase of Genesis 32:26.

CHRIST LEARNING OBEDIENCE

undoubtedly that if he would have to pass through death, God might not leave him in the power of death but might help him safely through the dark pit of death and hell. But this also tells us what was the occasion for his prayer and fear. Christ was in the fear of death and hell.

And this is corroborated by the whole history of Jesus' life in the flesh and upon the earth. It is true, we first of all receive the impression from the words of our text that what happened in the garden of Gethsemane was chiefly before the mind of the author of the epistle to the Hebrews. By Jesus' suffering in that garden of Gethsemane the words of our text are most emphatically and literally realized. There, in that garden, he was sorrowful even unto death. Sorrow got such a strong hold upon our Lord that he would die of fear if help did not presently come to him. There indeed he prayed to him who was able to save him from death. And he prayed not only that he might be saved from death but also that he would not have to pass through all this suffering of death and hell. He so feared that he prayed to the Father that if it were possible, this bitter cup of suffering might be taken away from him. There, in Gethsemane, he cried aloud in agony with supplications. There indeed he cried loudly and with tears. Although the gospel narratives do not express this, according to our text this was true nevertheless. In Gethsemane Jesus wept as never before, and he wept in the anticipation of his awful suffering through which he had to pass.

Nevertheless, although it is true that the words of our text remind us immediately of his suffering and crying and tears in the garden of Gethsemane, yet this was only the climax of all his fear throughout his earthly life. This is also evident from the words of our text. For it tells us that he so feared and cried to him who could save him from death "in the days of his flesh." This phrase does not merely refer to his human nature: for that human nature he still possesses now in the highest glory of heaven. But it refers to his weak human nature, the human nature in which he came and dwelt in the likeness of sinful flesh.

In that frail human nature Jesus was always deeply conscious of his hour. All his lifetime he anticipated that final hour. All his lifetime he dreaded that hour. And all his lifetime he prayed to him who could save him from death. Nevertheless, the consciousness of that suffering

39

that was to come and the fear of that hour gradually deepened. As the cross approached, the shadows of death and the fear of death deepened and grew darker. A short time before his suffering on the accursed tree, the Lord said: "Now is my soul troubled; and what shall I say? Father, save me from this hour: but for this cause came I unto this hour. Father, glorify thy name" (John 12:27–28). And again, at the last Passover we read that Jesus' spirit was troubled, evidently because Judas Iscariot was still at the table of the Passover. For we read: "When Jesus had thus said, he was troubled in spirit, and testified, and said, Verily, verily, I say unto you, that one of you shall betray me" (13:21). All this suffering and trouble in soul and spirit came to its climax in the garden of Gethsemane. There, evidently, he is enveloped in the deepest darkness and night of fear, so that he is afraid to go on.

Yet in all his trouble and in all his fear that had its ultimate climax in the cross of Golgotha, our Lord Jesus Christ was never disobedient. Of this we read in verse 8 of the words of our text: "Though he were a Son, yet learned he obedience by the things which he suffered." The Son of God learned obedience. What does this mean? The expression is somewhat surprising. Christ was, as it is even emphasized in these words of our text, a son. Indeed he was the perfect Son. He was the Son of God in our nature.

We would hardly expect that this perfect Son had to learn obedience. How is this possible? As the Son of God, he certainly knew how to be obedient to the Father without any question. Yet we read in the text that although he were a Son, yet he learned obedience from what he suffered. Can this mean that after all he was sometimes disobedient and that he had to be corrected? This indeed we do and have to do in regard to our children. When our children are naughty and stubborn and disobedient, we use, if necessary, the rod; and we punish them in order to teach them obedience and to correct their rebellious spirit. Thus we correct our children.

But this certainly cannot be applied to our Lord Jesus Christ. For he was, in fact, never disobedient. Always he walked in and loved the way of his Father. Always he asked for the will of the Father. And always he performed that will in perfection. We may never suppose that even the desire to do the Father's will was ever absent from his mind and heart, even though that will of the Father led him in the way of deepest suffering and agony. We know that he had no sin and that not even for the smallest moment did he fail to love and to do the will of his Father. Also in all his prayers, even in the prayer he uttered in the garden of Gethsemane, even though he expressed in that prayer the desire that this cup might pass from him, he nevertheless was obedient, as is evident from what he said in this prayer: not my will, but thy will be done (Luke 22:42).

And therefore, we must not even think for a moment that his suffering was necessary in order to correct a disobedient disposition or a disobedient act on the part of our Lord Jesus Christ. It certainly was never the desire, even, of our Lord to refuse to walk in the way of obedience, which for him was the way of suffering and agony. That very desire certainly would have been sin, but that very desire was also absolutely impossible.

Yet we read that our Lord learned obedience by the things that he suffered. But I would interpret this not as if he ever had need of learning to be obedient, but rather that he learned by experience what it was to be obedient to the Father. Remember here, too, as we said before, that step by step the way became deeper and more difficult to travel. Accordingly, we may also say that the exercise of obedience became harder and more severe even as he traveled in the way of his suffering. As the hour approached, his suffering became more severe. And as he walked in the way of suffering, he certainly learned what it meant for him, as the head and mediator of his people whom the Father had given him, to be obedient even unto the end. Remember, as we said, that Jesus dreaded suffering. With all his mind and soul and heart he certainly could fear that awfully dark way of the cross.

Remember, too, that he had to set his foot voluntarily on that very way of suffering and agony. He was not compelled. He undoubtedly had the power to return, rather than to advance on that dark way of physical and mental and spiritual suffering. And therefore, every time the way became deeper and darker the Lord had to exercise a new measure of obedience. With every step on that way of suffering he tasted what it meant and what it was to be obedient to the Father as the suffering servant of the Lord. More and more he tasted what it was to be obedient. More and more he practiced, so to speak, the art of obeying.

Hence, he learned obedience. That is, he learned what it meant to be obedient. He learned practically. He learned by practicing obedience. This he learned in all his way. And in learning the deep way of obedience, he was not for a moment disobedient to the Father. He practiced obedience to the very end, even into the suffering of deepest death on the cross. He tasted what it meant to be obedient to the Father because he tasted the wrath of God against sin, against the sin of his people. He tasted God's righteousness and justice. All this he knew. But he also learned to know more fully as he proceeded on the way to the cross. By experience he learned to know what it meant to obey the Father. By experience he learned to know the real meaning and the real nature of perfect obedience, even under the wrath of God.

Oh, to be sure, he also learned to know the reward of obedience. For God delivered him as a reward for all his bitter and willing suffering. He set him on high in everlasting glory. He tasted not only the wrath of God; but he also tasted the sweetness of obedience, the saving help of God in suffering. And therefore, we may say that Christ indeed learned obedience, even in and through all his suffering unto death.

And Christ, walking the way of obedience and trusting in God who could deliver him from death, was not put to shame. For we read in the last part of Hebrews 5:7 that he "was heard in that he feared." As we have explained, this fear does not refer to the fear of God, although Christ certainly also had the fear of God in his heart. But it refers to his fear of the way of suffering. He feared the way of the cross. And especially in the garden of Gethsemane he was for a time overwhelmed by that fear. And in that fear he could never face the enemy. And therefore, he needed new courage and new strength to do the will of the Father. And it is evident, as he arose from the dust of Gethsemane, where his fear was so great that he sweat drops of blood, that he was delivered from that fear.

Still more, he was also delivered from death. He prayed to him who could deliver him from death. And also in regard to that prayer he was not put to shame. Oh yes, the Captain of our salvation was made perfect as such by and through his suffering. He was made perfect through the cross and through the resurrection and through his exaltation at the right hand of God. He was made perfect because, as the Captain of our salvation, he was empowered to save his own from sin and death and to highest glory in heaven and in the new creation. And thus we look upon Jesus. And looking upon him, by his grace we follow in his steps. And even as the Captain of our salvation was made perfect through suffering, so we, too, suffer in the world and suffer for Christ's sake. And when we thus suffer, we shall also be glorified with him.

# Chapter 7

# HOPE:
# THE ANCHOR OF THE SOUL

19. Which hope we have as an anchor of the soul, both sure and stedfast, and which entereth into that within the veil;
20. Whither the forerunner is for us entered, even Jesus.

*—Hebrews 6:19–20*

The soul of the Christian in the midst of this world has need of an anchor. And the only anchor that can possibly serve the purpose is the sure and steadfast hope. Let us not forget that the saints in Christ Jesus are frequently admonished not to be weak in the faith and not to be slothful, but to be followers of those who through faith and patience inherit the promise. Such is also the case in the context in the words of our text. It is through faith, but also through patience, that they must and can only inherit the promises.

The promise, you understand, concerns the things that are not seen as yet. In ages of yore some of the saints obtained a glimmer of the promise as they stood on the mountaintops of prophecy, whence they might anxiously and eagerly gaze into the distance. They would return from the mountain peaks of prophecy and inform those who lived in the valley below of what they had seen. And in the new dispensation we see Jesus, crowned with glory and honor, raised from the dead and received in the highest heavens, having all things subject unto him. But even so, we do not yet behold the full realization of the promise. But faith is "the evidence of things not seen" and "the substance of things hoped for" (Heb. 11:1). By faith we understand and are assured, while dwelling in the valley of the shadow of death, that over and beyond the mountains that surround us on every side there are the unseen things of life and glory and that our hope is not in vain.

For those things, however, the saints who are in the midst of the world wait with patience. The valley in which the saints in this present time still dwell is characterized by suffering, by the sufferings of this present time. All things are against those who are followers of those who inherit the promise. There are the sufferings of this present time both in general and the sufferings for Christ's sake. These sufferings would fill the soul of the believers with gloomy despair and induce them to give up the battle of faith, while the promise is tarrying and God appears to be slack concerning his promise. There are the cutting sarcasms of the scoffers, who loudly proclaim—and apparently not without reason—that all things remain as they were from the beginning, and who ridicule those who hope for the promise of his coming. There are the tempting offers of riches and pleasures, if the soul will but decide to cease from following after those who inherit the promise. There are the false philosophies that confuse the soul as to the direction in which she ought to proceed. And there are the actual sufferings of the body for Christ's sake in the midst of this world, when the believers are cast into prison and into death.

Thus, it is by patience only that we can be followers of those who inherit the promise. For patience is strength to endure unto the end in spite of all opposing powers. That endurance is the strength of the soul that is securely anchored in hope. The soul of the saint, therefore, in the words of our text is pictured as a ship that is waiting near the harbor for the favorable tide, which the strong current would carry far back into the sea, were it not that it is securely anchored. And that "anchor of the soul" is the hope that entered "into that within the veil" (Heb. 6:19), whither the forerunner, even Jesus, is entered.

Jesus is the object of the hope of the believer, and that, too, Jesus as he is already entered into the glory of God's eternal tabernacle. Such is the sense of the text. It is not the act of hoping, but hope itself, the object of the hope, that for which the Christian hopes, that is meant in the words of our text. From the word of God we know that sometimes hope is referred to as the action, the hoping itself, while at other times hope is referred to as the object for which the Christian hopes.

In the former sense, in the sense of the action of hope, it is the power and tendency of the believing soul, that is born from above, to seek its own level. It is the stretching forth in longing, by the assurance of faith, toward the city that has foundations, the heavenly country, the ultimate realization of the promise. But in the latter sense, that is, in the sense of the object of the hope, it is the realization of the promise itself, the inheritance incorruptible, and undefiled, and that fades not away, the glory of God's eternal tabernacle, in which there shall nevermore be night and death and sin, but God shall be our everlasting light, walk among us, eternally call us his sons and daughters, and we shall see him as he is and know him as we are known. Such is the object of our hope. It is of that object of the hope that the text speaks. And it is that object of our hope that is the anchor of the soul of the believer, secure and steadfast.

To that hope-object, that is in the heavenly sanctuary, the soul of him who follows after those who inherit the promises is now anchored. The object of the hope is now realized. This was not the case as yet in the old dispensation. Then the anchor of hope had not as yet been sunk in the solid anchor ground of the inner sanctuary. To be sure, even in those days the saints had a sure consolation, the same consolation, principally, that is ours in the new dispensation. For the promise was always sure by two immutable things. There was the immutability of God's counsel to give the eternal inheritance to the heirs of the promise, the elect in Christ. And there was the immutable oath that God would bless Abraham and his seed.

To that promise even the saints in the old dispensation looked forward. But even so, there was in the days of the Old Testament no tangible realization of that immutable promise. There were shadows and pictures of the hope that was to come. But Jesus was not yet. The blood of atonement had not been shed. There was as yet no resurrection of the dead. And no one had ever entered into that which is within the veil. But now Jesus has entered into that which is within the veil, the inner sanctuary. And it is not the place of the inner sanctuary but the idea that is meant here.

That sanctuary of God is indeed a definite place. When the glorified Lord in his resurrection body left the earth to enter into that sanctuary above, there certainly was a change of places. The resurrected Lord did not merely become omnipresent; he went from one place to another. He left the earth to enter into the house of many mansions.

Yet, not the place, but rather the idea and the significance of that place must receive all the emphasis. That which, according to the words of our text, is within the veil is the holy place, the holiest of all, where God dwells as he dwells nowhere else, the eternal and heavenly realization of the shadow and picture of it that was once seen in the earthly temple in Jerusalem. Of course, the meaning is not that even the highest heaven, that central realization of the glorified cosmos, could ever contain God. For the heaven, yea, the heaven of heavens, cannot contain him. Neither may we conceive of that highest heaven as if it were the place where God dwells by himself. For God is not confined to any place.

Nevertheless, it pleased God to establish his temple, his dwelling place with men, through Jesus Christ our Lord. That within the veil is the highest realization of his blessed covenantal dwelling with men, the revelation of his perfected friendship in Jesus Christ our Lord, that revelation of himself according to which we shall see him face to face in Jesus Christ our Lord. On earth we only see his picture, the reflection of his face as in a glass darkly; in heaven we shall look at his face directly (1 Cor. 13:12). On earth, as it were, we stand with our back to God and the mirror of his revelation in the Scriptures confronting us. In that mirror we can see a faint reflection of God's face. But in heaven, in that which is within the veil, we shall turn about and behold the face of God as it is revealed in the glorified Jesus, who is now gone before us into heaven.

There, in heaven, is God's blessed presence. There is the highest possible realization of that blessed fellowship in which we shall know even as we are known. That is the object of our hope. And that object of our hope, according to the text, is now realized principally by Jesus entering into heaven, into that which is within the veil. Thus the hope is the anchor of our soul.

Do not forget that the text speaks of Jesus having entered into that which is within the veil, into heavenly glory, and into the presence of God, as our forerunner. Only when we see and believe in the Lord Jesus Christ having entered into heavenly glory as our forerunner can hope be the anchor of our soul. Of ourselves we could never have entered into that which is within the veil and into the presence of God. We would not even be able to conceive of the possibility for man by himself and of himself to enter into the house of God in heaven. Let us never give way, even for a moment, to the philosophy of modern theology, which would present the ascension of Jesus as a proof and token of man's ability to enter into glory and into the presence of God.

Of ourselves, first of all, we have no right to be in heaven. Nor could we ever obtain such right for ourselves by our most serious efforts. We are guilty, and worthy of eternal death, and nothing else. Exiles we are from the presence of God. Children of wrath and perdition we are, by nature. Not only so, but second, we are also corrupt, so corrupt that it would be but torture for us even to be in heaven, where all is purity and holiness, and those who dwell there are constantly reminded of the presence of the Most High. In heaven every moment of the experience of those who dwell there is filled with the consciousness of his presence. But by nature we are also so foolish that we never would or could even desire to be in heaven and to dwell in fellowship with the ever-blessed God. Heaven as such could never be the object of our hope.

But thanks be to God, Jesus our forerunner has entered into that which is within the veil. A forerunner blazes the trail, prepares the way for those who follow him, secures the right for them to enter into the place whither they must go. In that sense Jesus is our forerunner into heaven. He blazed the trail. He prepared the way. He secured the right for all his people. He draws them for whom he thus prepared the way and the place unto himself, that they also may be where he is. All the way he prepared. He descended into the lowest parts of the earth, into our state of sin and guilt and condemnation, that there he might choose his starting point for the race he was to run into that within the veil, the state of perfect and eternal righteousness and glory.

And the way that lies between that state of guilt and damnation as the starting point and the glorious inner sanctuary as the point of arrival was the way determined by the righteousness and justice of God, the way of death. And the running of that way of death was the act of perfect and loving obedience to the demands of the righteousness of God, so that the justice of God with relation to sin might be satisfied forever. It was the way of blood. That blood our forerunner, even Jesus, shed on the accursed tree of Golgotha. He carried his own blood into the inner sanctuary of God, into that within the veil. He is the forerunner indeed. In perfect, willing obedience he poured out his life before the face of the Father for those whom the Father had given him. And now for them the way is opened forever.

Such indeed is the object of our hope, the anchor of the soul of the believers, an anchor of hope that is secure and steadfast. For we know by faith that he entered into that within the veil for us, on our behalf.

What good would there be in an anchor, however securely it may be sunk in solid anchor-ground, if it is not also securely fastened to the ship that is to be anchored? Of what avail would it be for the heirs of the promise if Christ had merely run before from guilt to righteousness, from death to life, from the depth of hell to the highest heavens, and in so running had merited for those who are his the right of the righteousness and glory, the right to dwell in the tabernacle of God, if he had done no more? Of what avail would it be if the truth concerning our hope and the glory of our heavenly tabernacle with God, merited by Jesus Christ our Savior, were simply proclaimed to us, and we were admonished and exhorted to hold fast? Would the anchor of our hope be secure and steadfast if indeed on its heavenly side it rested immovable because God's work in Christ Jesus our Lord was perfect, but if on our side its security must be measured by our strength to hold fast?

Oh no! But Jesus our forerunner entered into that which is within the veil in our behalf, for us. He does not simply wait for us there, but he works for his own, whom the Father has given him. As our forerunner he prays for us. For he is not merely a mediator who merited for his people the right to follow him into glory. But he also mediates in actually drawing them into the blessed state of glory that is his own. He prays. He prays not for the world, but for those whom the Father gave him out of the world (John 17:9), the heirs of the promise, on whose behalf God swore by himself that they should inherit the blessing. And he prays: "Father, I will that where I am, there also may be those whom thou hast given me. Fill me as their head and mediator with all I merited for them, in order that I may bring them here, and they may be with me forever."[2] This prayer is always heard, because it is a prayer according to the will of God. For it is the Father's will that of all he gave unto the Son he should lose none.

Therefore, the forerunner, even Jesus, who entered into that within the veil, receives from the Father all he asks of him. And what he receives of the Father he bestows on us through the Spirit he has given us. He blesses us with all the spiritual blessings of salvation, makes us partakers of his resurrection life, justifies, sanctifies, and preserves us even unto the end. He draws us unto himself even through death and resurrection. And he works within our hearts the hope that is fastened to the object of the hope within the veil. And that object of the hope, as well as the act of hoping whereby we are fastened to the anchor, is sure and steadfast. It can never fail.

---

2    A paraphrasis of Jesus' priestly prayer in John 17.

## Chapter 8

# CHRIST
# OUR HIGH PRIEST

3. Without father, without mother, without descent, having neither beginning of days, nor end of life; but made like unto the Son of God; abideth a priest continually.

17. For he testifieth, Thou art a priest for ever after the order of Melchisedec.

*—Hebrews 7:3, 17*

I would like to call your attention to the priesthood of Christ. Christ is not only our chief prophet, but also our only high priest, who by the one sacrifice of his body redeemed us and makes continual intercession with the Father for us. And it is certainly true that Christ was priest also according to the order of Aaron. For also the high priest in the old dispensation sacrificed and made intercession for the people. Only, the Scriptures teach us that the priesthood of Christ was not limited to the priesthood of Aaron. He was more than Israel's high priest. And this greater excellency of Christ's priesthood is expressed in the scriptural statement that he was priest after the order of Melchizedek. And we do well to try to answer the question, first of all: What does this statement concerning the priesthood after the order of Melchizedek mean?

This is an important question, as is evident from the repeated emphasis of Scripture on this excellency of the priesthood of Christ. That the Messiah would be priest after the order of Melchizedek was already revealed in the old dispensation. For David spoke concerning him:

1. The LORD said unto my Lord, Sit thou at my right hand, until I make thine enemies thy footstool.

2.  The Lord shall send the rod of thy strength out of Zion: rule thou in the midst of thine enemies.
3.  Thy people shall be willing in the day of thy power, in the beauties of holiness from the womb of the morning: thou hast the dew of thy youth.
4.  The Lord hath sworn, and will not repent, Thou art a priest for ever after the order of Melchizedek. (Ps. 110:1–4)

We may notice at once that the priesthood of Christ is here presented as an everlasting priesthood and that it is closely connected with the royal exaltation of Christ to power and glory. This truth is repeatedly expressed in Scripture, and especially in the epistle to the Hebrews. The fact therefore that Christ was a priest not after the Aaronitic order, but after the similitude of Melchizedek, is strongly emphasized in the word of God.

Let us try to answer the question, first of all: What is implied in this for the priesthood of Christ? Who was this Melchizedek, and how must his excellency and peculiar priesthood be explained?

As I said before, in the epistle to the Hebrews we are told many things concerning this Melchizedek and concerning his priesthood, things that sometimes are hard to be uttered. This Melchizedek was king of Salem, priest of the most high God. And he blessed Abraham as the latter returned from the slaughter of the kings. And Abraham acknowledged his superiority, the superiority especially of his priesthood, by giving him tithes of all. Moreover, it is explained that his name denotes him as a king of righteousness, while the fact that he was king of Salem designates, of course, that he was king of peace. Stranger still, we are told that he was "without father, without mother, without descent, having neither beginning of days, nor end of life; but made like unto the Son of God; abideth a priest continually" (Heb. 7:3.)

In view of all this, we need not be surprised that the person of Melchizedek as he appeared in Genesis 14 has been variously explained. One theory has it that this Melchizedek is the son of Cainan (Gen. 5:12), who guarded the hill Golgotha, where Adam was buried, who died in the days of Cainan. According to others, he is the same as Shem, the son of Noah, who certainly was living in the days of Abraham. Still others dare not make Melchizedek, of whom such wonderful things are written, a mere man. They make him an angel or some kind of incarnation of the Holy Ghost, or of the Word, or some higher God. All these allegorical interpretations and conjectures, however, have no sound basis in Holy Writ. There can be no question about it that Scripture in Genesis 14 pictures Melchizedek as a real man of flesh and blood, who lived in the days of Abraham and who was king of Salem and a priest of the most high God.

There are also those who explain the priesthood of the historical Melchizedek as a remnant of the original priesthood of Adam in the state of rectitude. Adam, too, was priest of God. His priesthood was, of course, not that of redemption and had nothing to do with atoning sacrifices for sin. It simply consisted in Adam's calling and ability to love God and to consecrate himself and the whole creation to the living God. And this priesthood, according to some, was not at once completely lost through the fall into sin. A remnant of that priesthood remained and continued to reveal itself and express itself even unto the days of Melchizedek, in whom there is an especially glorious manifestation of this priestly office and function. With this interpretation we cannot possibly agree.

First of all, it is not in harmony with Holy Writ. In the light of Scripture, such a remnant of the original priesthood of Adam certainly is not in harmony with what the Bible teaches us concerning the state of fallen man, who is totally depraved. True, as we have stated before, in this original state of rectitude man certainly was priest of the most high God. He was God's officebearer, his friendservant; and he lived in covenantal fellowship with God. And as such, it was his calling not only to know and glorify the name of his God in the midst of all the earthly creation, but also as priest to offer himself and all things as a living sacrifice to the Most High. About this there can be no dispute. There was an original priesthood of creation.

But through sin this whole relation to God was turned into the opposite, into reverse. Man not merely lost the image of God, but his knowledge of God changed into darkness; his righteousness into perversion; his holiness into pollution and love of sin. We must certainly say that even as through sin man became the false prophet, loving the lie, so also he became a false priest. Instead of consecrating himself and all things unto God in love, he became an enemy of God and devoted himself to the service of sin and the devil. There is therefore no remnant of his original priesthood left in man.

Nor is it historically correct to maintain that after the fall there was a manifestation of this priesthood of creation in the line of fallen man, that this beautiful afterglow of man's original glory disappeared only slowly and gradually, and that in the priesthood of Melchizedek we find a final and marvelous reflection of this priesthood. Also that is not true. On the contrary, history as revealed in Scripture clearly traces another line of development after the fall with respect to this original priesthood of creation, the line of a false and wholly corrupt priesthood that has its commencement with Cain, continues in his generations, reaches a climax in the vainly boasting Lamech, and perishes in the flood. And after the deluge, there is the same line of development. In the world of heathendom, outside the covenantal line that runs through the generations of Abraham, men turn away from the living God, corrupt the glory of the Invisible One, make themselves gods after their own hearts, consecrate themselves through their idolatrous priests and shrines to gods of wood and stone, worship sun, moon, and stars, man, beasts, and creeping things, corrupting themselves in the lusts of their flesh, in immorality and bestiality of every imaginable sort.

But even among Israel there is found alongside the central line of the covenant and of the true priesthood a continuous line of carnal and wicked priesthood, represented by a veritable multitude of official priests who defile the sanctuary, make of God's house a den of robbers, lead the people in their worship of golden calves, and introduce into the holy land literally all the gods of the nations round about Israel. And when, in the fullness of time, the true high priest comes to his temple, it is this line of false and corrupt priests that hates him, rejects him, and ultimately nails him to the accursed tree.

And as it was in the old dispensation, so it still is in the new. Always the great majority of mankind still makes its own gods. Paganism is polytheism. But also in the midst of nominal Christendom the line of the false priests continues. The Christ of the Scriptures is rejected openly or transformed into the modern Jesus. The blood of atonement is despised and trampled underfoot. And although the man of modern culture does not make his gods of wood and stone or literally bow himself before calves and oxen, he is nevertheless an idolater whose carnal mind is enmity against the true and living God and who prefers to corrupt himself in the worship and service of the gods of his own imagination. In this historical line of development from the fall in paradise to the final manifestation of the man of sin in the antichristian dominion, there is no room for the priesthood of Melchizedek.

The place of Melchizedek and his priesthood will therefore have to be found in the line of grace. His historical origin must be traced, not to paradise and the state of original righteousness, but to the ark and to the grace Noah and his seed had found in the eyes of the Lord. Not in the line of reprobation, in which by the power of a certain so-called common grace a remnant of original integrity is preserved, but in the line of election, in the generations of the people of God, saved by sovereign grace, the priest-king Melchizedek, as Abraham met him after his victory over the allied kings, must be placed and interpreted. Historically, Melchizedek was a real man of flesh and blood. And all the strange things that are written of him in the epistle to the Hebrews dare not be applied to his person but must have reference to his peculiar priesthood as typical of the priesthood of Christ. As priest he stands without father or mother, without genealogy; but as a person he has his descent in the generations of the sons of God.

In the abstract it is quite conceivable that Melchizedek, even as a person, was called forth by a wonder of God's grace, simply for the purpose of creating an altogether unique type of Christ, so that even as a historical person he appeared suddenly and inexplicably, without any historical connection with his contemporaries, as a priest of the Most High. There are those who prefer this interpretation of this exalted figure. In that case, he simply appears as a wonder of God's grace. He cannot be explained in connection with the history of his time. There is no relation between him and the world of his day and environment. As a unique individual, as a marvelous exception, he appears in the midst of a wicked and perverse nation. And in the midst of a world full of iniquity, he appears as a priest of the most high God, a wonderful manifestation of the wonder of God's grace.

But there is no need of such an interpretation. And the sober narrative of Genesis 14 leaves quite a different impression. He was a real, historical person. He certainly was king of Salem, and he must have ruled over a real people. As king, he was also priest of God in the midst of his people; and in a sense, the people over whom he ruled as king-priest must have been people who were themselves consecrated to God as priests. The narrative of Genesis 14 leads to the conclusion that at the time when Abraham sojourned in the land of Canaan there still was a group of people, a small nation, who knew Jehovah and who worshiped the Most High, and who through Melchizedek as their high priest brought their sacrifices to the God of Shem. Indeed, the Canaanite, too, was in the land; and the Canaanite was accursed and had long trampled the covenant of Jehovah, established with Noah and his seed, underfoot.

But in the midst of a wicked generation there was also a remnant of God's people according to the election of grace, a people who knew and served the Lord, and who were headed and represented by the priest-king Melchizedek. But if this is true, it is but natural to look for a historical interpretation of this marvelous priest-king and his people. Only, this explanation must not be sought in the line of the wicked reprobates, but in the line of the generations of the people of God, in which, even outside of Abraham, God still preserved his covenant in those days.

Nor can this present any special difficulties. If we only bear in mind the organic development of God's covenant and its continuation in the line of generations, then it is at once evident that Melchizedek, as a priest of the most high God, together with the people over whom he ruled, has his origin in the ark. In the ark and through the flood the church of God had been saved out of the wicked world. With Noah and his seed God had established his covenant—not a certain covenant of common grace with all men, but his covenant in Christ in the line of election.

But as always, so also from the loins of Noah there developed a twofold seed: the seed of the promise and the carnal seed. The main line of the covenant, according to election, ran through Shem and was afterward more specifically limited to the generations of Abraham. But this may not be understood as if with the calling of Abraham God's covenant was strictly limited to him and his family, so that the father of believers was a lonely remnant of those who knew Jehovah and called upon the name of the Lord. He who would thus explain the situation at the time of Abraham's calling would fail to reckon with the organic development of the covenantal line in history.

Not at once and all of a sudden was the fear of the Lord limited to the generations of Abraham. For, first of all, during Abraham's life many of the old patriarchs from the generations of Shem that culminated in Terah, the father of Abraham, were still alive; and even Shem was still living when the father of believers was called. Even though the immediate ancestors of Abraham apostatized and turned to idols, there must have been thousands of others in the earlier generations who kept the covenant of Jehovah. Besides, although the generations of Shem had been mentioned as those who were destined to receive the covenantal blessing in a special sense of the word, for a long time the fear of the Lord must have been preserved also in the generations of Japheth. And it is not even improbable that also in the line of Ham there were still found those who called upon the name of God.

In view of all this, it is by no means strange that even in the land of Canaan at the time of Abraham a group of people is found who have the knowledge of the true God and who are ruled and represented by a priest-king like Melchizedek. Although, therefore, Melchizedek stands outside of the generations of Abraham, and perhaps even of Shem, Melchizedek as a historical person must be explained as belonging to the generations of those who fear the Lord and with whom God still continued his covenant. He was a priest of the Most High by grace; and as such he was a type of Christ.

# Chapter 9

# AFTER THE ORDER
# OF MELCHIZEDEK

3. Without father, without mother, without descent, having neither beginning of days, nor end of life; but made like unto the Son of God; abideth a priest continually.

17. For he testifieth, Thou art a priest for ever after the order of Melchisedec.

*—Hebrews 7:3, 17*

We already mentioned Melchizedek, who was a priest-king at the time of Abraham. Here we may have to repeat something; nevertheless, our chief subject is that Christ was priest according to the order of Melchizedek. This is mentioned more than once in Scripture. This is the teaching of that beautiful Psalm 110, to which we already referred. And this is further interpreted by the epistle to the Hebrews. Distinction is made between the priesthood of Aaron and the priesthood of Melchizedek. And with this distinction in view, Christ is said to be a priest after the order of Melchizedek.

This does not mean that there is an antithesis between the two. It does not mean that the two priesthoods exclude one another. It is evident that in a certain respect they were alike. Also the priesthood of Aaron foreshadowed that of the great high priest who was to come. Aaron, too, was a type of Christ. The situation is rather thus, that while the priesthood according to the order of Melchizedek included that of Aaron, the former is of a far more exalted character than the latter.

We may ask therefore, first of all: What is the distinction between the two orders of priesthood? In what respect was the priesthood of Melchizedek of a higher order than that of Aaron? Scripture emphasizes especially two points of difference. The first is that while among

Israel the priestly and royal offices were separated, so that one and the same person could not function in both offices, in Melchizedek they were combined. Melchizedek was a royal priest. And the second point of difference is that while the priesthood of Aaron in its specific meaning was temporal and must come to an end as soon as the perfect sacrifice was made, that of Melchizedek is everlasting. In both respects Christ was a priest according to the similitude of Melchizedek.

That this is true is evident especially, first, from Psalm 110. There we read: "The Lord hath sworn, and will not repent, Thou art a priest for ever after the order of Melchizedek" (v. 4). From these words it is evident that the priesthood after the order of Melchizedek was distinct from that of Aaron, as I already mentioned. In Psalm 110 the Spirit of Christ in the psalmist does not at all express his own personal experiences and circumstances but speaks directly of Christ. Its content can in no wise refer to the psalmist.

That this is true is evident, first of all, from the very first verse of the psalm: "The Lord said unto my Lord, Sit thou at my right hand, until I make thine enemies thy footstool." Christ in his controversy with the Pharisees refers to this word as proof that he is the Son of God:

41. While the Pharisees were gathered together, Jesus asked them,
42. Saying, What think ye of Christ? whose son is he? They say unto him, The son of David.
43. He saith unto them, How then doth David in spirit call him Lord, saying,
44. The Lord said unto my Lord, Sit thou on my right hand, till I make thine enemies thy footstool?
45. If David then called him Lord, how is he his son? (Matt. 22:41–45)

And we read that the Pharisees were not able to answer him a word (v. 46; see Mark 12:35–37; Luke 20:41–44). From the very first verse of the psalm, and from the application made of it by Christ, it is evident therefore that David is not at all speaking of himself; but he refers consciously and objectively to the Messiah. Him he calls his Lord. And to him Jehovah said: "Sit thou on my right hand, till I make thine enemies thy footstool."

This is evidently also true of Psalm 110:4, "The LORD hath sworn, and will not repent, Thou art a priest for ever after the order of Melchizedek." These words must not be interpreted as meaning that they were spoken by the people and addressed to David. That is not the case. First of all, this explanation is contrary to the tenor of the whole psalm, which, as has been shown, speaks of the Messiah directly. It is quite in harmony with the context to say that also these words are addressed to Christ. And second, they could not have been spoken of David: for the offices of priest and king were not combined in him. He was king of Israel; but the priesthood was found in the generations of Aaron, not in those of Judah and David. Hence, these words cannot have reference to David.

Nor can the interpretation be accepted that one of the priest-kings at the time of the Maccabees is the author of this psalm, and that the reference is to him. Oh, it is true that in some of the Maccabees the two offices of priest and king were combined in the same person; but the one great objection to this interpretation is that the psalm is Davidic, as is sufficiently proved by the Lord's own reference to it in the words quoted above. Hence, there is only one possibility, and that is that the words concerning the priesthood after the order of Melchizedek are immediately and directly messianic. They are put in the mouth of Christ. And this is also corroborated by the reference to them in the epistle to the Hebrews.

From the words that we quoted before, it is evident that the priesthood of Melchizedek was distinct from that of Aaron. First of all, it is distinct because the priesthood of Christ was a royal priesthood, as was, in a typical sense of the word, the priesthood of Melchizedek. In him, and therefore also in Christ, the kingship is combined with the priesthood. To Christ it was said: "Sit thou on my right hand, till I make thine enemies thy footstool." Moreover, to this victorious and exalted king, that is, Christ, it is promised by oath: "Thou art a priest for ever after the order of Melchizedek." Even as Melchizedek was a royal priest, or a priestly king, so also Christ will combine in himself the kingly and priestly office, and that, too, in final and highest perfection, at the right hand of God.

Second, in close connection with this combination of the royal and priestly offices, the priesthood after the order of Melchizedek is distinct in that it is forever: "Thou art a priest for ever." That cannot be true of the priesthood of Aaron. His priesthood came to an end; but that of Melchizedek is realized in Christ, and Christ is everlasting. He is everlasting also as priest-king.

We may also refer to the prophecy of Zechariah. There, too, the priesthood and kingship are combined in one person. Thus we read in the prophecy of Zechariah that the prophet is enjoined to take silver and gold of those who are of the captivity and have come from Babylon to Jerusalem. And of that silver and gold the prophet is enjoined to make crowns. And the crowns are set upon the head of Joshua the high priest, thus indicating prophetically that the priest shall be crowned king.

And now I quote Zechariah 6:12–13,

12. And speak unto him [that is, Joshua], saying, Thus speaketh the Lord of hosts, saying, Behold, the man whose name is The BRANCH; and he shall grow up out of his place, and he shall build the temple of the Lord:
13. Even he shall build the temple of the Lord; and he shall bear the glory, and shall sit and rule upon his throne: and he shall be a priest upon his throne: and the counsel of peace shall be between them both.

It is evident that in this prophecy we have a further prediction of what was already promised in Psalm 110. The passage I quoted has no reference whatsoever to an alleged covenant of redemption in the eternal decree of God, but it refers to the harmonious union between the king and the priest, united in one person, the person of the Branch, that is, of the Messiah.

All this is rather elaborately developed in the epistle to the Hebrews. Of Melchizedek as a type of Christ the author of this epistle is speaking and calling attention to his name and to the place of his reign. He explains that as a typical figure Melchizedek was both king of righteousness and king of peace. This is deduced from the name Melchizedek. For, according to the epistle to the Hebrews, Melchizedek signifies "King of righteousness," and as the noun *Salem* means "peace," king of Salem signifies "King of peace" (Heb. 7:2). And concerning this priesthood the author of the epistle to the Hebrews reminds us, first of all, that Melchizedek was a "priest of the most high God" (v. 1). And further, he describes him as appearing "without father, without mother, without descent, having neither beginning of days, nor end of life; but made like unto the Son of God; abideth a priest continually" (v. 3).

You understand, of course, that all that the author of the epistle to the Hebrews describes of Melchizedek and interprets cannot be applied to Melchizedek as a historic person, but only as a type of Christ, and with reference only to his priesthood. He appears in Genesis 14, as we have already pointed out, as priest, without any reference to his descent or genealogy. Nor is anything said about his end or about the continuation of his priesthood in his generations. He had no need, as did the Aaronitic priest, to prove that he descended from the priestly family. And in all this he is typically, not personally, made like unto the Son of God, the Christ, in whom all these typical traits are realized in highest perfection. And here again, the same two elements of the priesthood of Melchizedek that were mentioned in Psalm 110 appear on the foreground. He was priest-king, and his priesthood is everlasting. This cannot be said of Melchizedek as a historic person, but refers to him as a type of Christ, the Messiah who was to come.

In both these respects, namely, that the priestly office and the kingship were combined in one person, and second that he was a priest forever, Melchizedek was a type of Christ. Christ is the real Melchizedek. Christ is the real royal priest, the king of righteousness and the king of peace. Christ functions in both the royal and priestly office. And Christ's office was without end: it was everlasting.

It may be said indeed that there was a figure, or image, of the priesthood in the first Adam, in paradise in the state of righteousness. Adam was an earthly image of the eternal, heavenly priest-king. For Adam was very really priest of the Most High. This we cannot understand as long as we see the essence of the priesthood and of the priestly function in the offering up of bloody sacrifices. For this there was no room in the original state of rectitude of Adam. This was added after the fall, and it became necessary because of sin. But bloody sacrifices are not an essential element of the priesthood at all. Even as the prediction of future events, though belonging to the office of a prophet among Israel, cannot be considered essential to the prophetic office, so the offering up of bloody sacrifices, though for a time necessary on account of sin, is not the essence of the priesthood.

The central idea of the priestly office is that of consecration of oneself and of all things to the living God. A priest is a servant of God. He loves God. He consecrates himself to the Holy One. He serves in God's tabernacle, in his house. And in this sense Adam was surely priest of the most high God in the midst of the earthly creation. All things must serve him, that he might serve his God and be consecrated to him with all his heart and mind and soul and strength. And as priest, Adam was also king. Dominion was given him over all the earthly creation.

The royal and priestly offices, therefore, were harmoniously united in his person. And this was but proper. Only the servant of God has the right to have dominion. For only as long as he stands in the right relation to his God, that is, in subjection and obedience, can he properly rule over all things in the name of the Lord and according to his will. Prostrating himself in the dust before the sovereign of heaven and earth, and consecrating himself and all his power, together with the whole earthly creation, to the living God, Adam in the state of righteousness might have dominion and sway the royal scepter over all creatures. He was priest-king, servant-king, under God.

This, however, was different among Israel. There the two offices were strictly separated. Aaron was priest, but he did not sway the scepter. On the other hand, the king might not minister at the altar. Hence Aaron, though he was prefiguring a phase of the priestly office of Christ, was not his perfect type.

The perfect type is found in the figure of Melchizedek, king of Salem and priest of the Most High. His priesthood is realized in Christ. For Christ is the most perfect priest. He is the most perfect servant of Jehovah, whose meat it is to do the Father's will, and who, as the Son of God in human nature, is consecrated to him with his whole being. He is the only high priest over his brethren and is set over the whole house of God, to accomplish all things pertaining to God. And having accomplished all, and having become revealed as the perfect servant of Jehovah who became obedient unto death, even unto the death of the cross, the accursed death, he is now exalted at the right hand of the Majesty in the heavens, and henceforth expecting till all things shall be put under his feet.

And therefore, it is very evident that the priesthood of Melchizedek is perfectly fulfilled in him. He entered into the sanctuary above, a sanctuary that is not made with hands, and constantly consecrates himself and all things to the Father. And he has all power and authority in heaven and on earth; and he sits on his Father's throne. As the perfect high priest, he is also king of righteousness. And on the basis of God's everlasting righteousness, he is also the king of peace.

This priesthood of Christ is, of course, without end. It is everlasting. This was not and could not be true of the priesthood of Aaron. It represented, as I said, but a phase of the priestly calling of Christ. That phase it represented that had become necessary on account of sin. And this priesthood of Aaron could not be everlasting. It belonged to the way that the high priest must travel to realize his everlasting priesthood, his everlasting covenant with God. It was part of the work of Christ that must be performed to build the house of God. It was accomplished in the perfect sacrifice of Christ on the cross. And there it came to an end. Of this phase of the priesthood of Christ that of Aaron was a mere shadow. Hence, while the priesthood of Christ could be typified in just one figure, that of Melchizedek, the priesthood of Aaron must be spread over a long line of generations. For the blood of bulls and of goats could never blot our sin; it must ever be repeated until the perfect sacrifice of reconciliation had been offered in the blood of the cross.

But this could not last forever. Not only must there come an end to the sacrifices of bulls and goats, but also the perfect sacrifice of the high priest himself could never be repeated. But the priesthood of Christ could not reach its end even on Golgotha. It is everlasting. Forever he consecrates himself and his people and all things in perfect love to the Father. Presently, when all things are finished, the tabernacle of God will be with men. And in that heavenly tabernacle all things will be sanctified to God, and Christ will be everlasting king-priest, the king of righteousness and the king of peace, after the order of Melchizedek!

*Chapter 10*

# THE POWER TO PURGE OUR CONSCIENCE

How much more shall the blood of Christ, who through the eternal Spirit offered himself without spot to God, purge your conscience from dead works to serve the living God?

*—Hebrews 9:14*

By the blood of Christ, our consciences are purged from dead works. Thus the Scriptures teach us in Hebrews 9:14. The context points to the excellency of the New Testament high priest above that of the Old Testament. The Old Testament high priest came and functioned in an earthly tabernacle, a figure for the time then present, in which were offered gifts and sacrifices that could never make one perfect as pertaining to the conscience. Christ, however, came as the high priest in a greater and more perfect tabernacle, not made with hands, the heavenly sanctuary; and he came, not by means of earthly gifts and sacrifices, but by his own blood. And thus, he did what the Old Testament high priest could never have done: he obtained eternal redemption for us. If there were the power of a typical and ceremonial cleansing in the blood of bulls and goats, and in the ashes of an heifer sprinkling the unclean, "how much more shall the blood of Christ, who through the eternal Spirit offered himself without spot to God, purge your conscience from dead works to serve the living God?" To purge our conscience from dead works belongs, therefore, to the power of the cross. Let us investigate, first of all, into the meaning of this power, in order then to see how this power is in the cross, or, as the text has it, in the blood of Christ.

The text implies that, by nature, apart from the blood of Christ, we perform nothing but dead works; and that these dead works are written in our conscience.

Now, what are dead works? First of all, they are works that have their origin in, that spring from, death. The expression implies that, by nature, we are dead and that, being dead, in our state of death, we still perform works. This appears to be a contradiction in terms as long as we entertain the philosophical notion of death. For then we ask: How can one that is dead be active? Death is the state of inactivity. It is the end of all work. But this is not the Scriptural conception of death. According to the word of God, all men are dead, not when they die, but when they are born; and they are so really dead that, unless they are born all over again, they shall never see life. This is the truth which our Lord impressed upon the mind of Nicodemus, and which that teacher in Israel had great difficulty to understand. "Verily, verily, I say unto thee, Except a man be born again, he cannot see the kingdom of God" (John 3:3). And he must be born again, not by entering a second time into his mother's womb and being born over, for even if such a thing were possible, it would be of no avail. That which is born of the flesh is always flesh, and in that flesh death reigns and has dominion. He must be born of water and of the Spirit. Then, and then alone, does he live, and can he enter into the kingdom of God.

Apart from this new birth, therefore, all men are dead. When man was created, he lived. For he was endowed with the image of God, in true knowledge, perfect righteousness, and spotless holiness. His mind so operated that he knew the mind of God, he thought the thoughts of God, he saw and had his delight in the glory of God, he loved to sing the praises of God. His will was in full accord with the will of God, so that he longed and chose and was capable to live and move according to that will, and to perform the commandment of life. His whole nature was consecrated to the living God, so that he loved the Lord his God with all his heart and his whole being. And being thus in harmony with the living God, he walked in the light of God's countenance, had sweet and most intimate communion with his God, and knew himself to be the object of God's blessed favor. Such was man's life.

From this state of righteousness and life, he fell into the state of sin and death by his willful disobedience. And this state of death does not mean that he was destroyed or annihilated. Nor does it signify that he became wholly inactive. On the contrary, he continued to exist, and to move about in the world. Moreover, he remained a moral, rational being. He could still see and hear, speak and work, think and will and desire. It is true, much of his original powers he lost. Moreover, the curse was laid upon creation. But the fact remains that his fall into sin and death did not change him essentially. However, his whole nature was turned into reverse from an ethical viewpoint. His love of God was changed into enmity, so that he now hates God and his neighbor. His knowledge of God became darkness, so that he loves the lie and pursues it, and no longer has his delight in declaring the praises of his Creator. His righteousness turned into perversion of will, so that he is no longer capable of loving and choosing the good, and is inclined to all evil. His holiness was changed into the pollution and corruption of his whole nature, so that, instead of thirsting after the living God, he seeks self and the satisfaction of his carnal lusts. He is an exile from God's house, and the object of his wrath. Such is man's death. In that death, all men are born. And all the works he performs in that state are dead works. They have their origin in death.

Besides, works that spring from man's corrupt nature not only have their fountainhead in death, they are also, as to their ethical character and value, dead works. Negatively speaking, they are dead because the life of the love of God is not in them; and, positively, because they are all motivated by enmity against God. "For they that are after the flesh do mind the things of the flesh...for to be carnally minded is death... because the carnal mind is enmity against God: for it is not subject to the law of God, neither indeed can be. So then they that are in the flesh cannot please God" (Rom. 8:5–8). And do not imagine that this is applicable only to some of the works of the flesh, of the natural man, while, for the rest, he performs many good works that are acceptable to God. The tree is dead, and all its fruit is dead. The fountain is corrupt, and all its water is polluted. The carnal mind is enmity against God, and all its works are characterized by that enmity. Whether a man holds up a bank, or whether he donates a million dollars to some charitable institution, if his act is not motivated by the love of God, it belongs to the category of dead works. Man that is dead through trespasses and sins can only perform dead works, void of the living vibration of the love of God.

Finally, dead works are so-called also because they are worthy of death, and they lead to destruction. The truth of this is evident even in man's life and development in this world. Man that departs from the living God seeks and rushes into his own destruction, and brings death and destruction upon the whole world. He makes a desperate attempt to stem the tide of sin and death. He tries to adapt himself as much as possible, in an outward sense, to the law of God. But this enmity against God and the neighbor—his lust of the flesh and lust of the eyes and pride of life, his greed and covetousness, his malice and envy—lead him astray, and he fails in his attempt. And thus, he destroys all life. He boasts of his wisdom, establishes colleges and universities, opposes the wisdom of God, and creates a race of atheists. He commits adultery and destroys the very foundation of society: the home, making laws that make a mockery of the sacred institution of marriage. He lusts after wealth and pleasure, and creates continual strife.

And what is true of individuals is applicable to the nations of the world: they talk of peace, but their covetousness and envy, their spirit of hatred and revenge, involves them in the most deadly conflicts that become more dreadful and destructive in scope and character in the measure that an ungodly civilization provides them with more effective instruments of destruction. But even so, all is not said. For these dead works also lead man to eternal death. By these, he increases his guilt daily, and gathers unto himself treasures of wrath in the day of wrath, and of the revelation of the righteous judgment of God. Their end is eternal desolation!

Now, what does our conscience have to do with these dead works? That there is some connection is plain, for the text tells us that the blood of Christ is powerful to purge our conscience from them. And that seems to imply that, somehow, all these dead works remain in our conscience, and pollute it. What is our conscience? In this connection, it may be sufficient to say that our conscience is our awareness of, and our agreement with, our consent to, the righteous judgment of God over all our works.

Let me offer a few words of explanation of this biblical conception of our conscience.

God is Judge. He always judges all our works. Constantly, from moment to moment, in all our life and activities, we stand in judgement before him. He declares his just verdict on every act we perform. And we are aware of his judgment. For we have a moral consciousness. We discern the difference between good and evil. And in that moral consciousness, God inscribes his own judgment and just evaluation of our every thought, desire, word, and act. He makes this inscription through his revelation, whether in nature and providence, or through the Holy Scriptures; and by his Spirit. And that inscription of his righteous judgment is indelible.

Hence, all our dead works are inscribed in that conscience, together with God's verdict of condemnation and our agreement with that judgment. Our conscience condemns us. We know that we are worthy of death. A thousand voices are raised against us from within. We may try to silence them, but it is in vain. We may try to justify ourselves, but in our deepest heart we know that we stand condemned in the judgment of God. Our sins rise up against us and shall be exposed in all their damnableness in the day of the revelation of the righteous judgment of God, when the books shall be opened, and every one shall be judged according as his work shall be!

Now, the marvel of the gospel, the wonder of the word of the cross, is that it speaks of purging our conscience of those dead works, that is, of completely blotting out that otherwise indelible handwriting that testifies against us! Just think of the wonder of it all! Those dead works are still there. For the purging of our conscience from them does not mean that we are made to forget them. What is more, we still commit them. For we are never perfect as long as we are in the body of this death. Daily we sin. As far as we are concerned, even when we are reborn, we still increase our sin. But God's sentence of condemnation against us is no longer there. We are forgiven! No longer can our sins rise up against us from our conscience to condemn us. Nay, what is more, we receive the very testimony of God that we are righteous, that we are clothed with an everlasting righteousness that makes us worthy of eternal life! Our conscience is purged from the guilt of sin, from the damning verdict of God's justice, and we receive the testimony from God that we are righteous before him forever!

The power so to blot out the damning handwriting of our conscience is in the blood of Christ. It is in nothing else!

In that blood it is surely! It never fails. When that blood is sprinkled upon your conscience, it surely purges it from the guilt of sin. The text emphasizes this. If the sacrifices of the old dispensation made one typically and ceremonially clean, *how much more* will the blood of Christ purge our conscience from dead works!

But why is there this cleansing power in that blood? The blood of Christ is the life he poured out on the cross in perfect obedience to the Father, and that, too, in our stead, as our Representative, and on our behalf. And the text emphasizes a few things about this act of self-sacrifice on the part of Christ, in order to make plain why his blood has this power to purge our conscience from dead works. First of all, let us notice that it is the blood of self-sacrifice. By shedding his blood, Christ offered himself to God. And this means that his act of dying on the cross was of his own free choice and determination. He laid down his life, no one took it from him by force. He willingly shed his blood, no one drew it from his body. His death was an act of obedient love to the Father on behalf of sin. Hence, it was a sacrifice. Secondly, and in close connection with the first point, he could offer himself *without spot* to God. He had no sin. No dead works were inscribed in his conscience. There was no judgment against him. Of him, the Father testified: "This is my beloved Son, in whom I am well pleased" (Matt. 17:5).

Hence, he did not have to die for himself. And he was able to offer the perfect sacrifice, to express the perfect *yes* over against the *no* of our sin. Thirdly, he offered himself up "through the eternal Spirit" (Heb. 9:14). This may simply refer to his Godhead, or it may refer to the Holy Spirit. It is best to understand the term as referring to both. He is the Son of God. And as the eternal Son, very God of God, and Light of Light, he suffered all the wrath and judgment of God against sin, the Holy Spirit preparing and sanctifying him to the task in his human nature. Hence, his sacrifice was not only without spot, and acceptable to God, but, as the death of the Son of God, it is also of infinite value, abundantly powerful to atone for all the sins of all his own. By that blood of the cross, the guilt of our sins was completely blotted out, and an eternal righteousness was obtained for us, on the basis of which we are declared worthy of life everlasting.

That blood is sprinkled upon our conscience, by his own Spirit, through his own gospel, the word of the cross, and by means of the faith he gives us. It is all of him, and none of self.

And through the sprinkling of that blood upon our consciences, they are purged. When the Spirit begins to apply that blood of the Lamb to our consciences, we begin by seeing our sins in a new light: we are filled with a true sorrow after God, and repent in dust and ashes. We cry out with the publican: "God be merciful to me a sinner" (Luke 18:13). And in that blood, we find the answer. In the blood of the Lamb, we experience the power of redemption, of forgiveness, of the purging of our conscience, of perfect justification, so that we have peace with God. We have experienced and do experience the truth of the word of God: the blood of Jesus Christ our Lord cleanseth us from all sin! That is the power of the cross!

Yet, this is not the end. Having thus been redeemed, and our conscience having been purged from dead works, we also experience a new freedom: the liberty to serve the living God! As long as we are under guilt and condemnation, we have no right to this blessed service. We cannot, we will not, we cannot will to serve God, nor do we have the right to be delivered from this spiritual bondage. But in the blood of Christ, there is the power to cleanse our conscience from the guilt of sin, and, therefore, also the right to be delivered from the bondage of corruption. Justified, we are also sanctified. Redeemed, we are also delivered. And standing in that new freedom, we fight the good fight against sin and the devil, and, with a new delight in his precepts, we serve the living God, till he shall deliver us perfectly, and take us with him in his blessed tabernacle. There we shall serve him day and night!

*Part Two*

# A CLOUD
# OF WITNESSES

*Chapter 11*

# FAITH: THE SECRET
# OF THE CHRISTIAN'S LIFE

Now faith is the substance of things hoped for, the evidence of
things not seen.

—*Hebrews 11:1*

## 1

Although there is no superscription above this epistle to the
Hebrews that informs us as to what place this letter was addressed
and delivered, yet the contents establish it beyond a shadow of doubt
that the epistle is addressed to a community of Jewish Christians,
that is, of Christians who were converted to the Christian faith out
of Judaism. Everywhere almost in the early church there were such
Jewish Christians in the congregations founded by the instrumental-
ity of the apostles. And sometimes these Jewish Christians seemed to
constitute a large majority of the congregation, judging by the influence they exerted upon the life of the early church. But the community
addressed by the author of this epistle was peculiar in this respect, that
it must have been unmixed. It was, as is very plain from the contents, a
purely Jewish Christian church to which the apostle is writing.

And the fact that so much mention is made of the Old Testament
temple service gives reason to believe that they were Jews, that is, Christians from the Jews, perhaps at Jerusalem or at least nearby Jerusalem,
so that they were well acquainted with the temple, and what is more,
stood in daily temptation of falling back into the bondage of the shadows of the old dispensation. It is plain, at least, that this danger was the
occasion for the writing of this epistle to them. They were somewhat
disappointed with the Christian faith at this time. The Lord tarried to

come back, as he was expected. And this delay in the coming of Christ caused them to waver in their faith. Perhaps they had expected him to return soon. And wavering in their faith, they were much exposed to the temptation of relapsing into their old faith, and of falling back into the worship of the shadows after the real body had been revealed.

Hence the epistle is, first, an earnest warning against this danger and an exhortation to remain faithful to the end and to hold fast to the profession of their faith. The old dispensation had served its purpose. The temple had seen its day. The priests of the Old Testament were but shadows and types of the real Priest, who offered himself once forever. And therefore, they could not cling to the shadows, now that reality had come. The day of types had passed ever since the new day of reality had appeared.

This the writer makes plain in the first part of the epistle, called the dogmatic part, and extending from chapter 1:1 to chapter 10:18. In the nineteenth verse of the tenth chapter he begins his hortatory part, admonishing the brethren to abide by the true faith and not to grow weary. He assures them that they may now boldly approach the throne of grace by a new and living way, consecrated in the blood of Christ. He admonishes them to hold fast the profession of their faith (v. 23), as was delivered unto them by the apostles, and not to fall back into the error of Old Testament shadow-worship. And since many had already fostered the bad habit of forsaking assemblies, the apostle [1]warns them not to do so (v. 25), since that would only tend to greater apostasy from the true faith, and there is no redemption possible if the true sacrifice is rejected.

As an encouragement in their struggle, he reminds them of former days, when they remained faithful in the midst of affliction and persecution (v. 32) and exhorts them now to practice that same faith without growing weary on the long way. And if it should seem to them that the Lord tarried to come, he strongly reminds them that the righteous do not live by sight, but by faith (vv. 37–38). They evidently wanted to see. And not seeing as soon as they had expected, they grew

---

1 Hoeksema at times refers to the author of the epistle to the Hebrews as "apostle." He does the same with James, the author of the epistle (for instance, page 160). However, both attributions are disputed.

weak and discouraged! But they must learn that the righteous does not live by sight, but by faith alone. And to live by faith means the exact opposite from living by sight and experience. For, according to the words of our text: "Now faith is the substance of things hoped for, the evidence of things not seen" (Heb. 11:1).

We can readily understand that the writer of this epistle does not mean to give an exhaustive definition of faith in this first verse of chapter 11. On the contrary, he merely means to consider the gift and power of faith from a certain aspect, namely, as the evidence of things unseen and as the substance of things hoped for. This, of course, is not all that faith contains. No more than I give a complete definition of the Scriptures when I say that the word of God is the delight of the children of God, no more does the writer of this epistle give an exhaustive definition of faith when he says: "Now faith is the substance of things hoped for, the evidence of things not seen." Faith implies far more. It is, as we know, also the power by which we appropriate our Christ. It is the means whereby we are ingrafted into him, so that we are one plant with him. It is the root of the entire spiritual life of the Christian, so that from it all the other Christian virtues spring forth as the fruit of the tree.

But here the writer views faith from a certain point of view. He views it as the secret of the life of the Christian in the midst of this world. So often it looks foolish, what the Christian does, and what he confesses and says. So often the world laughs at his simplicity. So often it seems to the world as if the Christian is foolish in denying himself the pleasures and treasures of the world for something he does not even see. And the question is asked sometimes: How is it possible that the Christian can do these things? Does he not follow after a mere phantom, while he forsakes that which is real, that which we can see and hear and touch? And the answer of Scripture is: the righteous shall live by faith (Heb. 10:38). And faith is the very opposite of sight. God does not want us to see, but to believe. And faith is all sufficient, for it is the evidence of things unseen.

"Not seen" in the words of our text, of course, is to be understood in a most general sense of the word, as of things that escape all our experience, our natural perception, entirely. There is a world that appeals to our sense, a world that can be perceived. God has created man in such a marvelous way that he stands in connection with the world outside of him in a fivefold way, through his five senses. God has given him the sense of sight, so that he can see the world; the sense of hearing, so that he can hear it. God gave him the sense of touch, so that he can feel the outside world; the sense of smell, so that he can smell it; and the sense of taste, so that he can taste it.

It is through the means of these five senses, by which man stands in contact with the world outside of him, that he becomes convinced, immediately convinced, of the reality of the world in which he lives. Man beholds a tree, and it is impossible to doubt that the tree is actually there. He believes his eyes. He becomes aware of a certain fragrance in the air, and immediately he draws the conclusion that there must be a rose in the vicinity. He believes his sense of smell. And thus it is with all our senses. Man stands in contact with the world outside of himself. He experiences, he perceives, that world in many ways; and he becomes assured that the world really exists.

But now our text speaks of things unseen. And then we must not merely apply this in a special sense, as if the things of which the writer speaks were merely invisible while perhaps they might be touched or heard or tasted or smelled, but in a general sense. There is a world that escapes our experience entirely. There is a world that entirely eludes our perception. There are things that we can neither see nor hear, things that cannot be touched or tasted or smelled—things the existence of which is entirely hidden from our natural perception. And if you ask the Christian how then he knows that this world of unseen things is real and true and actually exists, then he answers: "By faith, and by faith only. For faith is the evidence of things unseen."

Those unseen things, the reality of which is evident to the believer, may be divided into three classes, namely, those of the past, of the present, and of the future. The entire past is hidden from our view in a certain sense of the word. It refers to things that were once, but that are no more except on record. And to a certain extent every historian must have faith in a general sense, in order to believe those facts. That past no one can see anymore.

Thus, but now in a special sense of the word, it is also with the Christian. The Christian believes as the author tells us in verse 3, that the world was created by the Word of God. No one was present at that creation. The creation as such, as an act of God, was unseen. Nevertheless the Christian believes it and understands it by faith. For faith is the evidence of things unseen. The Christian believes that this world was once good and without sin and imperfection and suffering and death, and that man lived in perfect harmony with the law and in highest bliss in the first paradise, although it belongs to the world of unseen things and although present experience contradicts it. For faith is the evidence of things unseen. The Christian knows that Noah was saved in the ark, while all the world perished; that Abraham was called to be the father of all believers; that Moses performed his mighty miracles in the land of Egypt; that Elijah was fed by the ravens, etc. All these things were once, and occurred once, but are no more, and are for that reason unseen, while at the same time the age of miracles is past, so that they are never seen anymore in this dispensation. But faith is the evidence of things unseen.

The Christian believes in the greatest of all wonders, the incarnation of the Word of God in Jesus Christ our Lord. He believes that the Son of God in the flesh came to take away our sins and transgressions upon his mighty shoulders, and that he died for them on the cross, that he rose from the dead, and that he ascended into heaven. He believes that the Spirit was poured out in that wonderful way on the day of Pentecost. All these things are invisible, not only because they belong to the past, but also because they are events that happen nevermore, so that we cannot see their like in our present day. They are things invisible.

But there is more. There also is an unseen world in the present, which is nevertheless very real for the Christian. The Christian believes that God is, although God is also absolutely invisible. No one, so the Scripture tells us, has ever seen God. And surely, to our natural experience he is invisible. We can never perceive him with our eyes. We cannot hear him with our natural ears. We cannot touch him and feel him.

He escapes our experience from the natural point of view, and it need not surprise us that there are men called atheists, who deny that God is. Even though it is true that God impresses that he is upon the heart and mind of every man in the world, these atheists, however, philosophize long enough to cover up that conviction. They argue that they cannot find out God with their natural powers. They can indeed scan the heaven; but they do not see him. They can examine the remotest stars, so they say; but he is not there. He escapes our vision entirely.

But the Christian can never be an atheist. To him God is real in the highest sense of the word, because he lives by faith in the revelation of the Most High. There is a heaven, and there are things heavenly. There is another world than ours. There is a city not built with hands, but eternal in the heavens (2 Cor. 5:1). There is a place of highest glory and bliss, a place where there is no sin and no misery, a place where the heavenly spirits surround the throne of God and sing their hymns of praise day and night to his glory, a place where also the saved souls in Christ Jesus dwell, and where Christ sits at the right hand of God.

All these things, and many more, are real to the Christian. That world exists for him. But that world is not the object of his experience. That world he has never seen. From that world he has never heard a sound. That world has always escaped his every perception. That world is hidden in the dark. That world belongs to the things unseen. Yet, to him, it is very real. For he believes. And faith is the evidence of things unseen.

Finally, there is also a very real world that is still future, that is real to the Christian, but that belongs to the things that are not seen. Even as the past, so also the future escapes our vision. We are children of the present. The past we cannot see because it is no more; the future we cannot perceive because it is not. And still the Christian tells you wonderful things about that future. He informs you that he expects to live after he has died. In spite of the fact that he sees the bodies of all his fellow Christians decay and pine away one after another, so that nothing but a miserable heap of dust is left of them, he maintains that there is a life after this life, that the soul never dies but passes on into higher spheres, and that also the body of the Christian, although surrendered to corruption, shall once inherit eternal glory and bliss.

No, still bolder are his expectations of the future. Not only does it stretch forth to things that pertain to him personally, but also to the world. That entire world shall once be delivered from the bondage of corruption. Christ shall return on the clouds of heaven, and he shall establish his kingdom. He shall cause a new heaven and a new earth to spring into existence, a world in which there shall dwell righteousness forevermore. That is the world in the future, which is real to the Christian—so real that already he lives in that unseen world.

In conclusion, I wish to emphasize that the things of faith are very real to the Christian. Do not say that for him it is a mere theory, and that in reality this world of unseen things is no more real to the Christian than it is to the unbeliever. For he shows in his entire life that this world of the future and the world of unseen things is very actual to him. He forsakes the present world for it. He denies himself for it. He does not seek after the things of the present and goes through this world as a pilgrim and as a stranger, expecting with uplifted head the world that is to come. And yet it must be said that this entire world belongs to the things unseen. No one ever saw it. No one ever had any perception of that world. No one ever heard a sound from it. But the Christian believes. And faith is the evidence of things unseen.

## 2

I emphasized especially that faith is contact with an entire world of invisible things—things in the past, things in the present, and things in the future.

Now the text emphasizes that faith is *evidence*, evidence of things unseen. This does not mean that faith is proof. For faith is never proof. A proof is something that is valid also for the other man. A proof is objectively valid. And if faith were a proof, the believer ought to be able to demonstrate the reality of his unseen world to the unbeliever, so as to convince him of it. And that is never possible. My faith has no value for anyone but myself and my fellow believer. It is no proof for anyone else. My faith is evidence only for me, and for all who believe.

When the text therefore tells us that faith is an *evidence* of things unseen, this must not be taken in the sense of proof, but rather in the sense of immediate assurance. The believer is immediately certain of the reality of that unseen world in which he believes. If it is true that he can never prove anything to the unbeliever, the reverse is also just as true, that the unbeliever can never argue long enough to convince the Christian believer that the world in which he believes is not real. Even as the sight of the tree convinces every man of the reality of that object, so the faith of the Christian is sufficient to assure him of the reality of that entire world that escapes his experience and that is no object of his perception. Can you prove that the tree is there? Of course not, you say. To maintain this is folly. That needs no proof. When I see the tree, I am convinced that it is real. Can you prove that this unseen world really exists? Surely not, neither is this necessary. I believe that it exists. And that is for me and for any believer sufficient.

Can you prove that God created the world? Not at all, but that is not necessary. I am convinced that it is so because of faith. And if you say a thousand times that this is not true, that does not affect me in the least. You demand proof that Christ is the Son of God in the flesh and that he died for sinners? This also is absolutely impossible, but also equally unnecessary. It is true, I cannot give any other evidence than the testimony of the word of God. But that is sufficient, for I believe that the word of God is true. I am assured that Jesus died for sinners like me, as you are that the ground on which you stand is real. But I believe it, and faith is the evidence of things unseen.

You want proof of the resurrection from the dead? Proof of the reality of heaven and of heavenly things? You want proof of the life after this present life, the life after death? You want proof of the final glory and the resurrection of the body? That is impossible. For these things do not belong to the world of seen things, to the world of weight and measure; and therefore I cannot prove them. Neither do I need proof. I assure you that all these things are very real, and I am inwardly assured of their reality. For I believe, and faith is the evidence of things unseen. So clear and positive an evidence is faith for me that I am more positive of this unseen world than you are of the things visible. I am so positive that the unseen world exists that this invisible world influences my entire life, that it is the motive of all that I do, so that I really already live more often in this unseen than in the visible world.

We understand, of course, that faith is not independent. It is not thus, that faith without anything else gives us the assurance of the reality of things unseen. Faith does not within itself carry the contents of things invisible. Or, in other words, ask the question whether we also derive the object of our knowledge from faith, and whether faith itself tells us anything about the invisible world, and you feel immediately that this is not the case. On the contrary, for its material, for its contents, faith is dependent on the Scriptures. Without the Bible, without that word of God, faith would be blind.

Without that word of God man might probably have the power to believe, the power to accept unseen things as realities, but there would be no world for him to accept. He would then be like a man who possessed all his five senses, but who stood in space absolutely empty. There would be no world to see, though his sense of sight were ever so keen. There would be no sound to hear, though his hearing were ever so sharp. There would be nothing to see and to hear and to accept. And thus would be the man with faith but without the word of God, if you can for a moment imagine such a person, which, of course, is impossible. He would not know anything of that unseen world.

Faith as the evidence of things unseen, therefore, clings to the testimony of the word. That word reveals that invisible world. But it reveals it only to faith. Without the word, faith is blind. Without faith, the word is empty. Without the word, there would be no unseen world to believe in. Without faith, that unseen world can never be reality to anyone.

But, you ask, if that is so, if faith is the evidence, that positive assurance of things unseen, why am I so often swung to and fro, like a reed shaken by the wind? Why do I live so little in that unseen world, if I by faith am so positively sure of its existence? And the answer is that the trouble lies not with faith, for faith cannot doubt, but with the lack of faith, with our old nature. Faith is the evidence of things unseen. It is absolutely positive. It is unshakeable. Faith itself can never doubt.

But that faith is often so small. It is frequently covered by the unbelief of our sinful nature. The things that are seen most frequently captivate our attention, fill our soul to the very brim, so that there is no place for the world of unseen things. Material things, things that can be touched and tasted, things that can be seen and heard and enjoyed by the flesh, are the objects of our diligent search. And the result is that we apply this fleshly method also to the unseen world. We want to see instead of to believe. We try to make the unseen world evident for our natural perception. And the result is that we fail. And as we are discouraged, we begin to doubt. We do not believe in the reality of the unseen world as firmly as we should.

And therefore, what we must do is exercise that faith, and always let it be in close contact, in living connection, with the word of God as we have it in the Scriptures. The faith that is the evidence of things unseen must constantly be fed by the word of God. And then, instead of trying to live by sight, we must live by faith as an evidence of things unseen. Then you shall live more and more in the reality of the unseen world. And accepting that reality, you shall hope firmly that once that unseen world shall be seen and possessed by all believers, by you personally. For faith, as true evidence of things unseen, is also the substance of things hoped for.

Hope—what is hope? In a certain natural and general sense of the word we may say indeed that hope is one of the most powerful factors in every human life. It is the strong support in suffering, the sustaining power in times of adversity, the inspiration of joy, the incentive to action and life itself. As children of time, we can live neither in the past nor in the present. But we always stretch ourselves spontaneously, involuntarily, toward the future. The past has not satisfied. And reflecting upon that past, we wonder how it was possible that we ever were as satisfied with it as we actually were. It looks at the very best stale and miserable. The present does not satisfy, for it is not the highest pinnacle of our ambition.

In the future: there lies our bliss, our happiness, our hope. The child longs for the time that he will be called a youth. The youth stretches longingly forth to manhood. And the man looks still to the future as his hope, till the days come of which we say: "We have no pleasure in them." Morning longs for the full day; and the full day for the eveningtide. Winter looks forward to spring; and the bosom of spring heaves with longing for the summer. The poor man hopes for improvement of his condition; the rich for more riches. All the world lives and labors in the future, and for that very reason, in hope. And that is the reason why death is so utterly hopeless for the world, since it has no longer any expectation. It is a cutting off of the future in its very idea.

But we must not confuse the Christian hope with this general longing and hope of the world. For it is essentially different. The hope of the world means little more than a certain longing for things in the future. There is no certainty in the hope of the world. Hope means a longing doubt. It is mixed with a painful uncertainty, all the more painful according as the longing is more intense. But that is not the case with the hope of the Christian. Also for the Christian hope is a stretching forth in longing after things in the future. Also in his case it implies a thorough dissatisfaction with the present state of things. But instead of the uncertainty of the world, the hope of the Christian, of the believer, is sublimely certain of the reality of its object.

For many things the Christian hopes, indeed, for things to hope for which the world deems folly and fanaticism. He hopes for a future world. He hopes that after this present house of his earthly tabernacle shall be dissolved, he will have a house with God, not made with hands, eternal in the heavens. He hopes that he shall be delivered from the body of sin in the future, that he shall once inherit eternal glory and bliss. He hopes that his Lord Jesus Christ shall return to deliver all his people and to establish his kingdom forever, a kingdom of peace and righteousness and glory. And in hoping for these things, which are all unseen, he is so certain that he passes by the things that are seen many a time, that he forsakes the world and all its treasures and pleasures, and that he walks his path with head erect, looking constantly toward the future, where he shall lay down the staff of his pilgrimage and receive the eternal crown of glory.

The Christian hope is certainty. It is the certainty of faith. And as it is the certainty of faith, so it is also intense spiritual longing for the object to come. Hope is indeed expectation; but it is not a cold expectation. It is the expectation of the longing to be with Christ: for that is far better.

But why is it, so we ask, that the Christian is so certain in his hope? And the text tells us that faith is not only "the evidence of things not seen," but also "the substance of things hoped for" (Heb. 11:1). Of course, that does not mean that faith itself is the basis of those things: for that is not so. Our faith is not the basis of the existence of heaven and of the heavenly things for which we hope. But it means that faith

85

is the inner confidence as an element of hope. Hope does not exist alone in the heart of the Christian. It is not thus, that hope is one power, and faith another, so that the two would exist independently of each other. It is not thus, that faith can be strong, but that there is little or no hope. Nor is it possible that there can be real hope where there is no faith.

No, faith is the root of hope. Take faith away, and you lose the very substance of hope. Take faith away, and you have no more that calm assurance that the unseen world really is there, and that it is for you. Take faith away, and you lose that assured confidence that you will inherit this world invisible that is to come, the world of everlasting life and glory. And therefore, not hope without faith, nor faith without hope can possibly exist. The two go hand in hand. They stand in most intimate relation to each other. Where you meet the one, you also meet the other. And if you should seem to meet the one alone, you may as well make up your mind that it is false, that it is an imitation.

Faith is the substance, that which gives support, that which lends certainty to hope. Hope is faith stretching forth to future bliss. And therefore, the believer is certain of the world of his hope, so certain that he lives as if that world were already in his possession. By hope he is saved. By hope he lives. By hope he is filled with joy not only when worldly prosperity envelops him as a cloud and when he meets but roses on his path, but also then, when the world visible becomes dark, when affliction is his portion, when all in the world that is seen seems hopeless—even when he must suffer for the sake of his faith, for Christ's sake. For even then he takes his flight above the world that is seen, and lives in higher spheres by faith, which is the evidence of things unseen and the substance of things hoped for. That faith, that hope, makes the Christian a real spiritual hero. It makes him the victor of the world in Jesus Christ his Lord.

Do we have that faith? Or rather, let me ask: Do we live in and by that faith? Are we partakers of that strong and living hope? Is the invisible world real to us? Does it exert its influence upon our life in the world that we see, in the present world? Oh, if not, how poor, how narrow, how miserably limited is our life.

Indeed, we hear much of narrowness and narrow-mindedness in our day. But how narrow is he who can take in his view only the things that are visible. He who lives for the things that are seen, that can be touched and grasped, that can be heard and enjoyed, that can be weighed and measured, he who lives for material things only, how narrow, how poor, how miserable is such a person. Limited by the material, he is bound on all sides. Measured by time, his hope ends with death. No God, no heaven, no eternal life and no eternal future, no hope beyond the temporal, no ideals beyond the material, he has. And therefore, without that faith and that hope, our life is poor and miserable.

But once more: Have we that hope? Have we that faith? Do we live in that faith and in that hope? It would seem that sometimes we possess but very little of it. If we have the firm faith in things invisible, why do we so often live entirely for the things visible, while the things unseen have no noticeable influence over our lives? Oh surely, we believe in the unseen world. But that unseen world is so often no living reality for us. And for that very reason our hope is so often weak, so often on the point of dying, as it seems. And therefore, if it is true that you possess that faith that is the evidence of things unseen and the substance of things hoped for, live in that faith. The apostle means to say that this faith is so great and such a tremendous power that it inspired all the heroes of faith he mentions in the rest of this chapter. And what they did is summarized exactly in the words of the Savior: "Seek ye first the kingdom of God, and his righteousness; and all these things shall be added unto you" (Matt. 6:33).

*Chapter 12*

# ABEL'S MORE EXCELLENT SACRIFICE

By faith Abel offered unto God a more excellent sacrifice than Cain, by which he obtained witness that he was righteous, God testifying of his gifts: and by it he being dead yet speaketh.

*—Hebrews 11:4*

## 1

We now turn to the first of what are called the heroes of faith. He is described to us in Hebrews 11:4.

We must constantly bear in mind, as we discuss the various heroes of faith mentioned in this beautiful eleventh chapter of the epistle to the Hebrews, that the writer considers faith not in general but from a certain particular point of view. He looks at faith from the viewpoint he announces in the first verse of the chapter, namely, as the substance of things hoped for and the evidence of things not seen. Or, if you please, he looks at faith as the power by which the Christian clings to things invisible. We discussed this in our last chapter, and we saw that as such, faith is the power through which the world that is invisible, that is, the world that escapes our natural perception, becomes real to the believer. It is the evidence of things unseen. The Christian is inwardly assured of the reality, of the real existence of a world he cannot see. He does not only believe in things he can perceive and things he can see and hear and touch; but he also knows that there is a world that eludes his natural perception, that baffles his every attempt to see or touch it.

And if you ask the Christian why and how he becomes assured of the reality of that other world, he tells you simply: by faith. That is

Scripture throughout the chapter we are discussing now. The Christian can give no proof. And yet he feels sure that the world of invisible things is real. And what is still more, he already lives in that unseen world, just as well as in the world that is visible, and that through that same faith. For that same faith is also the substance of things hoped for. He hopes for many things. And those things are all unseen. He hopes for what never eye has seen, or ear has heard, and what is still more strange, which really contradicts everything in the world visible.

That hope is not a mere longing, filled with doubt and uncertainty, but it is the firm hope of which faith is the substance. By faith he is inwardly confident that the things he hopes for are real, and that they shall once be given into his possession. That they shall once be realized he does not doubt. From that point of view the author of this epistle considers faith.

Now it ought to be very clear that this power of faith causes a difference in life between him who possesses it and him who lacks that power of faith. There is an inward difference between the believer and the unbeliever. And this inner difference is bound to manifest itself in outward life. The believer is the one who sees by faith the invisible world, who consequently is also influenced by that world. He lives not merely for this world, but he also lives for the world of unseen things. He even is dominated in his entire life by that world invisible. That world also claims his thoughts and his willpower. That world molds his life-view and all his actions, so that actually it becomes evident in his whole life that he believes and lives in a world not visible to the natural eye.

The unbeliever, however, has only the world of visible things. He knows of no other world than the one he can see and hear and lay his hands on. He cannot understand the life-view of the believer. He does not comprehend the glitter that shines in the eyes of the believer, but that is nothing more than a reflection of the light and glory of the world invisible. He thinks the Christian foolish when he walks as a pilgrim on earth, with head erect, in expectation of a world to come. And he lives for no other world than the one he can weigh and measure. In a word, there is a fundamental difference between the two, and the faith of the Christian is bound to distinguish him from the unbeliever in his entire life. An illustration of this difference we find in the words of our text. And we will study this difference in the first of the two brothers, as we treat Abel's more excellent sacrifice.

In the discussion of Cain and Abel we are very apt to forget that they were both religious men and that they both brought their offerings to the Lord. Yet that is exactly what our text tells us. And that is also what we read in Genesis 4, where the history of Cain and Abel is recorded. We are accustomed to look upon Cain as a very wicked man, as a downright infidel, as thoroughly irreligious. And we are used to compare him with people who must have nothing of God and his service, with people whom we in our day probably would place behind prison doors or send to the gallows. But this is not the case.

Oh, essentially this certainly was the case. And this also becomes manifest when he kills his brother Abel. But that is not by any means the case at first. If that had been the case, the matter would have been very plain and easy from the start. Then Cain would have been very wicked, and Abel very pious. Then Cain would have been a manifest unbeliever, an atheist, an infidel of the worst sort, while Abel was very clearly a child of God. Then the faith of Abel as an evidence of things unseen does not become so evident, nor is it so clear from this point of view that it was exactly this that Cain lacked.

And therefore, we will have to revise our view of Cain somewhat and begin with the fact that Cain as well as Abel brought his offering to the Lord. And whatever else may have been expressed in the offering, certainly that sacrifice was an element of worship and service. You must not classify Cain all at once with the outcasts of our time, with the wicked people, with the robbers and thieves and drunkards. You must not classify him with the downright infidel, who does not believe in God and who thinks that it is foolish to serve him. Then you can never explain why Cain also brought his offering. Unbelievers, infidels, are they who openly say: "We care not about God, and we regard it as folly to serve him." Cain did not say so. He believed in God. He also wanted to serve him. And therefore, he faithfully brought his sacrifice, as well as Abel.

An offering was at any rate the expression of service and devotion and love, the expression of willingness to acknowledge that all good gifts come from above, come from God. It is the expression of total dependence upon the Most High. It is the expression also of thankfulness. If Cain had lived in our day, he would have been called a Christian. He would have been full of the idea of service. He would have been the first one to proclaim a day of prayer or a day of general thanksgiving. He would have been a faithful churchgoer, and he would have put large gifts in the collection. I think that if Cain had lived in our century, he would have been classified by many as a model Christian, as a man who was filled with the idea of the fatherhood of God and the brotherhood of man.

For never should we forget that Cain offered a sacrifice to God. And according to Genesis 4, he was even the first one who brought the offering. We read that Cain brought his offering unto the Lord, and that Abel brought his offering also. And instead of classifying Cain simply with the manifest unbelievers and wicked people, we will have to classify him with the people who bring sacrifice to God, that is, with people who serve him. Both Cain and Abel were religious people, as is evident from their offerings.

And yet there was a fundamental difference between the two men. And this radical difference consisted exactly in this, that Abel possessed faith, faith as an evidence of things not seen and the substance of things hoped for; but Cain did not. We must remember that the author means to say that Abel possessed faith as such. Abel therefore saw things that Cain did not see. Faith is an evidence of things unseen. And Abel hoped for things of which Cain had not the slightest idea.

What then, so we ask, did Abel see? As becomes evident from the difference in their sacrifices, Abel, first, saw the holiness and righteousness of God. And over against this, he saw his own sinfulness and condemnation. Of this Cain had no idea whatsoever. Cain and Abel differed fundamentally in their view of life and of the world and of God. Cain did not see anything abnormal in the world, did not see anything abnormal in himself, did not see anything abnormal in his own relation to God.

We imagine that it must have been difficult at that time to detect sin even from the natural point of view. Things were all so different than they are in our time. If it is impossible to detect sin as such without the power of faith, if it is impossible in our day to come to a true realization of sin by mere natural understanding, by mere natural vision and power, how much more difficult it must have been in that early morning of creation. In our more intricate relations, now we daily hear of theft and robbery, of murder and suicide, of hatred and war, of adultery and corruption, it is impossible to convince the world of its sinfulness. How much more must this have been the case in that early dawn of the history of the world. Even now, when the world is, as it were, in agonizing misery because of sin, people keep on talking of a great future, of universal peace.

And they do not acknowledge that at the bottom of all questions and problems of the age lies the guilt and sin of man. Oh, man is not so sinful, even though he is not perfect. Man is essentially good, if only he develops in the right direction. There is no such thing as total depravity. There is no such thing as regeneration necessary for man. And there is no need of an atoning sacrifice. God is still our Father, and we are all brothers, whether we be regenerated or not. All this is fundamentally only a denial of sin as guilt. God is not a God of wrath and righteousness and holiness, but he is the God of love. And if we only offer him our service, he will accept us and not condemn. Thus the world reasons today. And the world is very religious.

But how much more, we repeat, how much more difficult it must have been in that early morning of creation to detect sin and evil. Why, all was still peaceful. Oh, it is true, once in a while a thistle and a thorn sprang from the earth, but was not this natural? Once in a while a lion would threaten destruction to the primitive family; but was that not in the very nature of the animal? There was no robbery, no theft, no war, no suicide. There were not those public evils we can see every day in modern society. The power of sin had not developed yet as it has developed today. And all creation must have looked rather pure and tranquil and attractive. Who could see the wrath of God? Who could detect the condemning curse of God over creation? Never a one had seen death as yet, and the misery of sin was practically unknown.

Cain therefore did not see and acknowledge the fierce wrath of God and his own sinfulness. He was a religious man. He brought his offering every so often. He served God. Surely, he must have been very acceptable. It was very narrow-minded to say that he was worse than Abel. Father Adam and Mother Eve must have told the boys of sin and of the wrath of God. For they knew by experience what it meant to be a sinner. But Cain thought they were mistaken. Cain simply could not see it that way. He only judged by what he saw. And according to all signs, this was a pretty good world, and he could probably make it a good deal better still. Cain did not believe. He did not have the faith as an evidence of things unseen and as the substance of things hoped for.

But Abel believed. When his father would tell him about their sin and condemnation, he would listen and say: "Yes, so it is. I'm a sinner, and God is righteous. And as I am, God can have nothing to do with me." He felt the wrath of God. He realized his own corruption and guilt and unrighteousness. He possessed the faith whereby he saw the reality of unseen spiritual things and whereby he lived in an invisible world. Abel believed God, and Cain did not. Abel had the faith as an evidence of things unseen; Cain lacked that faith. Abel had the faith of which he hoped for the coming of another and glorious world; Cain lived in the present world of things that are seen. He lacked the faith that is the substance of things hoped for.

And this inward difference manifested itself naturally also in their outward life, particularly, according to the text both here and in Genesis 4, in their offering. We must not make a mistake. I have seen pictures of Cain and Abel offering that completely misrepresented the fundamental idea of their sacrifice. Cain and Abel are both offering the same sacrifice. But the smoke of Cain's offering dissipates and is scattered by the wind, while that of Abel's offering ascends beautifully heavenward as a sign of God's favor. This is a fundamental mistake. It proceeds from the idea that the offering of Cain was in itself just as good as that of Abel, and that the only difference between the two was that Abel's offering was brought in faith, and Cain's in unbelief. If Cain had only believed, he might have brought the very same offering he did now, and it would have been accepted. The offerings of the two brothers were the same essentially and in themselves; but Abel offered in faith, and Cain did not. And hence, the one was accepted and the other rejected.

But this is erroneous. Our text emphatically states that "by faith

Abel offered unto God a more excellent sacrifice than Cain" (Heb. 11:4). Faith was therefore merely the inward principle by which Abel offered a different sacrifice than Cain. There was, in fact, a difference in their sacrifices—a difference so great that the sacrifice of Abel was accepted, and that of Cain was rejected. The one was good, the other was no good at all. And fact is that if Cain had only believed, he would not have brought the same sacrifice. What then was the difference in the sacrifice of both? Of this we must elaborate.

Let me say now, in conclusion, and partly in anticipation, that Cain's offering was unbloody; Abel's sacrifice was a blood sacrifice. In other words, Cain's sacrifice was a denial of Christ and of his cross; Abel's sacrifice was more excellent because he looked forward by faith to him who was to come and who would offer the perfect sacrifice for all our sins and all our transgressions. Cain's sacrifice was antichristian; Abel's offering was the Christian offering, which is only acceptable to God.

## 2

We remarked that the greater excellence of Abel's offering consisted exactly in this, that in sacrificing an animal, in offering a blood sacrifice, he looked forward to the Christ and his perfect sacrifice that was to come. He believed the promises of God.

History tells us that Abel brought a bloody sacrifice; Cain did not. God must have taught the first parents to bring the sacrifice of animals. So we may gather from the third chapter of Genesis. He must have taught Adam and Eve by object lessons that there was reconciliation only through the death of the innocent. For we read that God made our first parents coats of skins. This presupposes the death of animals. It presupposes the shedding of blood. And thus he taught them early that they could have communion with him only when their shame, the shame of their nakedness, the shame of their sins, was covered by a bloody sacrifice.

Symbolically God must have taught our first parents that no sinner can have communion with the holy and righteous God as long as he stands in his unrighteousness. No gifts, no service of any kind could avail after they had once fallen into sin. They might live ever so purely and apparently holily and righteously, they might serve him with all their powers; but it would be of no avail. Their guilt had to be removed. God's righteousness is to be satisfied. His wrath had to be appeased. And since he had threatened death as a punishment for sin, our first parents had to know that God could have communion with them only through death, through blood; only through the death of one righteous could a state of righteousness be attained. And until that state was actually created, no sinner could have communion with God.

This Adam and Eve must also have taught their first two boys. And Abel believed. He therefore offered a bloody sacrifice not merely because he was a shepherd, as some have it, for he could undoubtedly have gotten some of Cain's fruit to offer. Cain would have been glad to give it to him. And if Cain had believed, he could have taken a sheep of the flock of Abel and sacrificed it. That therefore was not the reason. But the reason was that Abel believed. He knew his sin by the power of faith. He knew that he could not serve God and be pleasing to him in his present sinful state. He was acquainted with the fierce wrath of God, and he knew that it would be an insult if he as being unrighteous would try to serve God nevertheless, and act as if there were no sin to be atoned. And therefore, he offered a bloody sacrifice. And sacrificing, he confessed: "I am a sinner, lost in sin and misery. I am worthy of death. I can have no communion with thee, O thou Holy One. I have deserved to die as this animal dies before thee. But thou hast taught us to sacrifice the sacrifice of atonement. Accept this sacrifice, O my God, with a view of the Righteous One who is to come. And so let it be a sign that my sins are forgiven in the blood of that Righteous One."

Faith is the evidence of things unseen. Difficult it must have been to see how the blood of a sacrifice could atone, far more difficult than it is today, now the true sacrifice has been brought. But Abel believed the word of God. And believing, he saw unseen things, and he hoped for forgiveness and righteousness in the blood of his sacrifice. His sacrifice was the acknowledgment of sin and righteousness and judgment. He sacrificed with the acknowledgment of the holiness of God and therefore to his glory.

Over against this we read that Cain offered of the first fruit of the ground. That was the difference. And the difference was fundamental. He offered a bloodless sacrifice. That was his sin. He also must have been acquainted with the bloody sacrifice. His parents must have told him. And besides, the sacrifice of Abel was a testimony against him. But he did not believe. He did not possess the faith of Abel. And he meant to serve his God without reconciliation.

He saw Abel kill the animal and place it on the altar, and he would say: "Ah, you fool; why are you doing that? What are you killing that animal for? I do not believe in your blood theology. We are not sinful. And God is not a God of wrath, but a God of love. And even if this was not so, don't you understand that the blood of animals cannot pay for your sin?" And then he would build his own altar. And he would pile up his fruit: grain and fruit of all kinds, the pick of his apples and figs and grapes and pomegranates, and fruit of all sorts, beautiful to look at. And after he had it all piled up, he would kneel down before his God, for Cain was very religious, and he would show God what a nice crop he had raised, and thank him, and offer it all to him. But of sin and righteousness and judgment Cain did not know. And in the blood theology of Abel he did not believe.

That was the difference. The difference between the two brothers was exactly like that between the Pharisee and the publican (Luke 18:9–14). They were both religious. But the publican knew his sin, and the Pharisee did not. They both went to serve. But the Pharisee thanked God for his own goodness, and the publican asked for forgiveness for his corruption. And the outcome was also the same. For as the publican, so Abel was justified; and as the Pharisee, so Cain was condemned.

If we bear this in mind, it will also become intelligible why we read in the words of our text that by that faith "he obtained witness that he was righteous" (Heb. 11:4). Why, so we ask, is the righteousness of Abel emphasized in Scripture? Also our Lord speaks of "the blood of righteous Abel" (Luke 11:51). Now *righteousness* does not necessarily mean to be without personal pollution. And it certainly does not mean this in this connection. Abel was in himself unholy and defiled, with the stain of sin upon him, as well as Cain and as well as all men born from Adam. When there shall be no more stain, no more defilement, no more pollution of sin upon us, we shall have reached perfection. But that was not the case with Abel.

No, *righteousness* in this case does not refer to Abel's actual condition, but to his relation, to his state, before God. Righteousness in this case answers the question: How does God consider us, and how did he consider Abel? Does he pronounce us guilty or free? If we are righteous, then the Almighty pronounces us free from the guilt of sin, innocent, right before his law. And with respect to sinners, it simply means that their sins are forgiven them. For how otherwise can they ever be declared righteous before God?

Once more: if their sins are forgiven them, then they must have a covering for their sin. For God cannot forgive sins without atonement. Unless someone had paid for our sins, that is, Christ at his cross, they could never have been forgiven by our heavenly Father. And therefore, when we read in the words of our text that Abel received witness that he was righteous, it means that God gave him testimony that he was without the guilt of sin, that his sins were absolutely forgiven, so that he was not condemned. God had forgiven him all his sins for the sake of Christ who was to come. Hence, Abel had a covering for his sin in the blood of his sacrifice. It means that Abel was justified before God.

And how was he justified? Our text tells us: through that same faith. Through that faith by which he offered up that more excellent sacrifice than his brother, through that faith by which evidently he looked forward to the perfect sacrifice that was to be brought by Christ, through that faith by which he had seen the holiness and righteousness of God and his own corruption and guilt and condemnation, through that faith by which he had confessed his sin and condemnation in his sacrifice, through that same faith he also received witness that he was righteous. He obtained witness, our text tells us. Essentially this is the same witness the Lord gave later to some of the penitent who followed him. Oft times he would say to them: "Thy sins are forgiven." It was to them a testimony, a witness that they were righteous. So it was with Abel. He obtained witness that actually his sins were forgiven and that he was justified before God.

How did he obtain that witness? As we have already said, he obtained it subjectively through faith. But there was also an objective witness. For in the words of our text we read: "God testifying of his gifts" (Heb. 11:4). And also in Genesis 4 we read that God accepted the sacrifice of Abel, but not that of Cain. The Lord "had respect unto Abel and to his offering," but not to that of Cain (vv. 4–5). There must have been two testimonies therefore. Not only Abel, but also Cain received testimony as to his gifts. In what way this testimony was given we don't know. Certain it is that the Lord made plain to Abel that his offering was accepted and that of Cain rejected. God testified, therefore, that he would have nothing to do with an offering like that of Cain. He gave witness that however willingly he might appear to offer his service to God, the Most High could not accept his services, because he was guilty and unrighteous before him. He cannot have communion with sinners in themselves, outside of Christ.

Cain acted as if nothing had happened. He acted as if creation lay still enveloped in its virgin purity and as if sin had never entered. He acted as if the relation between God and the world, between God and him, was still normal. He was sinless. God was still the God of love, also for him. And hence, he was bold to come with a sacrifice of thanksgiving. He obtained no witness of his righteousness. He could not. Had God accepted the sacrifice of Cain also, he thereby would have testified that Cain was righteous, that there was no sin in him, and that man on the natural basis of things, without the blood of atonement, without Christ, could still serve God. And that was not true. Hence, Cain received by the rejection of his offering testimony that he was unrighteous, that he was a sinner, and that a real and a radical change had to be established in his relation to God before God could accept his service.

But Abel received testimony, for God accepted his sacrifice. He assured Abel thereby that his offering was righteous, and that he possessed the true faith, and that his sins were actually forgiven. No, there must have been many things that Abel did not understand. How the blood of an animal could be atonement for sins he could only vaguely see, with a view to the promise of him who was to come. But although his conception was by no means as clear as ours now can be, he nevertheless accepted the word of God by a true, living faith. He longed for righteousness; and righteousness he received.

The text tells us that by it, that is, by that faith, Abel, though he is dead, yet still speaks (Heb 11:4). He speaks also in our day, and that, too, very clearly. That faith of Abel is still a testimony. Oh, he must have spoken to Cain in his day. We read so significantly that the brothers talked together, just before Cain commits the heinous crime of fratricide. I imagine that they often talked together. And as they talked with each other, Abel must have spoken in faith and warned his brother Cain. He must have been a testimony, a living testimony of the word of God he accepted by faith. Often, we imagine, he spoke to Cain of sin and of righteousness and judgment. He must have warned him of his own wrong attitude. He must have spoken of their sinful condition, of their guilt, of the wrath of God, and of the terrible judgment of death. And besides, his very sacrifice was a testimony against that of Cain, every time they offered.

But it was of no avail. Cain was self-righteous. He thought the anxiety of Abel sheer folly. He was self-sufficient. He served God as well as Abel. And he did not think it necessary to change his views of his life and action. He believed in service, in good works; and God would have to accept his service sometime. And because of this self-righteousness of Cain he could not stand the condemning testimony of his brother. And as his wrath was set boiling by the continual witness against him both from on high and from his brother, he killed Abel. Abel is the first martyr of faith. He died as a witness, as a living testimony of the faith that God had given him. Boldly he testified of the faith. And testifying, he died a hero of that same faith.

But once more: thus he spake, and thus he still speaks, very loudly, also in our day. Our age is the age of Cain. What do we mean by this? This: that it invents its own way of serving God Almighty. Sin and guilt are denied. It is denied that man was placed very high by his Creator, and that he fell very low through his own sin. And instead of this man has developed his own theory of evolution. This world is not a world of sin under the wrath of God and doomed to his terrible condemnation. The present dispensation is not an abnormal one. All things have normally developed from lower to higher, under the universal fatherhood of God.

We speak no more of a kingdom of God in distinction from a kingdom of the world and of Satan. On the contrary, the world as such is the kingdom of God. It has not yet reached its goal. It is still defective. And therefore, it needs development. We must all help along to make the world the kingdom of God. It is not true that the world needs atonement. It is not true that God is filled with wrath. No, God loves us all. And what we must do is serve him. And how can we serve him? By serving mankind, of course. By bringing our offerings unto God and thus helping God to make of this world a kingdom of God.

In a word, the world of today brings the same offering that Cain brought: service without atonement. The so-called blood theology is denied. And of the righteousness of God we hear no more. Of universal brotherhood, fatherhood, love, etc., our age is full. But the vicarious suffering of Christ is denied. And of God's wrath and righteousness we hear nothing. It is a service of God without atonement, a sacrifice without blood, a service on the basis of man's own righteousness, which is the righteousness of corruption, the righteousness of the devil.

And therefore, Abel still speaks in our days. He speaks warningly. God will not accept such service, however nice and faithful man may appear. There is but one way of serving God, and that is: after his righteousness has been satisfied and the sins of man have been forgiven. Only on the basis of the atoning blood of Jesus Christ, only around the cross of Jesus, can we approach our God. Only in his offering can we be justified and receive testimony that we are righteous. Only in that blood can the eternal kingdom be established. If sin had not come, there would have been universal fatherhood and brotherhood. Now there is no more. God is our Father in Christ Jesus only. And only as believers in him are we truly brothers. In him we can offer the service, as believers, the service of gratitude, but without him all our offerings will be rejected. He who believes on the Son has everlasting life. But he who believes not the Son shall not see life: the wrath of God abides on him (John 3:36).

*Chapter 13*

# ENOCH, THE LONELY WITNESS, TRANSLATED BY FAITH

By faith Enoch was translated that he should not see death; and was not found, because God had translated him: for before his translation he had this testimony, that he pleased God.

*—Hebrew 11:5*

## 1

For man in general, and also for the Christian from a natural point of view, it is quite a general characteristic and tendency to take his place with the majority. That stands to reason. For he is a social being. He feels his oneness with the human race. And therefore, he usually does not like to stand alone, by himself, in the face of an overpowering majority. When the great majority is against us, we begin to doubt our cause and we are inclined to forsake the stand we took at first and to swing over into the opposite camp. In battle it is not easy, and certainly not pleasant, to fight on the side of the weaker army and of the weaker nation and with the feeling that all our good will and all our courage, all our undaunted bravery is of no avail, seeing that against the overwhelming host of the enemy we can never make a stand successfully.

From a natural point of view, it is thus also with the Christian over against the world. It is certainly not true from a natural point of view that one ever likes to stand alone for the truth over against the lie. The presence and the support of other fellow Christians, who share the same faith with us, is a mighty comfort for us. And the conviction that we do not stand entirely alone over against the enemy, even over against those who confess to be members of the church of Christ and deny the truth, fills us with more courage to be faithful and to testify of the name of our Lord Jesus Christ. It requires courage of faith, self-sacrifice, and self-denial to stand alone. And it requires above all the strength of confidence in the Lord our God through Jesus Christ our Savior.

Yet this has throughout the ages been the precarious position of the church of Christ. It comprised but a very small minority of the entire human race. This was true even in the community and countries in which it lived. For even there it could not depend on the support of the great majority of people. The church of Christ is small, always small. And according to the very prediction of our Savior, it is not destined ever to become powerful in numbers. It is called a small flock. It is often presented to us as a lonely witness in the midst of the world.

And the result for that faithful church is that, according to the words of the Savior once more, it must bear the reproach of the Master. They hated him; they will also hate his church. They persecuted him; they shall also persecute his people (John 15:18–20). Those are the very words of Christ himself. And those words have been verified by history a hundred times over. In the midst of the world the church is small. In the midst of the world, unless the church allies herself with the world about her, in whatever way that may be, she will have to bear the reproach and the shame of our Lord Jesus Christ.

Thus it is today, however beautiful the world may look and however aptly many so-called Christians can get along in the world without self-denial, without the reproach of our Lord. Thus it was at the time of the Reformation, when the faithful believers were persecuted in a severe manner and when faithfulness meant certain death in a cruel way. Thus it was at the time of the early church. Thus it was at the time of the apostle Paul. And thus it was at the time of the old dispensation. You have but to call before your imagination figures like those of Jeremiah and Isaiah, like Daniel, and in fact all the prophets of the old dispensation to find the verification of this fact.

All the prophets of the old dispensation were persecuted. They stood alone. They bore the reproach of their God. They were put in prison, and even deprived of their lives, merely because they would not deny the truth but were faithful unto the end, according to the word of God. Thus it was at the time of Elijah, who was a lonely witness for the name of Jehovah, his covenant God. Thus it was at the time of Moses, who denied himself for his people and his God, simply to be repaid with the shame and reproach from those very people. Thus it was in Noah's time, who stood all alone in the midst of a sinful and God-forsaken world. Thus it was also at the time of Enoch, whose faith we are to study in our next two chapters.

We speak on Enoch, a lonely witness, translated by faith. Let us first of all notice that according to Hebrews 11:5, Enoch pleased God; second that, pleasing God, he revealed his strong faith; and finally that thus revealing his faith, he was gloriously rewarded and taken into eternal bliss without death.

The wording of our text is somewhat intricate and involved. The sense, however, seems to be that Enoch was translated because he pleased God. His translation was a reward for his faithfulness and confession of his God in the midst of an opposing world. It is clear that this pleasing of God is a clear proof that Enoch possessed the true faith, and that, too, especially from the point of view that the author considers in this eleventh chapter to the Hebrews, namely, as an evidence of things unseen and as a substance of things hoped for (v. 1). This is evident, namely, in the fact that Enoch possessed this faith: for it is impossible to please God without this faith, seeing that he who comes to God "must believe that he is, and that he is a rewarder" of those who seek him (v. 6). This faith Enoch therefore possessed. And possessing this faith, he pleased God. He was acceptable to him. And being acceptable to God by faith, he was translated. Hence, it may indeed be said that Enoch was translated by his faith, so that he did not see death. And therefore, the first question, which is rather an historical one, arises in our minds: What is the import of the words, "He pleased God"?

Our text tells us: "Before his translation he had this testimony, that he pleased God." Now, if we look up Genesis 5, we find that this pleasing of God, or rather, this being acceptable unto him, is a commentary on the words that Enoch "walked with God." In Genesis 5:22 we read: "And Enoch walked with God after he begat Methuselah three hundred years, and begat sons and daughters." And therefore, if you want an answer to the question, how did Enoch please God, you may indeed say that he did so by walking with God.

Now this latter expression, that Enoch walked with God, has often been misunderstood by good and pious children of God, who found it their highest joy to be with their God and to live in close communion with him. They conceive of Enoch as a sort of mystic. He walked with God. That means, so they imagine, evidently that Enoch was a very pious man, that he had very intimate and close communion with his God, and that he was near to the Lord his God. According to them, he was a sort of mystical figure, a man who was extraordinarily pious, who lived strangely close to his God, who was far above this present world and really had no communion with this world at all anymore. It may be that some of the other people of his time were also God-fearing men; but Enoch was extremely pious. And this, then, is further maintained as an example of how our religious life should be. We must separate ourselves from the world entirely and try to find close communion with the Almighty and with our Savior Jesus Christ. And when our soul finds this communion, we must just enjoy this.

But we may say from the outset that this idea of Enoch is not in harmony with the text, nor with Scripture in general. Oh, surely, there can be no question about it, that Enoch lived near to his God and that by faith he had close communion with him. We may indeed depend on it that he spent much time in prayer, as all the people of God should do, and that his God was his strength from morning to night. In that true sense of the word Enoch was a very religious, a very pious man. But this must not be understood in a mere and false mystical sense of the word. Scripture nowhere teaches that the ideal of a Christian life is selfish enjoyment, no matter how beautiful and spiritual this may appear.

Our Father in heaven does not tell us anywhere that we should always, as much as possible, sit quietly at home by him and fear to go out into the world. However necessary sound and healthy prayer may be, and is, and however true it is that the Christian has moments that he lives in sweet and blessed communion with his God, Scripture nowhere teaches that such a mystical communion is really the whole of the Christian's life. If that were the purpose of the Christian's life,

and if God actually meant to save him for no other purpose, it is difficult to see why he still leaves him here upon the earth and why he does
not take him immediately with him to everlasting glory.

Once more I say: communion with God is good, and very necessary. The Christian must live in fellowship with God. Our soul must
know something of that panting after God as the hart pants after the
water brooks. Besides, from this true communion with our God we
must derive strength to fight the battle of faith. We are not yet in the
church triumphant but still in the church militant. The Christian must
fight. He must be a soldier. The battle that he fights is very frequently
severe. And true fighting power is one of the best virtues of a good
Christian. Also for this purpose, that he may fight that battle, he needs
continual, healthy communion with his God, because without that he
would surely suffer defeat. But the selfish and sickly communion of
the mystic is always condemned in Holy Writ.

Surely, we do not have a true picture of Enoch in our mind when
we make of him such a sickly mystic, who lived in literal separation from the world. First, the expression "Enoch walked with God"
denotes far more than mere fellowship with God, even though this
fellowship is presupposed. In Holy Writ the idea of walking with God
is something entirely different. It refers to our entire life in the midst
of the world, and that, too, in relation to God. As we know, man's life
in Holy Writ is represented as a path, and his proceeding through life
as a walking upon that path. Hence, this walking refers to our entire
active life in every sphere from a spiritual, ethical point of view. And
although it is true that walking with God denotes a special intimacy
with the Almighty, denotes close communion and intimacy with God,
this is by no means all.

We must remember that this expression, "walking with God,"
occurs but three times in the Old Testament. In the chapter following
ours (Genesis 6), we read that Noah walked with God. And in Mala-
chi 2:6 we read the same thing of the tribe of Levi. It is true that every
time it seems to denote special and direct intercourse with God, but
not for the joy of sickly mysticism, but to derive strength from him for
an arduous task and for a battle in the midst of the world. That was
the case with Noah. He had need of special strength in the time in

which he lived, when all the world had become wicked and he alone was upright and feared the Lord, and when to stand required special strength from the Lord his God. Hence, God must have revealed himself to him in a special and more direct way.

The same thing was also true with Enoch. That he walked with his God means that by faith he had direct intercourse with God in his entire life. In all that he did he had communion with the Almighty, so that it was his greatest desire to live according to the will of his God in uprightness and equity. Also in his time he had special need of strength. Constantly, by faith, by that living power that is an evidence of things unseen, he was privileged to have direct intercourse with God, in order that he might be able to stand in the wicked world of his time.

Then it is also plain why we read that Enoch walked with God after he begot Methuselah for three hundred years. This cannot refer to the sickly and mystical communion that we just mentioned. Man cannot always be in ecstasy. He cannot always recline on the bosom of the Father in sweet idleness. But surely, living in the midst of the strife of this present world, fighting the battle of faith, the Christian has need of constant intercourse and close communion with his God, so that he may derive strength from him. And that is the communion here referred to.

Enoch walked with God three hundred years. And those three hundred years were not a time of sweet and idle enjoyment, during which he took pleasure walks with his God. But they were a time of hard battle. They were a time of tremendous struggle. They were a time in which Enoch was called to testify of the name of his God in the midst of a wicked world. Instead of being a time of enjoyment, they were years, three hundred long years, of test and trial. And in this trial Enoch remained faithful. In communion with his God, walking in his strength, he was competent for the arduous task. He was a lonely witness for the name of his God. Thus Enoch was acceptable to God indeed.

Let me apply the thought I just expressed for a moment. We, too, are called to walk with God. We, too, have fellowship with God in our Lord Jesus Christ through his Spirit and word. But by that fellowship we, too, are called actively to walk with our God in all our life and in every sphere of it. Not only in the church and in our public worship, when we pray and sing our psalms and hear the preaching of the word, but also in our daily life we are called to walk with God. We are called to walk with him actively in our home, in the instruction of our children, in our Christian schools, where our children are educated in order presently to take their place in the midst of the world. We are called to walk with God in every sphere of our active life, in factory or office and wherever our place in the world may be. Then indeed we will fulfill our calling and live in the midst of the world to the glory of him who called us out of darkness into his marvelous light.

**2**

I called special attention to the statement that Enoch walked with God. I emphasized that this walking with God did not merely imply that he had close communion and fellowship with God, but also that in his whole active life in the midst of the world he stood for God's cause, fulfilled his will, and testified of his God in the midst of a wicked world.

In this connection we must still make one or two remarks. We must consider two more facts that undoubtedly must be taken into consideration in this connection. First, it is a fact that it is only of Enoch in connection with the prediluvian patriarchs that we read that he walked with God. Genesis 5 gives us the genealogy of the prediluvian patriarchs. Again and again we read that they were born, lived a certain time, begat sons and daughters, and died. But in the midst of this strange record, we all of a sudden read of Enoch that he walked with God. This certainly does not imply that all his ancestors were wicked, for that evidently was not the case. That would have been the case had Enoch been in the line of Cain instead of in the line of Seth. We may well accept that from Seth to Noah the general line of patriarchs were God-fearing men. Nevertheless, the fact that only of Enoch we read that he walked with God, and not of the others, tells us that he was a person of unique importance at the time, who issued a strong testimony against the wicked world.

And second, in connection with this fact we must bring the testimony that Enoch was a faithful witness, according to Jude 14 and 15. There we read:

14. And Enoch also, the seventh from Adam, prophesied of these, saying, Behold, the Lord cometh with ten thousands of his saints,
15. To execute judgment upon all, and to convince all that are ungodly among them of all their ungodly deeds which they have ungodly committed, and of all their hard speeches which ungodly sinners have spoken against him.

This certainly is not the picture of one who idled his time away in sweet dreams and mystic communion. Mystics are generally bad fighters. They are unfit for practical life. They live to dream and to enjoy.

But Enoch was a born fighter in the true sense of the word. He lived in close fellowship with his God. By faith he clung to him. By faith he derived his strength from him. And in that strength that he derived by faith from his God, he would go forth to fight the battle of faith and to testify against the wickedness of his own time. Enoch pleased God, once more, not by living in sweet and selfish communion with him for three hundred years, while doing nothing for the cause of his God, but by fighting the actual battle of faith and by being a champion for the name of Almighty God.

Thus we can understand why Enoch is so worthy of his place among the heroes of faith who are mentioned in the entire chapter of Hebrews 11. If he had been merely a pious mysticist, it would be difficult to see why he should be mentioned with these heroes of faith, with Abel and Noah and Abraham and Moses and others. But as soon as we understand that Enoch was a faithful witness in the time in which he lived, we can thoroughly grasp the entire situation. Enoch had the faith that is an evidence of things unseen and the substance of things hoped for. Such is the idea of our text (Hebrews 11:5).

And how is it evident that Enoch possessed that faith? The author says Enoch pleased, was acceptable unto, God. And this is impossible, except from the principle of faith. "Without faith," according to verse 6, "it is impossible to please him: for he that cometh to God must believe that he is, and that he is a rewarder of them that diligently seek him." That is the faith that Enoch possessed. In his deepest heart he was convinced that God is. And he revealed this by testifying of his name. He never had any doubt in his heart that God is, and that God is God, and that he is the God of our salvation. For by faith he clung to him. In that same faith he had communion with him. And again, by that same faith he testified of the glory of his great name in the midst of a wicked world for three hundred years.

And the power of this faith becomes still more evident if we consider for a moment the nature of the times in which Enoch lived. He was the seventh from Adam, in the line of Seth. Now, Lamech was seventh from Adam in the line of Cain. Enoch therefore must have lived contemporaneously with Lamech and his family. The picture we receive of that time concerning the descendants of Cain is that they were masters of the world. It was they, and not those in the line of Seth, who had developed the arts and trades, cattle raising and industry, music and the arts. All these were to be found among the descendants of Cain, and among them only. Even as it is today in the world, so it was also at that time.

In general, we may certainly say that it is not the people of God who become great according to the measure of the world. It is not among the people of God that you find the great inventors, the masters of land and sea. Oh, there are exceptions, we know; but nevertheless, it is generally among the children of this world that you find these things. Thus it was also at the time of Enoch. The line of Cain was a line of great and powerful men. They had developed. They ruled over the world.

But at the same time, it was a line of wicked men, of men who forsook God and did not believe in him. This is very plain from the arrogant speech of Lamech to his two wives, Adah and Zillah (Gen. 4:23–24). He reveals himself as a mighty despot. He is a tyrant. For an insult to his person he kills his fellow man, and seventy and sevenfold is his sore revenge. He was a mighty tyrant, who cared not for the life of his fellow human beings, and who sought his strength not in God, but only in his sword. And that this is only a picture of the times in general is evident from the subsequent development of the world, from the fact that even at Noah's time we read that there was a race of wicked giants on the earth, and from the fact that Jude pictures to us the general character of the time as one of ungodliness. We may safely assume that they did not believe in God but rejected him. They lived for the things visible, and for them exclusively. They had no eye for the things that are unseen. They never acknowledged their utter dependence upon God. They never confessed that he is, and that he is a rewarder of those who diligently seek him.

But Enoch believed. And to this wicked race of despots, which would inflict death upon a person for the slightest injury, Enoch testified. He testified not once, or twice, but untiringly. He testified in spite of their threats and insults. He testified for three hundred years that God is, and that he is a rewarder of those who diligently seek him. He testified against their ungodliness and their wickedness and maintained before them that they were in duty bound to live for God and to his glory. By faith Enoch walked with God. By faith he clung to his God and testified of him in a time of great wickedness and atheism. He was a very lonely witness.

But there was still more. Enoch revealed his faith also when he spoke of the future and of things to come. For Jude tells us that he did so. He spoke of judgment. He told his wicked generation that the Lord would come with ten thousands of his holy angels to execute judgment upon them, and to convince every one of them of their ungodly deeds and blasphemies. We can easily imagine that when Enoch testified thus, the wicked called him a fool. They laughed at him. They scorned his words. And if we do not misjudge the time in which he lived, a time of despotism and tyranny, we may safely draw the conclusion that they also persecuted him. They would not listen to his talk forever. They could not stand to listen for three hundred years to his nonsense. What? The Lord come for judgment? Nonsense, according to them.

Day after day Enoch went about testifying. Day after day they continued to scorn him and to mock his belief in the existence of God. Day after day he would testify against them, would tell them of the day of judgment. And day after day they would continue to perform their wicked deeds and to blaspheme the name of the Lord. And the Lord tarried indeed. Perhaps Enoch sometimes would look for the coming of the Lord and expect that presently he would appear. Perhaps sometimes the thought would arise in his mind, which later arose in the heart and mind of the poet: "Is there then really no knowledge with the Almighty?"[1]

But he believed in things unseen. Although the Lord tarried to come and although the mighty, wicked people continued to perform their deeds of wickedness as if there were not a God in heaven, Enoch persevered by faith. By faith he knew that God is a rewarder of those who seek him. He trusted that he would not be ashamed. He knew, on the one hand, that God would come to judge his enemies and convince them of their wickedness. And on the other hand, he also was well aware of the fact that he would finally receive the reward of grace.

I earlier remarked that it is human nature to like to be with the majority and to dislike to be numbered with the minority. This is especially true if that minority is very small. Man does not like to stand alone. And for the Christian it is a severe test when he must stand alone in the midst of the world. But we may add that in spite of that fact, the majority in the spiritual, ethical sense of the word is not often right but is generally wrong, while throughout history the minority take the side of the truth and of righteousness. Nor is this surprising in a world of sin. Nor is it surprising in view of the fact that God from eternity did not choose the majority of men, but that his elect were usually in the minority. Also this is evident from history. And it may be a reason for encouragement if we are called upon to take sides with the minority, or even if we have to stand alone in the midst of the world.

Scripture pictures to us men who stood alone for years and years and who must have made the impression of fools upon the people of their time. Yet they were right; and the masses were wrong. Elijah

---

1   Hoeksema is either translating or paraphrasing a section of Psalm 73:11, "And they say, How doth God know? and is there knowledge in the most High?" Similar references to the same verse appear also in *Behold, He Cometh! An Exposition of the Book of Revelation*, 2nd ed. (Jenison, MI: Reformed Free Publishing Association, 2000), 507, 535.

stood all alone, and he was right. Jeremiah stood alone. And he sometimes spoke prophecies and counsels that would make him look like a traitor in the eyes of the people. Yet he was right, and the people were wrong. Noah stood alone, and with a clear sky above him, and no rain in sight, he built a great ship; for a great flood was coming, according to his testimony. And the people would laugh at him and call him a fool. Yet he alone was right, and all the rest were wrong.

Faith is the evidence of things unseen and the substance of things hoped for. And as such it is never put to shame. Never yet was faith disappointed. Nor will it be. Thus it was also with Enoch. He believed that God is, and that he is a rewarder of those who diligently seek him. And the people around him told him every day that there is no God. And though they blasphemed his name, yet Enoch believed and manifested his faith by the fact that he walked with God in the midst of an ungodly world. He believed that God is, and is a rewarder of those who seek him, and that he would judge the ungodly and justify him. And although it seemed to the natural eye as if there were no God in heaven, and although these wicked people were faring well and were powerful and prospering, while he himself had to endure their shame and mockery and persecution, yet faith was also in this case the substance of things hoped for. He believed and persevered in his faith for three hundred years.

And his faith was rewarded. Again it became evident that the crowd was wrong, and he was right. For as a testimony of his faithfulness God translated him, so that he did not see death. Enoch saw no corruption. In the very first period of history we have one of the two or three men who did not see the corruption of their bodies but were translated like those who shall live at the end, when Christ shall take his church to heaven. That was the reward of his faith. But it was at the same time a testimony that he was right. Enoch walked with God, and he was no more.

By faith Enoch was translated. You understand, of course, that this does not mean that he was translated because of his faith. For faith has no meritorious value. Because of our faith we receive nothing. Nor does it mean that he was translated by the power of his faith. His faith did not translate him but the power of Almighty God.

But rather must we say that in the way of faith Enoch was translated, so that he did not see death. Just as God saves his people not because of their faith, but rather by means of it and in the way of faith, so Enoch was also translated in the way of faith. It is clear, of course, that his being translated was the reward of grace. Everything was of grace, also with Enoch. By grace he was regenerated. By grace he was called. By grace he received the power of faith. By grace he received the faithfulness to testify of the name of his God in the midst of a wicked world. It was all of grace. And therefore, the reward that Enoch was translated was also of grace only. But if this is so, then it is also clear what faith has to do with his translation. Without faith he could not have pleased God. Without faith, without that strong faith given unto him by the Almighty, he could not have witnessed and walked with God for three hundred years. And had he not witnessed and been faithful to the end, he certainly would not have been translated. By faith, therefore, Enoch was translated. His faith was not ashamed. And his hope was realized. For faith is the substance of things hoped for.

May I ask the question: Do we possess that faith that Enoch had? By that same faith Abel offered unto God the more excellent sacrifice. By that faith Enoch pleased God, and by that faith alone. Without that faith it is impossible to please him. Without that faith there would have been no reward for Enoch. And without that faith there is no reward of grace for any one of us. Therefore, the question is an important one: Do we have that faith, which is the gift of God?

But if we possess that faith, which is an evidence of things unseen and the substance of things hoped for, then we surely are called to reveal it in the midst of the world. Then we will please God and be acceptable to him, even as Enoch pleased him. Enoch denied himself in the midst of a sinful and wicked world. He took his place with the minority, with the despised, with those who had to bear the reproach of Christ. And he was not ashamed. That, then, is also our calling. If we are ashamed to confess our God, ashamed to bear his reproach, ashamed to testify of his goodness and grace and to glorify his name and his truth, then it is not possible that we please God. Faith without works is dead. And you can please God only by a living faith. Let us then walk by that living faith in the midst of a wicked world.

*Chapter 14*

# NOAH BY FAITH BUILDING THE ARK

By faith Noah, being warned of God of things not seen as yet, moved with fear, prepared an ark to the saving of his house; by the which he condemned the world, and became heir of the righteousness which is by faith.

—*Hebrews 11:7*

## 1

That we are living in extremely serious times is a fact denied only by the most superficial mind. By universal consent our age is admitted to be one of great significance. This is true, first, because we are living in an age of continual war and rumors of war and fear of war on every side. Disappointment must be the lot of those who hoped for and dreamed of universal peace.

Yet, on the other hand, some are still optimistic and assure us that this is simply an age of transition and that presently we will enter upon a much greater age, an age in which the human race shall have made a decided upward climb on the ladder of evolution. Many, indefatigable in their belief in the essential and fundamental soundness of the world and of the human race, are not at all discouraged, so it seems at least, by all the present unrest—social, political, and international—that is evident in the world of our time. And they continue to assure us that in the near future all war and unrest will cease, and that perhaps all the nations of the earth will unite in one great world-nation, so that international differences will simply be abolished, and strife and war shall be banished from the earth.

In fact, this doctrine is preached today from many a pulpit.

Preachers today assure us that the kingdom of God will come, not by a great crisis but by gradual development. Evil of all kinds will be opposed and abolished by concerted action of church and state, and sin will be banished from the world before long. Men themselves must cooperate to usher in the kingdom of God. Such, in brief, is the spirit of many an optimist even in our day—a spirit that is preached from many a pulpit and is incorporated in many a book.

Others, however—and among them also we ourselves—have an entirely different conception of the world and its future and of the coming of the kingdom of God. They do not believe in the essential goodness of the human race but maintain that the world is ethically and spiritually corrupt. They emphasize that only personal regeneration can possibly save the individual and that the state of final righteousness of God can be ushered in only by a great crisis. Not by gradual development of what is essentially evil do they expect the kingdom of God but by an uprooting and destruction of the present world and the establishment of the new heavens and the new earth, in which righteousness shall dwell.

Hence, they see in the present era not a transition to a brighter age, but rather a dark prologue of the great final scene that is still to be played on the stage of the world. They warn the church of God to keep aloof from the present world spiritually and to aim at nothing less than to be a testimony of the name of Christ and of the word of God in the midst of a wicked generation. These take the standpoint of faith, based upon the plain word of God in the Scriptures. And believing its testimony, they must have nothing of the shallow talk and optimism of those who refuse its message. They believe and emphasize that the world as such is sinful, and that man is depraved by nature, and that salvation can come only by Christ, through his cross and resurrection, and by his Holy Spirit.

Such is without any question the testimony of the word of God in Holy Writ. We must not look for a development of the kingdom of God here upon earth by human efforts. Scripture gives us a different picture. The Bible tells us plainly that the man of sin must develop, that the power of antichrist must first reveal itself, that the kingdom of darkness must receive new power, such as it has never had before.

Then Christ will come to make an end to this present dispensation and to establish the everlasting age and the kingdom of God in the whole world, that is, in the new creation. Scripture warns the church of God not to stem the tide of this development, for that is impossible, but rather to watch and pray and to be ready when the Lord comes, and to be faithful witnesses even unto the end.

Scripture gives us a clear picture of these days and informs us that they will be like the days before the flood. People shall eat and drink, marry and be given in marriage, till the great destruction be upon them, just as the flood came suddenly upon an unbelieving and mocking world. And since even as in the time of the composition of this epistle to the Hebrews, so also now Christians, what is called the church, forget that the Lord will come because he tarries so long, it may be well to contemplate, on the basis of our text for a few moments, the faith of Noah as it was revealed in the building of the ark and as it is pictured to us in the words of our text.

Our theme, therefore, of this chapter is: Noah by faith building the ark. We will first of all consider his faith as it was revealed in this building of the ark. Second, we will contemplate the testimony that by faith Noah issued to the entire world. And finally, we will consider the reward, the great reward that Noah received by faith.

We ask, first: How come Noah built the ark while as yet there was no flood whatsoever, and therefore there seemed to be no earthly use for a ship of this kind? The answer to this question is twofold. First of all, he did so according to the word of God that came unto him; and second, because he possessed the faith that is an evidence of things unseen and the substance of things hoped for.

First of all, then, Noah acted upon the revelation of the word of God to him. Thus we read, first of all, in Genesis 6:13-14, "And God said unto Noah, The end of all flesh is come before me; for the earth is filled with violence through them; and, behold, I will destroy them with the earth. Make thee an ark of gopher wood." And thus we also read in the words of our text in Hebrews 11:7, "By faith Noah, being warned of God of things not seen as yet." He received therefore a divine revelation concerning things that were about to occur in the near future.

But this objective revelation as such would not have induced Noah to obey the word of God and to build the ark. The testimony of this revelation, in fact, had been sent forth many centuries before and was well-known to the whole world, not only to those who feared the Lord but also to those who were wicked and must have nothing of him. The word of God respecting this future judgment, regarding these things that were not seen as yet, had come to the wicked world already more than five hundred years ago. Enoch, as we have seen in our last chapter, had preached to them about the final judgment of the Lord. He had been a living witness in the world of his time, and by the word of God he had bravely and faithfully condemned their works and spoken to them of the judgment to come. It was therefore by no means anything altogether new.

The word of God was not the special possession of a few. That word of God did not come only to those who were saved, but also to those who were lost. All the world knew, that is, were acquainted with, the word of God that there was to be a judgment. Just as the gospel is preached to all the world, so the testimony of the destruction of the world and of the judgment, of the final judgment of God, was openly proclaimed to all men; and they could know it.

Besides, and second, more particularly with a view to the time of Noah we may say that the world had a respite of 120 years.[1] And during those 120 years Noah must have been a preacher of righteousness unto the world of his time. Having received the word of God definitely, Noah also preached that word in a very definite manner. And he must have told the world of his time that there would still be 120 years of respite, and after that God would destroy the world by a great flood.

Nor is this a mere conjecture. Although in the account of Genesis we do not read that Noah preached the word of God concerning the judgment to come to all the world, the rest of Scripture clearly testifies to this fact. In 2 Peter 2:5 we read: "And spared not the old world,

---

1 Hoeksema is likely referring to Genesis 6:3, "And the LORD said, My spirit shall not always strive with man, for that he also is flesh: yet his days shall be an hundred and twenty years."

but saved Noah the eighth person, a preacher of righteousness." This leaves no doubt that Noah, being instructed of the things not seen as yet, preached sin and righteousness and judgment unto the world of his time. And still stronger testimony we have in 1 Peter 3:19–20, where we read in so many words that Christ himself preached to those people who were disobedient before the deluge and whom the apostle in his time calls "the spirits in prison." This also can mean but one thing, namely, that Christ as the great prophet also in the old dispensation preached his word and that in this particular case he did so through Noah. Finally, we also know that the very preparation of the ark was a symbol and a living testimony to the world that presently judgment would come unto them and that they all would be destroyed. We know, therefore, that not only Noah, and not only the people of God, as many as were with him at the time, received the testimony concerning the final judgment and destruction of the world; but also the entire world, though they did not believe, nevertheless were acquainted with this testimony.

And therefore, in addition to the fact that God revealed to Noah his word concerning the flood and the destruction of the world, we must emphasize that Noah received this warning of God *by faith*, as also is emphasized in Hebrews 11:7. It is by faith that Noah, being warned of God, built the ark. By faith Noah received and accepted the word of God. He believed that word and acted accordingly. Had Noah not possessed the faith that is an evidence of things not seen and the substance of things hoped for, he would not have received the word of God in his heart and would not have acted upon it. It must have been in his 480th year.

He had already been a witness of the great wickedness of his own time. The instruction he received at this time was not that the world should be destroyed, for that he knew already by faith. The idea of a coming judgment was by no means foreign to the world of that time, as we have already expressed. Years ago Enoch had preached that same message; and Noah must have believed in that coming judgment. Just as the idea of the second coming of Christ is well-known today all over the Christian world and is believed by the children of God, so also at that time everyone knew it, though only the people of God believed it.

And everyone knew that there was such an idea among some narrow-minded people, that the world should be destroyed and that God would come for judgment. But those narrow-minded people had gradually grown less in number. The old story that had been preached for so many years already was believed by gradually fewer people. Things remained just as they always were. More than fifteen hundred years the world had stood already. More than five hundred years ago it was that Enoch had preached the story of the coming judgment. But nothing had happened.

At first there were quite a few of those narrow-minded people. It is true, they did not all preach it so boldly as Enoch, and as Noah did after him. They were not all so strong in their condemnation of the present order. Nevertheless, there were rather many of those people who believed in the coming judgment and who for that reason separated themselves from the wicked world. But in course of time this faith had worn off. You cannot always keep people in the way of superstition. And especially when the world developed and became stronger in power and all kinds of accomplishments, the number of those who believed in this coming judgment gradually grew smaller, until finally Noah and his family only were left.

Of him alone we read that he walked with God at this time. He and his family at this time consisted exactly of eight members. At the time of Enoch this was still different. He also was alone as a witness but not as a child of God. Then there must have been more. Adam even was still living at the time, and many others were still children of God. And the great amalgamation of the time immediately before the flood had not yet been accomplished. But Noah and his family stood all alone, not only as witnesses, but even as children of God, as believers. And it required therefore a tremendous faith, as the evidence of things unseen, to believe the word of God when it came to Noah, this time definitely, in the 480th year of his life, that the world would be destroyed within 120 years, and that it would be done by a flood. This word, then, revealed to Noah and preached by him to all the world, all men received outwardly; but Noah only believed and acted upon it by faith.

Another element we must consider is this, that Noah revealed by faith a godly reverence for that same word of God. This is according to the text in Hebrews 11:7. We read that Noah was "moved with fear" and prepared the ark for "the saving of his house." This being moved with fear must not be misunderstood. It does not mean that Noah all of a sudden received a warning of things unseen, a warning of future judgment, that never before had he thought of such a possibility, and that now, receiving that divine warning, he trembles with fear of that terrible judgment in the relatively near future. In that case the expression "moved with fear" would have reference to the judgment as its final object. But that is not the truth. It cannot mean this.

First, as we have said already, the idea of the judgment cannot have come as a surprise to Noah, seeing that it had been preached centuries ago and that he as a child of God must have believed in it. Second, it must be admitted that the translation is very unhappy, and that it would have been far more correct had it been rendered "moved with godly reverence." And finally, it is spiritually untrue that one by faith can be moved with fear if the reality of the judgment is presented clearly to his consciousness.

It is characteristic of faith that it does not fear. I do not say that the children of God never fear. They can perhaps tremble quite often with fear of the great day of the Lord in the future. But it is not true that faith can fear. It is in this respect one of the greatest characteristics of faith that it has no fear, that it drives out all fear. That is but natural. For what is the relation? This, that there is indeed reason to fear if we know that we may be condemned. Only for those who know that there is condemnation to be expected in the day of judgment is there reason to fear, and to fear greatly. But that is not true of the believers. Who are the believers? They are those who are in Christ Jesus. They are for that very reason those for whom there is no condemnation, and who know the same by faith. But if that is true, if faith knows that there is no condemnation in the day of judgment, how can there be a reason for faith to fear? No, that is absolutely impossible. Faith cannot have fear of judgment.

Now the author wants to picture Noah to us exactly from the point of view of his faith. He says: by faith Noah, receiving divine warning, by faith Noah, moved with godly reverence, prepared the ark. And for that very reason we may not conceive of this fear in the unfavorable sense of the word. The object of this fear was not the flood, not the

NOAH BY FAITH BUILDING THE ARK

judgment. For besides all that is mentioned, we ought to remember, too, that not only the message of judgment was brought to Noah, but at the same time the assurance of personal salvation, so that all reason for fear in the unfavorable sense of the word was removed.

But the author speaks of fear as it so often occurs in Scripture, of fear in the favorable sense of the word, of the fear of faith, of the fear of God's name, of the fear of the word of God, of the fear that is the motive-power of all true religion, of the fear that manifests itself in true obedience. Noah received the word of God, and by faith he accepted that word. And by that same faith he was filled with godly reverence for that word of God. No, not as a convict fears the sentence that shall presently proceed out of the mouth of the judge did Noah fear. But even as a child has respect for the word of his father, so Noah by faith was filled with godly, though childlike, fear because that word of God had come to him in faith.

And this is the distinction between Noah and the world about him not only, but also between the children of God of all times and the ungodly. No, Noah did not fear the idea of judgment; neither do the people of God fear the final judgment that shall come upon the world. In fact, they look forward to it. But both Noah and the people of God at all times, even we, are filled with the true godly fear of faith, reverence of love, of the love of God in Jesus Christ our Lord. That is exactly the great difference between us, the people of God, and the children of the world. The former have again by faith learned to have respect unto the word of God; the latter have not the slightest respect for that same word. The children of God cling to that word while the ungodly attack it. Therefore, also now, in that true fear of God, in that true reverence of love, the children of God walk and testify in the midst of the ungodly world. And they do so by faith.

## 2

I discussed the faith of Noah, by which he built the ark while as yet there was no sign of the flood. I did so on the basis of Hebrews 11:7, which I wish to quote once more: "By faith Noah, being warned of God of things not seen as yet, moved with fear, prepared an ark to the saving of his house; by the which he condemned the world, and became heir of the righteousness which is by faith."

Throughout our discussion we must emphasize that the building of the ark by Noah was an act of faith. He believed that God is, and that he is a rewarder of those who diligently seek him (v. 6). As we emphasized earlier, the building of the ark was not an act of fear in the bad sense of the word, although by a superficial reading of the text we might receive that impression. But it became plain to us that this is not the case. On the contrary, the building of the ark was an act of pure faith, faith as an evidence of things unseen and the substance of things hoped for. This is also evident from the text itself, for we read that Noah was warned of God of things not seen as yet. And therefore, he built the ark.

By faith Noah accepted the warning as a word of God. By that same faith he had respect unto the command of God that told him to build the ark. And that faith, filling him with godly fear, culminated in an act of obedience: he built the ark. He did not question. He did not figure that the same message had come so often, the message, namely, that the world would be destroyed. He did not doubt. For had he doubted, he would never have obeyed the word of God in the building of the ark. Let us never forget that Noah, in obeying the word of God, put everything at stake. He and his family were the only children of God in the world. He was the lone preacher of righteousness.

Now it may very well be that those powerful giants who lived in the world in Noah's day, and who must have been personifications of wickedness at the same time, bore with him all the time that he built the ark. But suppose that his faith would not be rewarded. Suppose that after all he was wrong. Suppose that he would build that ark and preach definitely: "One hundred twenty years more, and the earth will be destroyed." Suppose that then, after 120 years, the sky would remain just as clear as ever, and never a flood of waters would lift the ark from the earth. Would not his fate be sealed in that case? Would he not become the object of mockery? And would not his life become unbearable? Would not all have been lost? Thus Noah might have reasoned very easily and very humanly.

The command to build the ark was at the same time a great test of Noah's faith. And he revealed his faith by obeying without reasoning. By faith he built the ark while nothing was yet to be seen of a flood, while no one believed in the coming judgment, while Noah lived in an age in which it might surely be said that the Lord had tarried to come. In spite of all this, Noah blindly obeyed. Unconditionally he accepted the word of God that had come to him, and he built the ark according to the instruction he received from his God.

But there is more. Faith must always be a testimony in the midst of and against the world. By that testimony the world must be condemned and God must be glorified. This is also true in the case of Noah's faith. It was God's purpose to condemn the world by the testimony of Noah's faith. If that had not been the case, God might have destroyed the world and saved Noah and his family in an entirely different way, rather than by a flood of waters and by having Noah be a preacher of righteousness for 120 years and publicly build the ark. But such was not the purpose of God. By building the ark, and at the same time by being a preacher of righteousness for 120 years, Noah must be the condemnation of the world. This is plainly expressed in the last part of our text. By building the ark to the saving of his house he condemned the world, thus the text has it.

And we may as well state at once that this is the only attitude a believer can possibly take over against the world in the sense in which it is meant in the text. It is evident that the meaning of the word *world* in the text is that of the whole of all wicked men as they exist in this present time and as they employ everything in the present creation—their bodies and their souls, their minds and their wills, their wives and their children, their goods and all their possessions—as means in the service of sin. Such is the meaning of the word in the words of our text. It is true, of course, that in Scripture the word *world* has different meanings. Sometimes it refers, particularly in the New Testament, to the world of men in general, in distinction from the Jewish nation in particular; and then it means, of course, all nations that exist in the earth. But this cannot be the meaning here. Quite frequently the word *world* refers to the product of God's hands, the world as created by God at the beginning. Also this cannot be the meaning in the words of our text.

No, when the author of this epistle speaks of Noah's condemning the world, then it evidently refers to the wicked world of men as it appeared outside of Noah and his family, or, if you please, to the wicked world of men outside of the church and the kingdom of God. That whole world has come under the influence of sin and corruption and under the spiritual power of Satan, the prince of the devils. And therefore, it denotes the entire kingdom of darkness. That world Noah condemned by his faith when he built the ark and became a preacher of righteousness.

It may be well to imagine for a moment, as far as possible, the condition of that world in Noah's time. First, the history-record in the book of Genesis informs us in very strong terms that the wickedness of that world had increased tremendously and had become very great, as well as universal, so that it became fast ripe for final judgment. For thus we read in Genesis 6:5, "And God saw that the wickedness of man was great in the earth, and that every imagination of the thoughts of his heart was only evil continually." And again, in verse 12 of the same chapter: "And God looked upon the earth, and, behold, it was corrupt; for all flesh had corrupted his way upon the earth." This means, of course, that the world was wicked thoroughly, was wicked only, and was wicked continually. Such is the judgment of God passed upon the world of that time. The power of evil, therefore, had developed tremendously already in the days of Noah. Besides, we may add that the wickedness of the world was absolutely universal. It was general, except for Noah and his family. There was not a man in the earth, outside of this family, who was not wicked.

We may probably ask: How had this come to pass in such a relatively short time? In what way had the whole world become wicked? And the answer to this question is, in one word: amalgamation. This is plainly stated in Genesis 6. Before this period there always had been a more or less clear distinction between the line of Seth and the line of Cain. Among the former were found the sons of God; the latter were the people of the world in its wicked sense. But the two lines mixed and became amalgamated.

Satan, we must remember, always hates clear distinctions. He does not like a spiritual separation between the church and the world, between his own kingdom and the kingdom of God. The tactics of the devil are always in favor of the obliteration of these lines of distinction. He wants no distinction between Seth and Cain, between the sons of God and the daughters of men, between the church and the world, between Christ and Belial, between the kingdom of light and the kingdom of darkness. What Satan likes is the false doctrine of the universal fatherhood of God and the universal brotherhood of man. He realizes very well that all obliteration of clear and distinctive lines is in favor of his own cause, the cause of the kingdom of darkness. He hates the preaching of sharp and definite doctrine in the church, such as the doctrine of election and reprobation; the doctrine of absolutely sovereign grace; the doctrine of total depravity, according to which man is totally incapable of doing any good and inclined to all evil; the truth that man cannot believe in Christ of himself, but that faith is a gift of grace; the doctrine of free justification, according to which the sinner becomes righteous in Christ only and has eternal life as a free gift of grace; the doctrine of sanctification, according to which God causes the life of regeneration to become manifest in the walk of his people in the midst of the world, so that they are a separate people.

All these doctrines the devil hates. He prefers the preaching of an Arminian gospel, according to which it is up to man's choice whether or not he will accept Christ or reject him, whether he will be saved or lost. For such an Arminian gospel, which is a denial of the truth of God, soon arrives in the sphere of total modernism. Thus the church gradually alienates from the truth, and the line between the church and the world becomes gradually more indistinct, until finally it is lost out of sight altogether. Then the devil seems to have gained his object, although this is only apparent, for God never causes his church to be entirely amalgamated with the world.

Thus it was in the days of Noah as well as it is in our present day. For we read in Genesis 6:1-2, "And it came to pass, when men began to multiply on the face of the earth, and daughters were born unto them, that the sons of God saw the daughters of men that they were fair; and they took them wives of all which they chose." Thus apostasy from the truth and the wickedness of the human race became universal. The people at that time must have nothing of the preaching of Noah that final judgment would come presently. They did not believe. They loved the world. They ate and drank, they married and were given in marriage; and they enjoyed all the things of this present world. Their wickedness became great and universal. The same is true in our present day. More and more the church departs from the fundamental truths of Scripture.

And what is our position over against that worldly-minded church? The same as that of Noah. We also take, like Noah, a noncompromising and a separatistic and condemning attitude over against the world and the worldly-minded church. Noah condemned the world by his faith. That does not mean simply that by quietly believing he condemned the world. But he condemned it by a living and active faith. By faith he condemned the world because he showed his faith in word and deed. In word he revealed his faith because he was a preacher of righteousness and a preacher of the coming judgment of God. He told the world of its great sin and corruption in no uncertain terms. But he also condemned the world by building the ark in obedience to God. The same is our standpoint over against the world and the worldly-minded church.

We must never be afraid of separating ourselves from the world. We often hear in condemning words about the fact that we build a fence, as it were, around ourselves. We must not build fences around the church. We must be in the world. But if Noah had not built a fence around himself and his house, if Noah had not listened to the command of God and built the ark, he would have perished with the world of his time. And therefore, once more: in word and deed we must reveal our faith in condemning the world and in condemning the worldly-minded church. We must build our "arks" as a testimony to the world. Our attitude over against the world in its evil sense is always one of condemnation.

What was the significance of this faith for Noah himself? Our text informs us that he became heir of righteousness that is by faith. What does this mean? It means of course, first, that Noah was justified, that through faith he was righteous before God, and that in the way of faith he became conscious of his justification. Noah is the first man of whom the Bible tells us that he was righteous (Gen. 6:9). And how was Noah righteous? He certainly was not righteous in himself, so that he had no guilt and sin. In himself Noah was just as sinful and just as worthy of condemnation as those other men of his time, whom he condemned. He also was a sinner, totally corrupt and guilty before God. But by faith Noah became an heir of the righteousness that is perfect before God (Heb. 11:7).

But how did Noah become righteous by his faith? Of course, this cannot mean that he was righteous because he believed. No man is a whit more righteous than any other man because of his faith. But this is the relation. First, God declares us righteous. He declares us righteous not because of our faith, but from eternity, in his sovereign counsel. That righteousness he also realizes objectively in Christ Jesus our Lord. The Son of God came into our flesh. He took our place before the tribunal of God. He took all our sins upon his mighty shoulders. And through the death of the cross he removed them forever. And when God raised him from the dead, he declared that he, as the head of his people, was eternally righteous. And all those who are in him are forever justified before God.

But how shall we know this? How shall we become righteous and justified before God in our own consciousness? The answer is: by faith. Only by a living faith in Christ Jesus our Lord, who died for our sins and was raised for our justification, can we be and are we forever righteous before God. As soon as we believe, as soon as we possess that true and living faith in our Lord Jesus Christ, by which we dare say, "My sins are forgiven me," we are heirs, possessors, of that righteousness that is by faith. And that justification includes especially two elements: we have the forgiveness of sins and life everlasting, now in principle, and presently, when our Lord Jesus Christ shall come in glory, in everlasting perfection in the new heavens and the new earth.

Thus it was with Noah. By his faith he became an heir of the righteousness that is by faith. And therefore, he became heir of the everlasting inheritance, which shall be revealed in the day of our Lord. In that faith, and as an heir of the righteousness that is by faith, he believed that God would come for judgment, that he finally would condemn the world. But he also believed that at the time when the world would be openly condemned, he would stand righteous before

God and before all the world and become heir of everlasting life and glory.

This revelation of Noah's faith, by which he became an heir of the righteousness that is by faith, is written, of course, for our consolation and instruction. It is also a warning. For the times before the flood are simply the historical type of the times before the coming of Jesus Christ our Lord. This is true according to the words of Christ himself (Matt. 24:37–39). Our time shows a good deal of similarity with the time of Noah. Let us be warned. Do not go along with the devil's scheme of amalgamation. Be a separate people. Remain diligent in searching the Scriptures. Rejoice in the full truth that alone will make us strong and able to stand. By faith alone are we assured of the things that are not seen as yet. By faith alone will we have respect unto the work of God and receive his sure promise in our hearts and minds. By faith alone will we have the courage to take the condemning attitude over against the world of wickedness. By faith alone will we build our arks. And by faith alone will we be justified and rejoice in the greatest of all facts, that there is no condemnation for us, neither now nor in the day of judgment, and that therefore we shall receive eternal life and glory in the day of our Lord Jesus Christ.

*Chapter 15*

# ABRAHAM'S BLIND OBEDIENCE BY FAITH

8. By faith Abraham, when he was called to go out into a place which he should after receive for an inheritance, obeyed; and he went out, not knowing whither he went.

9. By faith he sojourned in the land of promise, as in a strange country, dwelling in tabernacles with Isaac and Jacob, the heirs with him of the same promise:

10. For he looked for a city which hath foundations, whose builder and maker is God.

—*Hebrews 11:8–10*

**1**

This passage speaks of several things. First, it speaks of Abraham's faith, which is an evidence of things unseen and the substance of things hoped for. Second, it speaks of the call that came to Abraham from God, a call that no doubt he received verbally, so that he could plainly understand it, but that, as evident from the fruit of that call, he also received in his heart, and that was therefore efficacious. Third, it speaks of Abraham's obedience to that call, an obedience that was blind, because the text tells us that he went, "not knowing whither he went." Fourth, the text speaks of Abraham's spiritual self-denial, for he did not immediately receive the object of the promise, and for the rest of his life he sojourned as a stranger in the land of Canaan, "dwelling in tabernacles with Isaac and Jacob, the heirs with him of the same promise." And finally, it considers the faith of Abraham from the point of view of hope; and in that hope "he looked for a city which hath foundations, whose builder and maker is God."

Faith, obedience, unconditional obedience, and self-denial belong together. Without faith we can never obey the word of God and walk before him according to the precepts of the gospel in the midst of the world. Again, without faith it is impossible not only for us to obey the word of God, but also to deny ourselves—something that is closely connected with obedience—in the midst of the world. For if we live in the midst of the world by faith and in obedience to the precept of the Lord our God and according to the gospel of Jesus Christ, we must expect suffering in the world; and therefore, we must deny ourselves. Faith, obedience, and self-denial, therefore, are most intimately related.

Everywhere in Scripture it is emphasized that without denying themselves it is impossible for the saints to live in the midst of a world that lies in darkness. The saints are called to let their light shine and to confess the name of their God in Christ Jesus their Lord. They may never be silent, but they must reveal their faith in word and deed in every sphere of life, in their entire conversation and walk. They are called to be witnesses of the name of God in Christ in their own midst, wherever they are, as well as in the world abroad. And if they are faithful in this respect, they may expect the reproach of the world and the suffering of this present time for Christ's sake. In the whole world, in every sphere of it—in business and industry, in the education of their children, in home and school and church, in fact, everywhere and always—they are called to let their light shine and to reveal themselves as saints in Christ Jesus their Lord.

And this necessarily means self-denial. For the world that is in darkness hates the light, and for that very reason they hate the children of light. The more faithful the children of light are, the narrower will become their place in the world, until at the time of antichrist, they shall be able neither to buy or to sell. In a word, if we imagine that the time for self-denial and suffering for the sake of Christ has passed, we are mistaken. Today as well as in Jesus' time the words of the Savior remain very true: "If any man will come after me, let him deny himself, and take up his cross, and follow me" (Matt. 16:24). Or again, also today it is as true as in the time of our Lord that we may not love father and mother, sister or brother, more than him (Matt. 10:37). But we need not be afraid. For faith is strong and has the victory. It is not only the evidence of things unseen, but also the substance of things hoped for. And even as Abraham, so also we may look for a city that has foundations, whose builder and maker is God.

It is from this point of view that we wish to discuss the words of our text. Abraham, as we hope to see, not only obeyed the call that came to him from the Lord, but in that faith and in the way of that obedience he also practiced self-denial all his life. But he was perfectly satisfied. For he did not look for the things of the world, but for the things above.

The righteous shall live by faith, and by faith only. This is the principle that the author of this epistle has announced in the preceding chapter (Heb. 10:38), and it is at the same time the principle that we find announced and exemplified throughout Scripture, both in the Old and the New Testament. We walk by faith and not by sight, the apostle Paul assures us in the fifth chapter of his second epistle to the Corinthians (v. 7). This truth becomes evident in the lives of all the saints who are mentioned in Scripture and also in the life of every Christian in the midst of the world. As we have already seen, this became evident in the life of Abel. For God did not reward his faith immediately and visibly here upon earth. For he had to seal his faith with his own blood. The same is true, as we have also seen, in regard to Enoch. He did not see the fruit of his preaching and of his faith immediately. For he had to testify against the world of his time three hundred years and speak of judgment and condemnation to that wicked world for centuries. The same is true of the Christian of today. He believes, but practically nothing of all the things that are the objects of his faith is realized unto him. We also live by faith, and not by sight.

This is true of Abraham. He had to perform an act of faith and blind obedience when he went to obey the call that came to him in Haran. For notice that, first, the call was both indefinite and trying. Indefinite the call was, because God does not even tell Abraham whither he will be called to go. For our text tells us that when he obeyed, he did not know whither he went (Heb. 11:8). God, of course, knew, and that was sufficient. God knew that he would bless Abraham, and that he would make a great people out of him, and that he would give him the land of Canaan for an everlasting possession. But at the time of his call not a word was told Abraham about this intention of God. There is nothing that can really induce Abraham to follow up that call. Nothing can induce him to leave his own country, to leave the land in which he was brought up and the community he undoubtedly loved. Nothing could possibly induce him to leave all that was dear to him and just to go to some other unknown place. For at the time of the call all was indefinite for Abraham. He did not know what would be his future.

He knew but one thing. And that was something that must have been rather definite, even before the consciousness of Abraham at this time. And that was the fact that God called him. He called him to leave his father's house and country. There was no promise. There was no inducement. There was no definite statement concerning the future.[1] All is left uncertain. He must simply leave because of the word of God. Hence, Abraham lives by faith—by faith as an evidence of things unseen, he obeyed the call.

We may ask the question: Why is it that God causes his people to walk by faith, and not by sight? Might not God have informed Abraham, at least to some extent, about the country whither he would have to travel? It would have been very easy to help him in the making up of his mind by showing him at least some of the blessings that would be showered upon him, in the future. But instead of all this, only the call to Abraham: "Leave thy kindred and thy father's house, and go to the land which I will show thee." He must live by faith only. The question may be asked: Why is it that God wants his people to live by faith, and that, too, by faith as an evidence of things unseen?

We answer that God wants to reveal through his people that he is true and faithful, and therefore his people must show perfect

---

1    However, the first time that God called Abraham (Gen. 12:1–3), God said to him: "Get thee out of thy country, and from thy kindred, and from thy father's house, unto a land that I will shew thee: And I will make of thee a great nation, and I will bless thee, and make thy name great; and thou shalt be a blessing: And I will bless them that bless thee, and curse him that curseth thee: and in thee shall all families of the earth be blessed." In fact, Hoeksema later says: "This promise had been given to her husband already when they had first left Mesopotamia" (page 148).

confidence in him and in all his promises. The people of God must reveal that they believe the word of God and nothing else. By faith they must unconditionally surrender to God in Christ. They must unconditionally obey the call of God unto salvation, and thus manifest that God is God, and that he is a rewarder of those who diligently seek him.

It is exactly this that man in Adam denied in paradise. Adam was undoubtedly placed as prophet, priest, and king in paradise and over all creation. But never forget: he was king, not absolutely, but only under God. God was his sovereign. And in all creation he had to proclaim the name of his Lord. Of this relation to his God he must be constantly aware. Constantly he was called to acknowledge and to reveal in his whole life that God is God, the only and absolute sovereign, and that he, man, was called to love the Lord his God with all his heart and mind and soul and strength. As king under God, man had to obey, obey unconditionally. This obedience of Adam was put to a test. And the test, too, was based upon the idea that man had to acknowledge God, receive him at his word, and obey unconditionally.

The test was that Adam might not eat of the tree of knowledge of good and evil. Adam might have looked to the tree and found absolutely nothing wrong with it. He probably could see no earthly reason why he should not eat of the tree. In fact, the devil caused Eve to look at the tree so that she saw that it was very beautiful and desirable. The only thing was that God had spoken: "Keep off. Do not eat." It was therefore a test of man's absolute and unconditional obedience to God and the unconditional acceptance of his word. The tree placed him very definitely before the choice whether or not he would unconditionally obey—obey simply because God is God, and he alone is absolutely sovereign. And when Adam violated this command of God, he made a very definite decision, a very definite choice. He revealed very definitely that he had no intention of upholding the word of God and submitting himself unconditionally to his lordship. He did not wish to obey merely because God had spoken. In other words, even Adam in paradise, when he sinned, acted not by faith, as an evidence of things unseen, but in unbelief. The mere word of the Almighty was not sufficient to make him obey.

Now, God through Christ, by his Holy Spirit, implants faith in the hearts of his people, faith which is an evidence of things unseen and the substance of things hoped for. And that faith is always implicit confidence in the word of God, the word as it came to Abraham and all his saints, as well as the word that comes to us from the Scriptures and that is preached unto us by the gospel. That faith does not reason. It does not demand of God to give an account of what he demands and what he promises. Faith simply obeys and follows the call of God, trusting that in that way it shall find salvation and everlasting glory.

That is the faith of Abraham. Abraham received the call. And that call was the word of God. And that word of God was sufficient to Abraham. For he had the faith that is an evidence of things unseen and the substance of things hoped for. That call at the time God did not explain. He did not inform Abraham about the future. At the time he did not even tell him about the country whither he was commanded to go. One step must be enough. And step by step Abraham must obey the call. Every step must be a step of implicit obedience and perfect confidence in the Lord his God. Thus is the text: "By faith Abraham, when he was called to go out...obeyed; and he went out, not knowing whither he went" (Heb. 11:8).

Nor is this all. We said that the obedience of Abraham to God's call was not only blind, implicit, and unconditional, but also that this call demanded of Abraham that he would deny himself. True self-denial and denial of the things of the world is possible only through faith. Unbelief can never practice self-denial for the sake of God in Christ. But this self-denial Abraham practiced when he obeyed the call.

For, first, it is evident that he was called to do something that was very indefinite, and therefore to rely solely upon God in childlike obedience and faith. He could not see one step ahead. All he had to do was follow where the Lord would lead him. On the other hand, he was called to leave, to forsake, something that was very definite and that besides was very dear to his heart. He was called to leave his father's house, to forsake his country, to leave the community in which he was born and bred. He was called to bid farewell to all that tied and attracted him in this world and to go he did not know whither. All that attracted him—his house, his friends, his country, his relationship—he had to forsake, in order to follow up the call wherewith the Lord called him.

Oh, we can easily imagine that by his fellow men he was considered a fool. We know that already at this time the world was once more fallen away from God. We receive the impression that Abraham and his kinsmen, his family, were the only ones who were left in the world. If we bear in mind that it was only four hundred years after the flood, and that except for some individual saints all the world had once more forgotten the name of the true God and bowed before idols, we can somewhat understand the situation. If we remember that according to Joshua 24, also the immediate surroundings of Abraham were filled with idolatry and superstition, so that the name of the true God was not known among them anymore, we can also easily imagine that they must have considered Abraham foolish to leave his home and kindred and to go to a land that he did not even know.

And perhaps as Abraham became ready to leave, some of his neighbors and kinsmen came to him and inquired where he would go; and Abraham could not answer them. All he could say is: "God called me. And I do not know where I shall ultimately arrive." Then perhaps they would come with all kinds of arguments to persuade him to stay. They would tell him that it was the height of folly thus to risk his life, his possessions, and his entire future, and follow an indefinite call of God. Would they not try to persuade him that he was the prey of his own imagination? Was he not the victim of deceptive hallucinations? Who ever heard of such a thing? A man is asked, when he is about to leave everything, whither he goes, and he answers, "I do not know"? He is asked, "Whither leads the way?" And again, he answers, "I do not know; I must obey blindly, step by step, and day by day"?

Yet Abraham answers undoubtedly, and he replies by an appeal to God. He would undoubtedly say to those who asked him: "I do not know whither I have to go. But one thing I do know. And of that I am absolutely certain in my heart and mind, and that is: I have received the word of God. That word of God called me. And that word of God is absolutely true and faithful. Moreover, I know that when God calls, I must obey, and follow in the way in which he leads. It may look foolish to the world. It may demand that I deny myself. It may require of me to forsake all things in the world. It may seem against all human reason. Nevertheless, I obey the call, and I will forsake all things if necessary, because God has called me. I know that you can reason on natural and rational grounds that I am foolish. And if you do so, I will admit. But it makes no difference. God has spoken. That is all I know. And that is all that is sufficient for me. Because he has spoken, I obey, entrusting myself to his marvelous grace and power, and confiding in him with all my heart. And therefore, I go, not knowing whither I will be led."

Such is the faith of all the saints. Such is the faith of the people of God in the world today. On the basis of the word of God, they believe in Christ. They believe in the cross. They believe in the resurrection. They believe that Christ presently will come again, to glorify them forever in the new creation. Such is their faith, as an evidence of things unseen, and as the substance of things hoped for.

## 2

We called your attention to the fact that Abraham was called by God to go to a land that God would show him, that he obeyed the call, and by obeying denied himself, for he knew not whither he went. And go Abraham did. We do not read that he had any reasons to go. Nor do we read that he asked for a sign, or that he asked God for information, in order that he might know whither the way would lead. But he simply goes. With Sarah and Lot and the souls he had gotten in Haran, Abraham left (Gen. 12:5).

Until the time of this call his life had been very definite. He had had a definite country. He had had a definite home. He had had a definite future, for he was rich. He had nothing to think or to worry about. But the call from God came. That call he obeyed. And from now on all would be different. No more on things visible could he rely; entirely on things invisible he had to depend by faith: an invisible country, an invisible future, an invisible way in which he had to go, a way that he could take only one step at a time, led by the Almighty. His faith was implicit. He had made no remarks. Nor was his condition one of a day or two. On the contrary, it was a long time before he even knew to what country he would be led. The way to Canaan was at least four hundred miles, partly through a trackless desert.

And if Abraham had reasoned, and if he had at all doubted the word of God, he must have had many a time that he would have wished to return. All this time he was placed before the definite choice between things visible and invisible. He might choose the former and return on the way he had come. He might return to his kindred and country instead of pursuing such an uncertain and unknown track and wandering aimlessly in a hopeless desert. But he did not doubt. He did not return. By faith Abraham listened to the call of God and followed it up all the way. And by that same faith he continued in the desert and through valleys and over mountains, all the time ignorant about his future. Every step he made was one of implicit faith. Surely, by faith Abraham obeyed when he was called.

Nor is this the end of Abraham's trial. That would have been the case if he had found a country all prepared for himself and for his family, so that he could definitely take possession of it. God had called him from his own country and from the midst of those who were dear to him in the earthly sense of the word. But perhaps he thought that presently he would receive something very definite instead. He might have had the idea that in that new country he would find an altogether different class of people, people with whom he was not related by blood, but with whom he could have spiritual relationship, while in the country he left they were idolaters. He knew, of course, that in Mesopotamia the people did not serve the true God but served idols. And probably he knew, too, that he was the only one left who believed in and served Jehovah. Perhaps as he was wandering through the desert on his journey to the new and strange country the idea had come to his mind that he was called to live in the midst of the people of God. Perhaps God would have all things ready for him as soon as he came to the new land. Perhaps the Lord might have prepared a home, a new home for him there, and he may have expected that presently his faith would be rewarded by finding himself in the midst of his spiritual kinsmen.

However, if that were Abraham's expectations, he certainly was disappointed. When he came to the country to which God led him, he found it partly inhabited by heathen tribes, by men far worse spiritually than those he had left. Not only did they serve idols, but they were positively wicked. They did not care for the name of the true God. And they were ripening for the day of judgment, as soon it came upon the cities of the valley. Besides, he could not call the country his own. Truly, when he entered the land, the situation changed. He received more definite information regarding his future. First, he received the promise of a seed. He was told that he would receive a son, and that he would become the father of great nations, yea, that in him all the nations of the earth would be blessed. He was told, moreover, that he could go through the land from the north to the south, and that all the land would be given to his seed for a possession, so that indeed he was possessor of the land of Canaan by divine right and according to the promise of God.[2]

However, do not forget that all this was merely by promise. Again, Abraham was called to exercise his faith. He simply had to believe the promise of God. We might perhaps ask the question: Why did not God actually and immediately give him the land? Why did he not drive out the peoples who lived in the country at the time? Why did he not give to Abraham the promised son immediately? Could that not have been done? Yet God did not do so. You ask, why not? The answer is: Abraham had to live by faith, and not by sight. That same faith he had shown when he was called from his own country to go to a land that God would show him, he was now called to exercise for years, and in fact, even to the end of his life.

Twenty-five years long he had to wait before he received the promised son. And these twenty-five years were simply a test of his faith. For in the meantime Sarah became older, and the possibility of the fulfillment of the promise gradually disappeared, from a natural point of view, as the years went by. And as to the land in which he dwelled, our text tells us that he was a perfect stranger in it, even to the end of his life. "By faith he sojourned," our text tells us (Heb. 11:9). And that means that he was a stranger in the land of Canaan. It means

---

2    Hoeksema is summarizing the events reported in Genesis 13:14–18 and Genesis 15–17.

not only that Abraham had never a foot of ground given to him of the promised land that he could call his own, but also that he felt himself a stranger in that country. He lived as a sojourner, as one who was never at home, and as a person upon whom everyone looked as a stranger.

He did not mingle with the people, although he might have done so. Abraham was a mighty man, and he was respected as such. He was so mighty that he could pursue the king of Elam after they had pillaged Sodom and Gomorrah and overcome them (Gen. 14). He was certainly a person who could have become mighty in the land. But he did not choose to be such. He lived entirely as a stranger and sojourner in the land of promise. He knew that the country was his. And he knew that he possessed the promise. And therefore, he also knew by faith that God would give the land to him in due time. And in that faith he lived in Canaan as a sojourner, as one who never mingled with the people about him, and as one who never felt at home. He was a poor mixer. He did not mingle with the world. He did not seek the honor of the world. He did not try to conform to the world.

He lived in separation, conscious of his high calling to serve the Lord his God, conscious that he had no business to mingle with the God-forsaking people of the land and trusting that in due time he would receive the land from his God. Hence, he continued to live as a sojourner in the country, in the country that was his own by right of the promise of God. He was a guest in his own house. And he was content to be such.

By faith, therefore, as the text tells us, Abraham sojourned. He sojourned in the land of promise. He sojourned in his own land. He lived as a stranger and remained a stranger until the very end of his life. If you would have visited him as he lived at Mamre, you would have noticed the contrast. He spoke a different language. He wore different clothes. He built different altars. He served a different God. In a word, he looked like a stranger. He never conformed to the life and habits, and above all to the religion of the country in which he dwelt. He dwelt in the land of the promise, but as in a strange land. It never became his own; and never did he attempt to make it his own. When the dispute arose between the shepherds of Lot and his own, he offered the latter the first choice (Gen. 13:5–12). He did not attempt to exercise lordship over the country, as if he were afraid that he would lose it.

God had called him to this country. God had promised this land to his seed. And although Abraham had to wait twenty-five years for the seed, and although he never had an inch of ground in the land that he could call his own, he was perfectly satisfied. That he dwelt as a stranger and a sojourner is also evident from the fact that he lived in tents all his life with Isaac and Jacob (Heb. 11:9). He did not have a permanent abode in the land of promise.

Although the whole land was his by promise, nothing was his in reality. If Abraham had not believed the promise, he would either have tried to gain possession of the country by main force or have returned to his own country. But he did neither. He dwelt in tents. He did not crave earthly possessions. He did not doubt the promise. He did not build a city in the land. Even Isaac and Jacob after him lived in the same land after the same fashion. In Abraham's time there was not a glimmer of fulfillment to be seen. The realization of the promise lay in the far future. But Abraham believed. And believing, he was perfectly content to live as a stranger in the midst of a strange people, simply because his God had told him to do so.

But, so we are inclined to ask, was Abraham's life then dreary and hopeless in every respect, and was he simply called to deny himself without any hope whatever? On the contrary, his faith was not only the evidence of things unseen, but also the substance of things hoped for. And that this is true is plain from the last verse of our text. For there we read: "For he looked for a city which hath foundations, whose builder and maker is God" (v. 10). It is evident that in this verse we do not only have a sort of reason or explanation for Abraham's apparently strange behavior and life, but also a very definite contrast with the preceding. In the preceding verses Abraham is pictured as a stranger in the land of promise, as having no home, no permanent place where he could live abidingly. He dwelt in tents, pitching his tent in one place only tempo-rarily, ready to leave and to move to another spot. He lived as a man who is conscious of the fact that he had no permanent abode in the laud.

But now the view becomes different. The scene changes. For Abraham looked for a city that has foundations. A tent surely has no foundations because it is not an abiding dwelling place. But the city for which Abraham looked was abiding, for it was built upon firm and stable and enduring foundations. Many interpreters will have it that Abraham at the time did not know anything about heaven and about the glory of the new Jerusalem. He could not expect, so they claim, a state of future glory since that is a truth that was revealed to the people of God much later in history. They therefore refer this expression not to Jerusalem that is above, but to the earthly city of Zion. He now dwelt in tents, so they say. But he looked forward to the time when he did not have to dwell in tents anymore. He now had no permanent abode. But in the future he expected to take definite possession of the land, according to the promise, and he looked toward Jerusalem, the holy city, where God would dwell among his people. In a word, they claim that this refers to the city in the land of Canaan that later played such an important part in the history of the people of Israel.

This, however, cannot be the truth. Many objections may be raised to this view. First, we might remark that this would after all be a very poor consolation for Abraham personally, since he never lived in that city. If he looked forward to living in the earthly Jerusalem, he certainly must have been utterly disappointed. For he never saw it and never lived in it. And it is evident that this last verse of our text means to be an explanation of the fact that Abraham could be content to live as a stranger all his life in a foreign land.

Second, this would introduce an element into the epistle that the writer means to combat and to avoid. For it was exactly against the idea of the earthly Jerusalem and against the earthly temple that this epistle is directed. Hence, it is extremely unlikely that he would now suggest that this earthly Jerusalem was the ultimate end of Abraham's expectations.

But finally, it is not true that Abraham would not know anything of the state of future glory. All the God-fearing people who had died before him had undoubtedly died in the hope of eternal life. And not only this, but Enoch had gone directly to heaven, something that cannot have been unknown to Abraham. We may say, therefore, undoubtedly that Abraham knew of that heavenly city that has foundations.

Besides, this is quite contrary to the words of our text. For in the last part of verse 10 we read that the builder and maker of that city that has foundations is God. This certainly does not leave the impression that it refers to Jerusalem on earth, but very decidedly to the heavenly city, of which Jerusalem on earth was a mere shadow. Not of Jerusalem on earth was God the architect and maker in the literal sense of the word, but of the city above he only is the founder. That glorious city is conceived and planned by the Almighty himself. And it is also built by him. No human architect had anything to do with the building of the heavenly Jerusalem. But God Almighty planned it in his eternal counsel for his people. And God Almighty built it through his Son, Jesus Christ our Lord. And therefore, it is to that city, permanent, having foundations, just because God is the maker and builder, that our text refers.

This was Abraham's reward for his blind obedience and for his self-denial in going to a land while he did not know whither he went and in living as a stranger in the country, dwelling in tents with Isaac and Jacob. We may say, first, that Abraham certainly looked for that reward, and that it was perfectly proper to look for it. For it means that Abraham after all looked for God and longed for the perfect fellowship with his God that now he could enjoy only in principle, but that then he would obtain in perfection.

Oh, to be sure, Abraham also had fellowship with God in his present life upon earth. In principle he knew God and loved him and was assured that God loved him. In principle, therefore, he had covenantal fellowship with his God even in this present life. But he longed and looked for the perfection of that fellowship. And that perfection he would find in the heavenly Jerusalem, whose builder and maker is God. The looking for that heavenly city, therefore, as a reward was by no means sinful on the part of Abraham, but was the expression of his faith, which is not only an evidence of things unseen, but also the substance of things hoped for.

Besides, and second, do not forget that even this reward was a reward of grace. It is all of grace. Nothing is of our own works. It is of grace that Abraham had the faith that is an evidence of things unseen, and the substance of things hoped for. God only had implanted that faith in Abraham's heart, as a gift of grace. It is of grace that Abraham heard the call to leave his father's house and country and to go to a land that God would show him. It is of grace that he dwelt in the land of Canaan as in a strange land, dwelling in tents with Isaac and Jacob. It is of grace that he heard the call and obeyed the call. And for that reason also the reward is a reward of grace from beginning to end.

In and through that same faith the people of God live today. In and through that same faith they also deny themselves, looking upon Jesus, the author and finisher of their faith, who died for their sins and transgressions and was raised for their justification. By that faith they deny themselves and live as strangers in the midst of the world, looking for the city that has foundations, whose builder and maker is God. And in that faith they will never be disappointed. God, who worked the faith in their hearts, and who leads them all the way as they walk as strangers in the midst of a wicked world, will also give them the reward of grace in the city that has foundations. There they will be delivered from all sin and corruption, from all suffering they endure in the midst of the world. And they will forever live in perfect fellowship with the Lord their God in Jesus Christ their Savior.

## Chapter 16

# SARAH'S FAITH: THE MEDIUM OF HER STRENGTH

11. Through faith also Sara herself received strength to conceive seed, and was delivered of a child when she was past age, because she judged him faithful who had promised.
12. Therefore sprang there even of one, and him as good as dead, so many as the stars of the sky in multitude, and as the sand which is by the sea shore innumerable.

—*Hebrews 11:11–12*

## 1

What is faith? And what is the relation between faith and salvation? This is rather an important question. And the erroneous answer to this question is fatal to our entire conception of the truth. This, I think, is the case especially with respect to the rather generally prevailing view that faith is a condition in relation to our salvation. This wrong conception has entered even into many of our Reformed churches. And it seems to be very difficult to root out. It is taught and preached in many churches that if we only will believe, then, and then only, God will save us. Faith is the check on the bank of heaven. And if only we go and cash the check, God will give unto us eternal life.

This, I say, is a very fatal conception not only to our Reformed faith, but, of course, to our entire conception of the truth as it is in the word of God. For, first, that false conception of faith does in no way fit in with the rest of the truth concerning our salvation and concerning man as a sinner, as it is revealed in Holy Writ. The two can never be harmonized. For according to Scripture, the sinner by nature is wholly "dead in trespasses and sins" (Eph. 2:1). That implies, of course, that he can never be saved, that it is absolutely impossible for him to believe in Jesus Christ our Lord unless God comes to him first. He does not even have the will to believe, or the desire to believe, or the inclination to come to God and be saved.

But if we say that faith is a condition that is to be fulfilled by the sinner, then, of course, we contradict the truth of Scripture that man is wholly incapable of doing any good and inclined to all evil,[1] and therefore also incapable of believing. If we claim that faith is a condition that man on his part must fulfill in order to be saved, we deny that the grace of God in saving the sinner is absolutely sovereign and free. For then indeed we must also maintain that God is dependent upon the sinner for his salvation. Man is expected to do something first: he must fulfill the condition of faith. And then God follows up that act on the part of man by saving him from sin and death.

It may be true, as it is very piously maintained, that there is nothing meritorious in man's fulfilling the condition of faith. The fact remains, however, that if faith is a condition that man must fulfill in order to be saved, man is first, and God is second. One can no more speak of absolutely sovereign and free grace. And therefore, we wish to emphasize also in the following chapter that faith is not a condition unto salvation whatsoever, but that it is a Godgiven power, which he sovereignly through the grace of the Holy Spirit of our Lord Jesus Christ works in the heart of the sinner, and that it is even so not a condition, but a means through which the sinner clings to the God of his salvation in Jesus Christ our Lord. Faith is not a condition, but a means unto salvation. This is evident from the text that is the basis of our present chapter, and that is found in Hebrews 11:11–12.

This is indeed a very marvelous passage of Scripture. It tells us that Sarah's faith was the medium of her strength, of her physical ability to conceive seed and to bring forth Isaac. So much is plain from the words of our text. The conception and birth of a child is, of course, first a physical act, an act of the body. Faith itself does not conceive seed and does not bring forth children. Faith is a spiritual power. And to

---

1    A reference to the Heidelberg Catechism, Q&A 12.

bring forth a son requires more than mere spiritual power: it requires the strength and the life of a body of flesh and blood. Nor is this the meaning of the text. The text rather emphasizes that the conception and bringing forth of a child is a physical act that requires the life of a body. But Sarah was dead as far as the possibility of bringing forth a child was concerned. She was past age. She did not have the power to bring forth children anymore.

The question therefore is: How did Sarah receive the necessary physical life and strength to conceive seed and to bring forth a child when she was already past age? And the answer of the author is simply: through faith. Through faith Sarah herself received strength to conceive seed, and was delivered of a child when she was past age (v. 11). This therefore must be evident first. Faith did not conceive seed; and faith did not bring forth Isaac. No, it was the physical power of Sarah through which she conceived seed and brought forth a child. But faith nevertheless was the means through which she received the physical strength to conceive seed and to bring forth Isaac. Faith was the medium of Sarah's physical strength to be delivered of a child.

In order to see that this was actually the case, and that the strength through which she gave birth to Isaac was actually derived through faith, we must, first of all, understand and clearly see that Sarah no more possessed this power by nature. The text also emphasizes this, as we have said before, very strongly when the author says that Sarah was past age, or as it reads literally in the original, that she brought forth Isaac *contrary to her age*. That she was very decidedly past the age to conceive and bring forth children is also evident from the history of the case as we have it in Genesis 18:1–15. There we read that the Lord visits Abraham as he was dwelling in the plain of Mamre, and Abraham invites the Lord and the other two visitors to tarry, prepares for them a meal, and stands by them as they sit under the tree and eat. Very plainly the main purpose of this visit is not so much to meet Abraham but to deliver a message to Sarah, a message of which Sarah was very much in need, as we shall see presently. The message was the word of the Lord that next year about the same time she shall be delivered of a son.

Leaving for a moment the significance of this entire visit for later mention, let us ask the question: What is in this scene revealed to us about Sarah? There is but one answer to this question, and that is that she was decidedly past the age to bring forth a child. It was not thus, that it was still doubtful, and that there might still be a glimmer of hope in the heart of Abraham and Sarah. But it was rather thus, that all expectation of a child had become impossible, that all hope had vanished from the heart of Sarah that she would ever have a son. The testimony of Scripture directly is that both Abraham and Sarah were "well stricken in age" (v. 11), an expression that simply means that both were old and that certainly they could not expect children anymore. And thus it was indeed. Abraham was at this time ninety and nine years old, and his wife was eighty-nine. And if it might still be objected that this was not so old at that time, at the time in which they lived, we may nevertheless remark that Scripture informs us that even at this time it was deemed an age in which one could not reasonably expect to become a mother. The Bible tells us that it had "ceased to be with Sarah after the manner of women" (v. 11).

And also Sarah reveals very plainly that she has given up all hope, and Sarah herself expresses the same idea when she laughs within herself and says: "After I am waxed old shall I have pleasure, my lord being old also?" (v. 12). And when the Lord nevertheless assures her that the next year about this time she will have a son, she laughs in unbelief. So incongruous, so impossible, seems to her the realization of this promise, that even in the face of the word of the Lord to her she laughs. And therefore, surely according to all the facts it was, as the writer of our text expresses it so delicately, certainly true that Sarah "was past age" (Heb. 11:11). Her age was such that from the natural point of view there was no possibility of conceiving and being delivered of a child. As a mother, Sarah was dead. She had no natural power either to conceive or to bring forth a child. Hence, from the point of view of reason and of natural perception, all was hopeless. In short, Sarah as she was could never bring forth a child.

Yet the writer informs us, as does also the account in Genesis 18 and 21, that this actually took place. Sarah conceived and bore a child. And the author of the epistle to the Hebrews informs us that this physical act on the part of Sarah was performed by the spiritual power of faith.

We would probably never have come to this conclusion if the author of this epistle did not inform us about this fact and give us his commentary on Genesis 18 by divine inspiration. For, at first sight, it is a commentary that contradicts the facts as they are recorded in that chapter of Genesis. For there we do not read of Sarah's faith but, on the contrary, of her unbelief. Judging from what we read of her in that chapter, we would say that it may be true that Sarah has no more physical power to conceive seed and to bring forth a child, but if she must derive that power and strength through faith, all seems hopeless. For faith in the promise seems to have disappeared altogether at this time. The record rather gives the impression as if there were no faith whatsoever in the heart of Sarah.

When the Lord expresses the definite promise that she will have a child the next year at this time, Sarah stands behind the door of the tent and listens and laughs at the very idea of it. We must not have the impression as if this laugh was a smile of joy and glad surprise, as it was in the case of Abraham shortly before this; but it was a smile of unbelief. She laughed in herself because of the apparent folly of the promise of God. She was wholly incredulous. She did not at all accept the promise.

Now this condition of Sarah at this time can easily be explained. She was undoubtedly well acquainted with the promise that she would have a son and that through her Abraham would become the father of a great and innumerable people and of a royal posterity. This promise had been given to her husband already when they had first left Mesopotamia. And several times after this the promise had been repeated. It is, of course, inconceivable that Sarah was not acquainted with this promise. On the contrary, also she well knew that promise of God, and also she had waited for years to see the fulfillment of the word of God. And she had lived in hope day by day to see the fulfillment of the promise.

On the other hand, however, we can also easily draw the conclusion from what we read about Sarah, especially in connection with the birth of Ishmael, that this hope was not founded exclusively on the power and faithfulness of God, but also on the natural possibility that some day she would bring forth a son. Had she simply believed the promise, had she simply relied exclusively on the word of God, her hope would have remained in spite of the fact that the natural possibility of receiving a son became weaker every day. But now it was different. Oh, to be sure, she had believed the word of God, and she had had hope of a child as long as there remained a natural possibility that her hope would be realized. But as the years went by, and as she grew older, and as it ceased to be with her after the manner of women, also this hope and faith waned, grew weaker and weaker, and gradually disappeared.

Almost fourteen years before this she had already had an attack of this unbelief, and she had given her handmaid to her lord, seeing that she would never have a child of her own. For thus we read in Genesis 16:1–3,

1. Now Sarai Abram's wife bare him no children: and she had an handmaid, an Egyptian, whose name was Hagar.
2. And Sarai said unto Abram, Behold now, the LORD hath restrained me from bearing: I pray thee, go in unto my maid; it may be that I may obtain children by her. And Abram hearkened to the voice of Sarai.
3. And Sarai Abram's wife took Hagar her maid the Egyptian, after Abram had dwelt ten years in the land of Canaan, and gave her to her husband Abram to be his wife.

And this might not be. This the Lord would not have. Faith must be based on the word of God only. For that reason the Lord removes that basis of reason and natural grounds. He waits with the fulfillment of the promise till all natural possibility of bringing forth a child is gone. And then he comes once more with the same promise and with his word: "At the time appointed I will return unto thee, according to the time of life, and Sarah shall have a son" (18:14). And when this word of God comes, and also comes to Sarah, now all the natural possibilities on which after all she had built her hope have disappeared, she laughs at the idea and shows that she possesses not the slightest remnant of conscious faith. In short, Sarah did not believe.

How then can the author of this epistle state so positively that it was through faith that Sarah herself also conceived and bore a child? We will emphasize once more, as is also plain from what we have stated already, that Sarah's faith certainly was no condition that she had to fulfill in order to be able to conceive and bring forth Isaac, but it was a God-given power that became the means whereby she received physical strength to bear a son. And as it is the case with Sarah, so it is also true of our faith. Our faith is never a condition. It is always the God-given power whereby we take hold of Jesus Christ, and through him of the God of our salvation. And through that means God gives us everlasting life, now in principle, and presently in perfection.

## 2

We quote the text once more: "Through faith also Sara herself received strength to conceive seed, and was delivered of a child when she was past age, because she judged him faithful who had promised. Therefore sprang there even of one, and him as good as dead, so many as the stars of the sky in multitude, and as the sand which is by the sea shore innumerable" (Heb. 11:11–12).

The author informs us here that it is through faith that Sarah conceived seed and was delivered of a child. And I said earlier that the historical record in Genesis rather leaves the impression that Sarah had completely lost her faith that the promise of God concerning her son should be fulfilled. But in spite of this historical record that would lead us to the very opposite conclusion, the writer of the epistle to the Hebrews assures us that Sarah conceived and brought forth a son because she had received strength by faith. In the light of this commentary, therefore, we ask: How then did this faith become manifest? How can the writer come to this conclusion that Sarah also herself possessed the faith? And how, in the light of these verses, must the history be explained as it is recorded in Genesis?

We may undoubtedly say, first, that the very fact that Sarah gave birth to Isaac is to him[2] sufficient ground for the assertion that she received the strength to do so by faith. This is the argument of the writer. Sarah possessed no natural hope and no natural power to

2    That is, to the author of the epistle to the Hebrews.

conceive and to be delivered of a child, for she was past age. Nevertheless she was delivered of Isaac. Therefore, the outcome shows very plainly that she must have received strength in some marvelous way. And this strength is the power of faith. Hence, the author emphasizes here that even Sarah herself received strength through faith.

The implication of this emphasis is that even she, although at first sight it might seem that she did not have the faith, that even she received strength through faith. In the case of all the other examples of faith who have been mentioned, the fact that they possessed the faith is rather evident. But even Sarah—even of her, the writer means to assert—in spite of the fact that for a time she revealed herself differently, even of her he says that she received the strength to conceive and bear a son only through faith. The fact that she brought forth her son is sufficient proof of this. And if we ask, second, how then must be explained the unbelief of Sarah, or rather, how must be explained her faith in spite of the apparent unbelief, then I would say that Sarah was called back to the true faith by that very visit of the Lord at Mamre. This, it is very apparent, was undoubtedly the chief purpose of that visit. Just let us read a few verses of that chapter, Genesis 18. We begin to read at verse 9:

9. And they said unto him, Where is Sarah thy wife? And he said, Behold, in the tent.

10. And he said, I will certainly return unto thee according to the time of life; and, lo, Sarah thy wife shall have a son. And Sarah heard it in the tent door, which was behind him.

11. Now Abraham and Sarah were old and well stricken in age; and it ceased to be with Sarah after the manner of women.

12. Therefore Sarah laughed within herself, saying, After I am waxed old shall I have pleasure, my lord being old also?

13. And the LORD said unto Abraham, Wherefore did Sarah laugh, saying, Shall I of a surety bear a child, which am old?

14. Is any thing too hard for the LORD? At the time appointed I will return unto thee, according to the time of life, and Sarah shall have a son.

15. Then Sarah denied, saying, I laughed not; for she was afraid. And he said, Nay; but thou didst laugh. (vv. 9–15)

Hence, I claim, in view of the historical record, that the Lord intentionally went to Mamre for the purpose of bringing especially to Sarah his promise of a son. Sarah was unbelieving. She evidently had no hope anymore of a child. If she did not change, she could never receive strength to bring forth her son. For that reason the Lord himself pays her a visit and brings to her his powerful word in the form of a promise, and at the same time in the form of a rebuke of her unbelief. That word was undoubtedly efficacious, as we learn from the outcome as well as from the words of our text. Ever after that visit, the unbelieving Sarah believed the word of God, and in that faith she drew strength to conceive and bring forth her son Isaac.

But we ask, second: How was this faith the medium of her strength? How could Sarah through faith receive strength that she did not naturally possess? In answer to this question we must first of all confess that the power of faith and the mode of its operation is ultimately a mystery. It is very evident from the text that through faith Sarah regained for a while youthful power. Through faith she was, as it were, transformed, so that she could bring forth Isaac. Through faith she received physical strength and life. From a natural point of view she was dead as a mother. Through faith she received strength and life. From a natural point of view she had no hope and no power. Through faith she received both. Through faith, we may say indeed, her youth was renewed as an eagle's (Ps. 103:5), in the literal sense of the word. Ultimately, I say once more, this is a mystery. We cannot see how this faith works and how this faith could actually transform Sarah so that she could deliver a child. We must here believe the word of God. And our text is not capable of a completely rational interpretation.

Oh, we have other instances in history, and even in the history of our own lives, that are also wonderful and mysterious, if only we stop to think. People there were in the past who suffered all kinds of torture for Christ's sake, who ultimately died in the flames. And while thus suffering unbearable agony, they sang songs of praise and joy to the God of their salvation, in the hope of everlasting glory. That, too, is a manifestation of the power of faith. And even today there are those who must suffer physically, till the suffering becomes virtually unbearable. And yet, in the midst of agony and affliction, they sing instead of groaning; and they are often cheerful witnesses of the name and grace of their God in Christ. Also this can be explained only by faith.

Faith gives strength. Faith is the power to draw strength from God, just as the tree draws strength from the soil. Faith is the channel through which this strength from on high can flow into our being and transform us. Without faith we have no living connection. By faith we're connected with the source of all life and strength. And therefore, also spiritually the first thing the Holy Spirit accomplishes in the work of salvation is the implanting of the faculty, the power, of faith in the moment of regeneration. This may give us a glimpse of the transforming power of faith in the case of Sarah. If she had had no faith, she could not have conceived and brought forth her child. By nature she possessed no strength, and without faith she had no connection with the source of all strength. Hence, it is by faith that she had direct and living connection with God on high. And from him she drew the strength to conceive and to be delivered of a child.

In a way, although we cannot fully elucidate the mystery of the power of faith, the fact that through faith Sarah drew her strength from the Lord her God, and that therefore her faith was a means whereby she received power also to conceive and deliver a child, is suggested by the text itself. For it tells us that Sarah deemed "him faithful who had promised" (Heb. 11:11). In other words, her faith as a power was also the evidence of things unseen and the substance of things hoped for. Because of this faith, she clung directly to the God of her salvation. For in this faith she drew the one and all-sufficient conclusion: God is faithful. For her this meant, first, that he surely would not make a promise if he had no power to fulfill it. And therefore, since now God had made that promise, by faith Sarah knew that God was powerful to realize the promise unto her.

This is exactly what the Lord explained unto her at Mamre. At that time she looked at all things from a natural and carnal point of view; from the point of view of her reason. And from that viewpoint the whole thing is an impossibility. But God fixes her attention upon himself and asks the question whether anything would be too wonderful for him. Sarah from this time forth keeps her eye of faith on God, and judges indeed that since God had made the promise, he also must be able to fulfill it, no matter how impossible it may seem to reason. And thus her faith becomes the evidence of things unseen. How was it ever possible that she would conceive and be delivered of a child at her age? This was a mystery to her. She could not possibly see it. But by this faith, that considered God powerful because he had promised, she knew and was sure that it was true nevertheless.

Second, she considered him faithful also in the fulfillment. He was not only powerful to do so, he would also surely accomplish it, once the promise had been given. On this she relied. On this she based all her hope. Her faith was not only the evidence of things unseen; it was also the substance of things hoped for. In short, her faith was faith in the promise; and therefore it was faith in God himself. By the power of that faith she clung to God directly. Her attitude, the relation of her entire heart, was such that she had intimate communion with God. Hence, she drew all her strength from him. By the power of that faith she also drew the strength to do what was seemingly impossible, namely, to conceive and bear a son. Faith is the power that draws strength from God. And for that very reason, it is the transforming power of our entire life.

Thus it was in the case of Sarah. Thus it was in the case of all the saints who are mentioned in this chapter. Thus it is always with all the believers in the world. Thus it is also with us.

Finally, we must still consider the glorious reward or, if you will, the marvelous outcome of this faith. To be sure, the immediate and personal reward of Sarah is that she became a mother and experienced a mother's joy, which she beautifully expressed after the child was born. For she said: "God hath made me to laugh, so that all that hear will laugh with me" (Gen. 21:6). And again, she said: "Who would have said unto Abraham, that Sarah should have given children suck? for I have born him a son in his old age" (v. 7). That was Sarah's personal reward of her faith.

But the ultimate outcome is far greater, as also the text indicates. For the author tells us: "Therefore sprang there even of one, and him as good as dead, so many as the stars of the sky in multitude, and as the sand which is by the sea shore innumerable" (Heb. 11:12). In a word, the outcome of this faith was that God realized his own purpose through the faith of Sarah, as well as of Abraham. God's purpose was to call into being a people who would be his own in a special sense of the word, a people who would at the same time be a fitting symbol of the spiritual people of God, in fact, who would be his people, gathered from all nations and tribes and tongues in all the world. That people would have to be his product in every sense of the word. It would be impossible for that people to boast of their own strength and power, of their own goodness and greatness. No, it would have to be very evident that God had made that people, and that he had made them through his almighty power. This, then, had to become plain from its very inception, from its very birth.

Therefore, that inception, that birth of the people of Israel and the birth of the whole church had to be most wonderful. It must be born not in the merely natural way, but in the supernatural way of one who is as good as dead. That was true of both Abraham and Sarah. Both were as good as dead, our text means to say, in regard to the founding of a posterity. By nature it was impossible that there could spring a people from those who were past age. But by the marvelous grace of God it could be realized; realized, however, only through faith. Through faith, also through the faith of Sarah, it became possible that this great purpose of God was realized, and that as many as the stars of the sky and as the sand of the seashore innumerable were born of those who were as good as dead.

But the form in which this twelfth verse of Hebrews 11 is put reminds us of still another point of view, from which we must not fail to look at the words of our text. This verse, namely, is a direct quotation of the promise as it had been given to Abraham, time and again. As the stars in heaven in number would be his seed, and as the sand that is by the seashore (Gen. 22:17). Thus God had promised him. And so we learn also this from the words of our text, that the realization of the promises of God to us is accomplished only through faith. Thus we understand also more clearly what we said at the beginning, that faith is not and cannot possibly be a condition that we must fulfill. Faith in Sarah's case was not the condition upon which God would fulfill his promise. On the contrary, the promise was sure; it was yea and amen. "Next year about this time you shall have a son."

Nevertheless, faith was the power through which this blessing of the Lord came into the possession of Sarah. And mark you well, this must not be understood in the sense that she possessed that faith of herself and by nature. On the contrary, God implanted in her heart the power of faith and called it to consciousness through his own word. Faith is surely the power through which the promises of God are realized unto us. But that faith is the gift and work of God himself. And thus it was through faith that she became the mother of that wonderful people who was promised to Abraham. And through faith also Abraham became the father of believers.

This, then, is the truth that we learn from the words of our text. First, only by faith can we become the actual possessors of all that God has promised unto us and, in fact, of our entire salvation. Second, that faith, as we said, is not the condition, but the means whereby we may appropriate that salvation. Third, that faith is not of ourselves. It is absolutely and only a gift of God. And by that faith we cling to God as the author of the promise, through Jesus Christ our Lord. In ourselves we are dead, we can do no good. But in the strength of faith that draws all from our Lord Jesus Christ, we fight the battle even unto the very end. And faith will surely have the victory.

# Chapter 17

# ABRAHAM'S SACRIFICE
# OF ISAAC

17. By faith Abraham, when he was tried, offered up Isaac: and he that had received the promises offered up his only begotten son,

18. Of whom it was said, That in Isaac shall thy seed be called:

19. Accounting that God was able to raise him up, even from the dead; from whence also he received him in a figure.

—*Hebrews 11:17–19*

## 1

The problem of the book of Job is the problem of trials and temptations of the children of God. It is the problem of their suffering in the midst of the world. It is the problem of the question: How can God allow his children to suffer? This suffering is often so severe that the children of God are almost ready to cry out: "Is there no knowledge in the Most High?"[1] This is true of the children of God throughout the history of the world, both in the old and the new dispensation. And it is true today. Why does God send his children into the depth of sorrow and grief and suffering and affliction while the unrighteous often have prosperity and peace? That, I say, is the problem of the book of Job.

This Old Testament servant of God was sorely tried. At first he prospered; he was rich and honored. Besides, it is said of him that he was righteous and that he was never weary of welldoing. Yet he is deprived of all that he has and visited with suffering and affliction of

---

1   See chapter 13, footnote 1.

body and mind. In the beginning of this trial Job is apparently strong and glories through faith in the God of his salvation. And sitting on the ruins of his possessions and by the graves of all his children, he cries out: "The LORD gave, and the LORD hath taken away; blessed be the name of the LORD" (Job 1:21). However, he does not remain on this pinnacle of faith. After all is taken away from him and also his own body is attacked, his wife comes to tempt him, and his friends provoke him with their wearisome and stinging addresses, he curses the day of his birth (Job 3:1). Then the faith of Job is weakest. But from that darkest depth he rises again to a new and stronger faith that is ready to acknowledge the sovereignty of his God and to accept his suffering without asking questions and in obedience to him.

Faith is the victory. This is the truth that Job learned. It is the truth that Asaph learned in the sanctuary of God (Ps. 73). It is the truth that all the children of God must learn to understand in the midst of trials and temptations, when the path they must travel becomes narrow and almost impassable. Only by faith we can conquer. Faith is the victory. This is true when loads of sufferings are laid upon our shoulders, so that they would almost seem to crush us. But more especially is this true when trials and obedience are inseparably connected. Then we are placed before the alternative: suffer and obey or escape suffering in the way of disobedience. It is especially through such trials that God tests our faith. It is this truth that is immediately and especially illustrated in the words of our text. After having passed comment upon the heroes of faith whom the author has already mentioned in the preceding verses, he returns once more to the patriarch whose faith he has already mentioned. Already he spoke of the fact that Abraham left his home country by faith, that he sojourned and dwelt in tents. Now he speaks of the very climax of the manifestation of Abraham's faith, which consisted in this, that he was ready to sacrifice his own son Isaac.

The text says: "By faith Abraham, when he was tried, offered up Isaac" (Heb. 11:17). Abraham was tried. And God tried him. It was God who told him that he must sacrifice his own son. We may ask the question: How is it possible that God tries, yea, that he tempts his people? It is evident that by tempting, or trying, them God places them consciously before the alternative of obeying God in the strict sense of the word and for his name's sake, or of disobeying him for some selfish reasons and personal advantages. Such is the meaning of trial. It always presupposes that a difficulty is placed in the way that makes obedience of God very difficult and seemingly sometimes almost impossible. Thus it is, evidently, in the words of our text. Abraham was tried. An obstacle was placed in his way of loving and obeying God. Let us say that in the ordinary course of life Abraham did not think of leaving the path of obedience. He lived in faith and obeyed his God. But now by this trial obedience was made extraordinarily difficult by placing Abraham before a very heavy demand: "Offer me thy son Isaac."

And the question that arises in this connection is, first of all: How is it possible that God himself places an obstacle in the way of obedience? In James 1:13 this is apparently not true, for there we read: "Let no man say when he is tempted, I am tempted of God: for God cannot be tempted with evil, neither tempteth he any man." Perhaps you will say that James speaks of temptation while our text speaks of trial. And so you come to the conclusion that God tries man and Satan tempts him. However, this is hardly true. In the original the same word is employed here as the word that is used in the text in James. We may just as well read in our text: "Abraham, when he was tempted, offered up Isaac."

However, the answer is undoubtedly to be found in this, that James looks at the temptation from the aspect of its evil result. He means to say evidently: "Let no man say when he is tempted to sin actually, so that he succumbs to the temptation, that this was of God." Sin is never of God. When we fall before the temptation, this is not of God but of our own lusts, as James declares in the following verse of the same chapter. God does not lead his people into sin; and he does not try, or tempt, them for this purpose. And therefore, if we actually are led into temptation in such a way that the result is our fall into sin, we must never attribute this to God. In our text, however, merely the fact of the test, the fact of the trial and temptation, is referred to. Abraham was tested, and in that sense he was tried. A heavy burden was placed upon his faith. And this heavy burden was placed upon

Abraham by God himself. And Abraham carried the burden even unto the end.

It is of this temptation that the apostle James says in chapter 1:12, "Blessed is the man that endureth temptation: for when he is tried, he shall receive the crown of life, which the Lord hath promised to them that love him." This is the difference between the trials and temptations that God sends to his children and those that have their origin in the devil. When Satan tries us, he does so in order to lead us into sin and, if possible, to destroy our faith. When God tries us, he leads us not into temptation, but through the temptation to victory. And thus he saves us and strengthens our faith.

This leads us to a second question: What is the purpose of the trials and temptations into which God leads his people? Why did God place Abraham before this demand: "Offer me thy son Isaac"? We understand, of course, that the purpose of God was not to find out whether Abraham's faith was strong enough to obey God even in this demand. God has no need of employing such tests in order to find out how strong we are in the faith. He knows us. He scrutinizes the very depth of our hearts. He has no need of proof to find out that we actually believe. Besides, we must never forget that faith is also a gift of God, so that God would after all only test his own work if he would try it in order to find out how strong it is. But this is not the purpose of trials.

The object of God in trying his people is always pedagogical. The purpose is always to strengthen that very faith that he tries. We must never forget that God has created us rational, moral beings. And as such he always deals with us, even as believers. Thus it is in the entire work of salvation. As we have always emphasized, and emphasize now, God saves us. He saves us not partly, but entirely, from beginning to end. But he saves us nevertheless in such a way that we always remain reasonable beings and that we clearly realize that we are. He leads us by grace and Spirit through his word in the way of repentance and faith, so that we always feel and know our sins and repent and flee to our God for salvation. Thus it is in the beginning of the work of salvation; and thus it is also constantly, even in the way of God's strengthening our faith. He might perhaps strengthen that faith immediately, for he undoubtedly would be powerful to do so. Nevertheless, this is not his way. He uses means, means as are in harmony with our ethical and spiritual nature.

Now it is well-known that a man becomes physically stronger by the exercise of his physical strength. But the same is true of our spiritual life. A Christian becomes spiritually stronger when he fights the battle, when he struggles in the spiritual sense of the word. For this purpose temptations are surely necessary. Remove all temptations from a man's way, so that you make it impossible, so to speak, for him to sin, and such a man will never become strong in the spiritual, ethical sense of the word. Only in the way of battle, when a man fights consciously against evil in his own heart and evil round about him, when he meets temptations and overcomes them, does he become spiritually strong. By facing temptations, he is called to exercise his faith.

Test and trial are therefore means of God, not for the purpose of leading his people into sin—for that is the purpose of the devil—but to exercise their faith and to make them spiritually stronger and better children of his. The Christian whose faith has never been tried does not know how weak this faith is. But the faith that is tried and tempted and that through the grace of God has gained the victory in all trials and temptations, that faith is strong. And therefore, God tries his children. And for that purpose he also tried Abraham his friend.

It was indeed a very heavy burden placed upon the faith of Abraham in order to test it. Scripture tells us that Abraham was to sacrifice his son Isaac. That means, of course, first, that he was to butcher his own flesh and blood. How heavy this burden was, and how severe this trial, only those can fully realize who have children themselves, especially those who have accompanied their children to the place of final rest and have stood by the graves of their dear ones. Those who have stood by the bedside of their beloved children, who have watched them as they struggled the hopeless struggle against that terrible enemy death, can somewhat realize what a heavy burden was placed upon the faith of Abraham. Those who have felt the keen pain of having their dear children torn away from their very heart can understand a little of this trial. They especially can somewhat realize what a heavy test Abraham was subjected to by his God.

If you wish to realize somewhat the reality of this temptation, you must imagine that you bend over the bed of your child and that you must not be a mere passive onlooker while your child is struggling with death, but that you must actually take the butcher's knife and cut the throat of that darling, who is dearer to you than all your possessions. To see our children snatched away by the cruel hand of death is very hard indeed. But what then would it be to be called to be instrumental in their death, and to be the very cause of their struggle and agony? That was the case with Abraham.

Strikingly this is pointed out to him in the command that comes to him from God. It is as if God would have Abraham clearly realize just what he is called to do. God does not merely say: "Offer up Isaac." But he gives a detailed description of the reality of this awful task. "Take now thy son, thine only son Isaac, whom thou lovest" (Gen. 22:2). Every word cuts. Every single syllable draws one terrible feature of the task before his imagination. And surely, Abraham realized what he was called to do. His son, his only son, all that he had, Isaac, whose very name suggested the joy he had caused to his parents when he had made his appearance in the world, the son whom he loved. Yea, upon all the earth there was nothing he loved more; and all the love of his heart had concentrated upon this boy. That son he was to kill. God did not merely announce his death. That would have been sad and awfully grievous. But now he must kill him himself. He must sacrifice him on the altar. He must tie him, cut his throat, the throat of his beloved, of his only child. That was the demand placed upon Abraham's faith. And that message Abraham clearly understood.

But even this is not all. Isaac was also the child of the promise. For him Abraham had waited twenty-five long years anxiously. From a natural point of view, there was no hope that he would ever receive another child and that there was another possibility of the promise being fulfilled. For both Sarah and he were dead and well-stricken with age. To butcher Isaac meant to butcher his hope. To cut his throat meant not only to pierce his own heart, but also implied that he would bid farewell to all the hope of the promise, the promise that he would become a great nation. Surely, the test was very severe, and never must we imagine that it was not accompanied with much struggle. For also this struggle is indicated in the words of our text.

Now we must close by repeating the truth that faith, and faith only, is the victory, the victory in all our trials and temptations, the victory in life and in death. And do not forget: because it is faith that is the victory, therefore the victory is not ours, although we may walk in the way of that victory, but it is God's. Faith is the gift of God. And the strengthening of faith and the upholding of faith is always the gift of God. And therefore, when faith is the victory, the victory is God's victory, in which we may walk and which we may enjoy now and forevermore.

## 2

I discussed the test to which Abraham was submitted when God told him to sacrifice his only son Isaac. I then said that this test of Abraham's faith produced, first of all, a struggle in Abraham before he had the victory. And of this struggle I speak now.

We read in the words of our text that Abraham when God thus tried him did some accounting, some considering, some logical reasoning and comparing, and that finally he came to the conclusion that it was good for him by simple faith to obey the injunction of God and to offer up his son Isaac. In this one word, "accounting" (Heb. 11:19), we have, as it were, indicated the entire struggle that was fought in the heart and soul and mind of Abraham before he went and obeyed the word of God. It indicates an act of the mind, an act of the intellect, and an act of careful consideration, of the weighing of all the factors that enter into a certain case, a careful comparison of pro and con. Abraham therefore did not go at it blindly, but after careful consideration. It was not thus, that the entire thing embarrassed and surprised him, so that he did not know what he was doing. But on the contrary, what he did was the result of deliberation and accounting.

This act on the part of Abraham presupposed that there were two sides to the question he faced, and that before he chose for either the one or the other, he compared the two as to their relative importance and value. Even as a family who deliberates about leaving the old world and coming to the shores of the Western hemisphere considers both sides—the leaving of home and country and relatives and friends, on the one hand, and improvement of the material conditions, on the other—and weighs those two sides in the balance before they take the step of emigrating from the fatherland, so also Abraham did some accounting, some considering. The outcome of the struggle, of this deliberation, the conclusion to which Abraham came, is told in the words of our text. The ultimate result was that Abraham accounted that God was mighty even to raise his son from the dead if need be, and that therefore he could safely go and obey God. But we can easily imagine that before Abraham reached this conclusion, he must have fought a fierce struggle within himself as he was considering the whole case from every aspect.

The different aspects of the problem that Abraham faced we can easily construe. We can without much difficulty form a picture of the battle that was fought in Abraham's mind at this time. It was the battle between faith and reason, between things seen and unseen. On the one hand, there were things that were very real from the point of view of reason, of the things that could be seen. If Abraham obeyed, he could expect that ever after he probably would repent, at least be steeped in sorrow and grief all the rest of his life. For he loved Isaac, and his father-heart could not be satisfied with the idea that he had killed his son with his own hand. If he obeyed, his reason could easily figure that this was besides the end of all his expectations and hope. For long years he had waited to see his hope realized. Now he was to extinguish the last and only ray of hope from his heart if he obeyed. In a word, if he obeyed, it would simply be the cause of his own and Sarah's grief and misery ever after. Anyone could see that. They were the things visible. And hence, according to the conclusion of reason, Abraham would have disobeyed surely.

On the other hand, there were the things invisible. God had given him the promise that in Isaac his posterity should be founded. And surely, God was powerful to fulfill that promise even though he should kill Isaac. That was not a conclusion of reason. It did not belong to the things that are seen. For Abraham could not see how his posterity could ever after be founded in Isaac if he once had cut his throat and burnt him as a sacrifice to God. But God was powerful to realize his promise, although Abraham could not possibly see how.

In a word, the things that Abraham considered were these. On the one hand, there was obedience, unconditional obedience, the loss and death of Isaac, invisible things, God's promise, and God's power. On the other hand, there was the possibility of disobedience: he could keep Isaac, could save himself and his wife the terrible experience and remorse of having been instrumental in killing his own and only begotten son; but at the same time he would cut himself loose from God and could not possibly expect anything from him in the future. Reason told him that by disobedience he could be instrumental in fulfilling the very promise of God himself. Faith informed him that he could obey and leave the fulfillment of the promise to God in spite of apparent impossibilities. These things he weighed carefully. These things were the cause of a terrible struggle. But the outcome of it all was that he accounted that God was mighty to raise his son from the dead.

In that faith, which is the evidence of things not seen and the substance of things hoped for, Abraham had the victory. He believed in God, and he believed the promise of God. And that was for him sufficient. For the text tells us that Abraham obeyed, and that he sacrificed his son Isaac. To be sure, he did not sacrifice him in reality. The knife that was about to butcher his son was not allowed to touch his throat. But that does not make the slightest difference for the test to which Abraham was submitted and for the reaching of God's purpose. Abraham surely did sacrifice Isaac as to his intention. There cannot be the slightest doubt about this fact. In his experience he went through the whole performance. As to his personal condition he obeyed God perfectly in this entire incident. He did obey God and was perfectly ready to surrender his son and to put him to death and sacrifice him according to the word of the Almighty.

So much is very evident. For, first, we must not forget that after Abraham was through accounting, he simply went early in the morning to accomplish what God had demanded. That was already the decisive step. That departure from his home without deliberating, no doubt, with Sarah his wife—that departure, with all that was necessary for the burnt offering—proves that Abraham had reached the conclusion of faith, and that God, if necessary, was powerful to raise his son from the dead. And if there might still be any doubt about the firmness of Abraham's intentions and about the strength of his determination and faith, we must remember that Abraham sacrificed Isaac a thousand times over in his own experience and mind. For do not forget, he had to travel three days with Isaac at his side and with the intention in his heart of killing that beloved son. To be sure, God tried Abraham sorely. Intentionally he told him to travel three days and to go to Mount Moriah, there to accomplish the deed of obedience.

Those three days were extremely hard days for Abraham. If he thought that he was all through accounting the moment he had left the house, he surely made a mistake. Time and again he must have figured it all over. He must have weighed the possibilities in the balance of his mind over and over again. He might still return. He might still save the boy. He might still save himself and his wife all this misery. He might still disobey. And Satan also must have followed this faithful servant on his way to Moriah. Surely, the fact that Abraham finished the three days' journey without wavering and without once turning back shows that he was perfectly ready to obey, and that all the time the conclusion remained firm in his mind: God is mighty to raise my son from the dead.

And finally, if all this were not sufficient to establish the fact that Abraham, as to his intention and experience, sacrificed Isaac, follow him then as he climbs the mount with Isaac on his side. Follow him, and listen to the question of the victim: "Where is the lamb for the burnt offering?" (Gen. 22:7). Consider that in spite of all this Abraham remained firm. Follow him to the very top of the mountain and see him bind his son on the altar. Watch him lift the murderous knife, that will the next minute pierce the throat of his only begotten son and that will deprive him of all that is dear to him on earth; and judge whether Abraham did not obey, and whether the expression of our text is any too strong: "By faith Abraham...offered up Isaac" (Heb. 11:17).

To be sure, Abraham gained the victory. And the victory he gained by faith, our text tells us. What was that faith? That faith was, first, faith in the sure promise of God. Our text tells us, or rather reminds us, that God had given him a definite promise. He had told him that he would be the father of many and of great nations. But that was not all. That promise as such would not have been sufficient at this crisis. But God had given him a far more definite promise. He had assured him that his posterity would be founded in Isaac, for he said: "In Isaac shall thy seed be called" (v. 18). In that promise Abraham had the assurance that Isaac would not die, but live. That promise he had *received*, according to the translation of the text; but the original uses the stronger word *accepted*. Abraham had not only received the promise, but he had by faith accepted it. He had embraced it. He was certain in himself of the promise of God. He had believed that God would surely fulfill it. And now he was called to do what seemingly made the fulfillment of that promise impossible. He was called to kill his son. How, then, could the promise ever be fulfilled? That was the problem Abraham could not solve by reason.

But that was also the problem he did solve by faith, which is an evidence of things unseen, and the substance of things hoped for. By faith he turned the order of the argument around. He did not start from things seen. He did not first ask the question: "How can Isaac live if I kill him?" But he first established the truth: "Isaac shall live. That is the promise of God." That promise he had accepted. To that promise he clung. That was simply a fact, the assurance of which no one could take from him. Isaac shall live. But how can that be if Abraham should first kill him? By faith the problem was easy to solve. And Abraham, having established, first of all, that Isaac should and must live, would answer that question, as he did: "God is mighty to raise him from the dead."

And thus we see that also in this case faith is the power that ultimately clings to the truth and faithfulness of God. That was the case with Sarah, as we saw before. For also she judged him faithful who had promised. And that was also the case with Abraham. Surely, his faith was first of all founded on the promise, the promise of God. But what would the promise have been to him without him who promised? If his faith had not clung through the promise of God to God himself, it still would have faltered and succumbed. But now he considered ultimately not the mere promise, but him who had promised. He judged him powerful and faithful to fulfill the promise, even though this would require the seemingly impossible. Even if it would be necessary to raise Isaac from the dead, Abraham knew that God would realize his promise.

By faith Abraham clung to God. By faith he had vital communion with him. By faith he drew all his strength from the God of revelation. By faith he received strength to obey. And therefore, it is utterly true that in the power of faith he obeyed and sacrificed his son Isaac. Faith is the victory of the Christian. Always, also in our time, in the midst of trials and temptations, we must exercise that faith, and by faith see the promise, and considering him who has promised, judge him powerful to accomplish what he has once spoken even though we cannot see.

This faith will never be ashamed. It was not in the case of Abraham. For our text tells us that he actually received his son back from the dead. Again, not in reality, but "in a figure," in a parable, the text says (v. 19). As to Abraham's feeling, as to his intentions, he had already sacrificed his son. As to his experience, he surely had already surrendered him, and therefore he had given his son over unto death. That son, whom he ties upon the altar, was his son no more: he had already given him to the power of death. For his personal feeling, that son was already in the power of death. And therefore, when at the crucial moment the voice comes from heaven and prevents the uplifted knife from cutting the throat of the victim, Abraham actually does receive his son back from the dead, even though it be in a figure. For him it was as if Isaac had been dead already. To him it seemed that his son had returned upon the voice of the Almighty from heaven from the realm of death. Faith is the victory. And faith is never ashamed.

Abraham returns, glad because he may go with his son, but infinitely more satisfied he is because he has been strengthened to obey his God unconditionally. A terrible struggle he had experienced in the last few days. But he conquered. And can you imagine that the faith of Abraham is not stronger than before? Surely, also this trial had worked together for his good. For his faith was much stronger. He was now ready to obey God always, to obey him blindly, firmly convinced that God was powerful to realize the unseen.

This, then, is the practical purpose of the words of our text. This is the great lesson we learn from this climax of Abraham's faith. The trials of life are for the strengthening of our faith in the way of obedience. But we must say still more. For also here it is the glory of God we must adore. In the trials of life God gives special strength, so that we may obey. Abraham did not obey in his own strength. For also this powerful faith was not his by nature. We know how Abraham could be afraid, and how he could in his own power even twice invent a story to escape death, and spread the false report that Sarah was his sister. That is Abraham by nature. But this victory of Abraham reveals the grace and the wonderful power of God. And therefore, it glorifies the God of our salvation, and not the patriarch. Thus it is also today and in our case. God also sends us trials. And he does so with an educative purpose. But this purpose would never be reached if he did not also give the power to stand and to overcome. Faith, to be sure, is the victory. But this faith is the power of God. And therefore, let us in all trials and tribulations sing by faith:

> For Jehovah I am waiting,
> And my hope is in His word,
> In His word of promise given;
> Yea, my soul waits for the Lord.[2]

---

2　No. 363:3, in *The Psalter*.

*Chapter 18*

# ISAAC BY FAITH
# BLESSING JACOB AND ESAU

By faith Isaac blessed Jacob and Esau concerning things to come.
—*Hebrews 11:20*

**1**

F aith is the victory in the midst of trials and temptations. That is the truth we considered in connection with the illustration of Abraham's sacrifice of his son Isaac. God, so we noticed, sends unto his children trials and temptations, not in order that he might find out how strong our faith actually is, for he knows all things and has no need of such external means to find out what is in the heart of man. But he sends them these trials in order that they might struggle with them and, by the power of his own grace overcoming them, might attain to a better and stronger faith in an ethical, spiritual way.

Faith, however, is also the victory over natural weaknesses and desires of our natural and sinful man, over what are often called the sins and weaknesses of character. We saw that there is often a sort of practical contrast between faith and reason, that faith tells us one thing while reason would dictate something quite different. Thus we explained the fact that Abraham did some accounting when he was called to sacrifice his son Isaac. And by faith he came to the conclusion that God could raise him up from the dead. In such cases the struggle is mainly one of our faith over against our intellect and our rational nature.

But there is also not infrequently a struggle between our natural inclinations and desires and our faith. Not only our reason but also our will, our feelings, and our desires, our entire character, must be dominated by faith. Faith must have control over our entire old man. It must have the victory whenever there is a contrast, whenever there is a sort of clash between our natural desires and faith. This struggle probably characterizes the majority of the people of God. There are not so many children of God who experience the conflict between faith and reason; but most of them will be able to speak of a struggle between faith and their natural desires and inclinations, between faith and their natural character.

They must always fight the battle, in order to subject their natural desires and inclinations, the desires of their old nature, to the power of faith. In that respect the children of God often have a fierce battle to fight. Their natural desires are strong. They are inclined to follow them, unless faith has the victory. Thus it is, for instance, in regard to the injunction of Scripture that we must forgive one another even as our transgressions are blotted out by the Lord our Savior (Eph. 4:32). This injunction militates against our pride and haughtiness. It is often a difficult thing for us to stoop so low as to be able to forgive and forget an offence against our person. But faith must have the victory and overcome our natural desires. I think it is especially this truth that is clearly illustrated in the words of the text we are about to discuss. "By faith Isaac blessed Jacob and Esau concerning things to come" (Heb. 11:20).

At a first reading of our text we are probably inclined to ask: How can the author of the epistle to the Hebrews refer to Isaac as an example of faith? How can he give this man Isaac a place among the heroes of faith? And above all, how can he quote this particular incident of the blessing of Jacob and Esau as a proof that actually he deserves a place among the other examples of faith mentioned in this chapter? Was not the blessing of Jacob and Esau a mere blunder as far as Isaac was concerned?

To be sure, as to the first question we asked, we would say that there is among all the patriarchs not a weaker figure from a natural point of view, not a personality that is less attractive than this man Isaac. If we would write his biography, we would be inclined to say, first, that he was a spoiled child. This was, to be sure, very natural. For, first, he was an only child. But besides, he was a child for whose birth the parents had long waited for many, many years. He was their only joy, a child of their old age. We can understand that the aged parents were very naturally inclined to spoil the boy from his youth up. We can imagine how carefully he was guarded. In early youth he would spend most of his time in Sarah's tent, where he was undoubtedly petted, and tell his imaginary troubles.[1] Perhaps he would still be with his mother when other boys already went out with their fathers to the field or accompanied the men when they would go to find pasture for their cattle. All his desires were immediately fulfilled. Never was he allowed to exercise his own willpower or to cope personally with the difficulties of life. He gradually became used to seeing things prepared for him without any exertion on his part. And the result was that Isaac, when he was already a man, knew nothing, or very little, of the difficulties of life. He never met with opposition and adversity and knew nothing of the joy of overcoming difficulties by personal effort.

When he was about thirty-seven years old, his mother died; and for many years he was grieved and filled with sorrow because of the death of Sarah. Ever after, he would continue to spend in Sarah's tent his days, in order to meditate on past occurrences and dream about the sweet memories of days gone by. When he was forty, his father considered it time that Isaac should be married. This marriage is all decided for him. He must not go himself the long way to Mesopotamia, to fetch his wife from thence. For Abraham knows full well that this man of forty is not acquainted with the hardships of life, and he is afraid that Isaac will not be able to endure the difficulties of the journey. He therefore sends his servant to find Isaac a wife and to bring her safely home to him. When Rebekah arrives, Isaac is meditating at eventide in the field, and he brings her to his mother's tent, that there they might live together. It is in the arms of Rebekah that Isaac is finally comforted over his mother's death.

But Rebekah, who is far stronger than Isaac, can never cure him of his weaknesses. He always remained a spoiled child. Never could Rebekah prepare his meals so as to suit his taste; and perhaps he would always maintain that Sarah, his mother, could do it far better.

---

1    The text is not clear here. Perhaps Hoeksema means to say that, like any other boy, Isaac liked to spend time with his mother and tell her about the things in his young mind, or about "his imaginary troubles."

And of nice meals Isaac was fond. It was only after Esau, his firstborn, had grown up that Isaac was reminded of the meals he used to get. For Esau could prepare his venison just as he liked it. For we read: "Isaac loved Esau, because he did eat of his venison" (Gen. 25:28).

At Gerar he imitated his father and told the lie that Rebekah was his sister, for fear they might kill him. And when on a certain day the fraud is detected, and Isaac is found sporting with his wife, he stands before Abimelech and says: "Because I said, Lest I die for her" (Gen. 26:9). When his servants dig wells and a controversy arises about them, Isaac moves and never makes an attempt to defend his rights, till finally he succeeds in keeping one without dispute and calls it "Rehoboth" (vv. 18–22). When he is one hundred thirty years, he feels so exhausted and old that he calls his son to bless him, before he may die, although he still lived fifty years after this (27; 35:28–29). We would say, therefore, that from a natural point of view there was nothing in Isaac that merits for him a place in this exhibition of heroes. We cannot understand that the author of Hebrews chooses Isaac as one of the heroes of faith.

On the face of it, this would seem to become still worse if we consider the particular incident quoted, and which, according to the author, is evidence that Isaac deserves a place among the heroes of faith. For the author quotes as proof the blessing of his two sons, Jacob and Esau. According to the author, it was by faith that he blessed them, and by faith that he blessed Jacob first, and then Esau. By faith, therefore, according to the author, Isaac blessed the second son instead of the firstborn.

Now if you compare this with the chapter that records the history of this incident, you receive a far different impression. We read that Isaac was old, and that he felt as if he soon would die. He loves his son Esau for the venison. And he wants to give him the first birth blessing. On the other hand, he also knows what has happened. He knows that Rebekah loves Jacob more than Esau and claims that the birthright blessing of the twins does not belong to Esau, but to Jacob. This had been revealed to her by the Lord before the twins were born. For according to Genesis 25:23, "And the LORD said unto her, Two nations are in thy womb, and two manner of people shall be separated from thy bowels; and the one people shall be stronger than the other people; and the elder shall serve the younger." This Rebekah had told Isaac, and the latter knew that she certainly would claim the birthright blessing for Jacob. Besides, Isaac knew, too, that Esau had sold the birthright for a mess of pottage.

Nevertheless, he wants to bless Esau. And he thinks about the best way of bestowing the blessing upon him till he finally gets restless and nervous over it. The shrewd and clever Rebekah is quick to notice that there is something brewing in the mind of the blind old man. And shrewdly guessing the truth, she takes her precautions to prevent the worst. First, she manages to procure an old suit of clothes of the careless Esau. And then she watches the two every day, to be ready in case of need. And when finally the day comes that Isaac calls Esau and tells him to go hunting and prepare some venison for him, in order that he may bless him, Rebekah stands around the corner and hears the entire conversation. She hurries to Jacob, commissions him to kill two kids, prepares some nice venison, makes a pair of rough kid gloves and piece of neckwear of the same stuff, and sends him to his blind father, to deceive him and receive the blessing.

When Jacob comes to his father, the latter is suspicious. He asks why his son is back so soon. He calls his son to him, to feel him. He even smells his clothes. And he is still in doubt. But nevertheless, being afraid to wait, and fearing still more to call Rebekah to verify the identity of the son who stands before him, he blesses him. And when he has bestowed the birthright blessing on his second son, Esau comes, and the fraud is detected. Esau bewails his miserable condition and is bitter because of the fraud. But it is now too late. He also receives a blessing, but it is not the birthright blessing. He must be content to receive what is still left. And he hates his brother Jacob.

This is the history of what is briefly recorded in the words of our text: "By faith Isaac blessed Jacob and Esau concerning things to come." And we are inclined to ask: Is this an act of faith on the part of Isaac? Is there indeed faith to be discovered in the whole transaction on the part of any of those concerned in it? Was it not a matter of shrewdness and deception from beginning to end? Rebekah is shrewd and not any too scrupulous as to the means employed to gain her end. Jacob is a deceiver and bears his name "supplanter" with honor. Isaac attempts to be smart but makes a serious blunder and is outgeneraled by his keenly perceiving wife. The only character who appeals to us from a natural point of view and has our sympathy in the whole scene is Esau, who gets the worst of it. How, then, can the author of this chapter tell us that it was an act of faith on the part of Isaac when he blessed his two sons, and blessed them in that order, first Jacob and then Esau? Apparently, as we said, this is a mere blunder.

However, we must begin by believing that the author of this chapter is right when he informs us that Isaac blessed his two sons by faith. For this is the word of God. Hence, we may never explain the text on the theory that it was a blunder on the part of Isaac that he blessed his two sons. If we take this standpoint, and from this point of view inquire how the faith of Isaac becomes evident in the blessing of his two sons, we do not have to look long for an answer to this question. For then it will become plain, as we hope to demonstrate later, first of all, that Isaac was a very weak person from a natural point of view. He was not accustomed to fight against self and to deny his own desires and natural inclinations. His natural desire was to give the blessing to Esau, for he loved him for the sake of the venison.

Fact is, however, that he gave the blessing to Jacob, and that, too, as we hope to see, not by accident or through ignorance, but consciously and willingly. This he could do only by faith. And therefore, after all the transaction was not a mere fraud, but much rather the result of a fierce struggle on the part of Isaac. And in this struggle Isaac gradually becomes the victor. He overcomes his natural desires and inclinations by a true faith.

## 2[2]

I asked the question: How does the faith of Isaac become evident in this blessing of his two sons? And briefly I also answered that question by saying that the blessing upon Jacob was not a mere fraud but rather the outcome of a fierce struggle in the heart of Isaac.

---

2 The transcript titles this sermon "Isaac Blessing Jacob and Esau." However, since it is on the same text and topic of the previous sermon, I have included both sermons in one chapter.

We must remember in this connection that Isaac loved Esau. Esau was a rough and tumble sort of man, a child of nature. He would not sit like Jacob in Rebekah's tent all the while, to be caressed and petted. Nor was it of his liking to take care of the flock and dream about the future. On the contrary, Esau loved adventure. He loved the chase. He liked to go out into woods and meet with dangers and hardships, as well as experience the charm and fascination there is in hunting. Physically he was a strong man; and as to his character, he was daring and rough, thinking little about the future but living day by day, acting recklessly without thinking about the results of his actions. He was the very contrast of his brother. Jacob was gentle and less strong; Esau was strong and rough. Jacob was shrewd and cautious; Esau was careless and without worries. Jacob was calculating and deceitful; Esau was open and honest. Jacob was a businessman; Esau was a happy-go-lucky child of the woods. It was a pleasure to meet Esau with his open face, his hearty laugh, and his big voice; to meet Jacob put one on his guard immediately. Esau was loved by his father, and loved he was because in a way he was the very opposite of Isaac.

Isaac certainly did not love Esau because of his spiritual attractions, for them Esau did not have. Spiritually Esau was, as Scripture tells us, a fornicator, who cared little about God and religion, who trampled underfoot the most sacred things, and who would for that reason sell his birthright for a mess of pottage, as he did (Heb. 12:16). He did not mind at all to mingle with the Canaanites, and in spite of the desires and prayers of his mother, he would marry the daughters of the land. Isaac was well acquainted with this side of Esau's life. His love for Esau was a mere natural love, a love that was all the stronger because of its admiration for Esau's strength.

It is a fact often observed that one man loves another because he perceives in him exactly those traits that he himself is lacking. And this was also true of Isaac. Isaac knew that he was weak. He knew that he had but little courage. He realized that he did not have the strength and the moral courage to cope with the difficulties of life. In short, Isaac perceived his own picture rather in the weak and gentle Jacob from a natural point of view; but in Esau he saw exactly those traits that he felt that he himself was lacking. Esau was a strong man, and Isaac admired him for it. Esau was a daredevil, and the more he saw it the more Isaac loved him for it. His soul became attached to his eldest son, just because he noticed the sharp contrast and because he realized that his son possessed admirable traits that he himself was lacking. Besides, he loved the venison Esau prepared for him. For Isaac was strongly attracted by the material side of life. The more he would regard his son, the more he would admire him. Every time Esau came home from the chase and brought home some more venison, his love to the man would grow stronger.

In short, Isaac's natural inclination was to give the birthright blessing to Esau. It would demand a tremendous struggle, it would demand a severe self-denial, if he would deprive his son, the son whom he loved, of the blessing and give it to his second son, in whose gentle character he perceived his own weakness. He would have to set aside all his natural love and affection. He would have to forget all about the nice venison his son had prepared for him in days gone by, before he could make up his mind to bless Jacob instead of Esau. In a word, from a natural point of view, from the point of view of his character and natural inclination, from the point of view of his experience, from the viewpoint of visible things, Isaac would never have blessed Jacob instead of his firstborn son. Add to this that Isaac was a weak person, that he was spoiled and self-willed, and that he was not wont to deny his own whims and fancies, and you draw the conclusion that Isaac will surely bless his son whom he loves, and not Jacob.

But from a spiritual, invisible point of view, from the point of view of faith, things were quite different. First, we must never forget that the pronouncement of the patriarchal blessing was after all nothing but an expression of what had been decreed by God himself upon the sons who were blessed. The blessing as such had no magic power, so that we may believe that Esau would have been blessed if by mistake Isaac had been allowed to bless him. No, it was of power only because it was given to the patriarchs to know the counsel of God with regard to the future of their sons, and to express that counsel by way of prophecy upon them.

According to the regular course of events, this was not so difficult, since the covenantal blessing was always bestowed on the firstborn.

But in this case it was quite different. Had not something special been revealed to the parents? And had not something extraordinary happened too? Most surely! First, when Rebekah is about to be delivered, and she inquires of the Lord concerning her condition, the Lord reveals to her that she will be the mother of two nations, that the one nation shall be inferior to the other, and that the elder shall serve the younger.

In other words, also the apostle Paul calls attention to the fact that it had been revealed to them that not the firstborn, but the younger should receive the covenantal blessing and should be loved of the covenant God (Rom. 9:12–13). This Isaac well knew, for Rebekah must have informed him of it. And especially when the boys grew up, and when the mother loved Jacob, the younger, while she perceived that the father loved the older of the boys, she must have often been anxious about the future and must have reminded her husband of the fact that by divine decree the blessing belonged not to Esau, but to Jacob.

But still more had taken place. Esau had shown himself to be completely indifferent to spiritual things. He had shown himself as without spiritual life and interest and without any spiritual inclinations. He married the daughters of the land, who were a grief to both Isaac and Rebekah. And to fully reveal his carelessness regarding spiritual things, he had sold his birthright for a mess of pottage. All these things made it very clear to faith that Esau was not the man whom God had decreed to have the blessing, that Esau was not the chosen of God to take his place in the covenant. All these things made it very evident that God had decreed that Jacob should have the blessing instead of Esau.

Hence, from the invisible side, from the side of God's counsel, it all looked very different. Then it was evident that the promise was upon Jacob instead of upon Esau. To faith it was very clear that Esau was not the man fit to receive the covenantal blessing. And that faith demanded of Isaac to set aside his natural love and inclinations, to overcome his weakness of character, and in spite of all to bless Jacob instead of the firstborn.

There, then, was the contrast, and at the same time the cause of a fierce struggle in Isaac's heart. What shall he do? Shall he believe, and act upon that faith, and bless Jacob? Or shall he follow his natural love and bless the older son? In the one case, faith conquers, and he denies his natural desires; in the other case, his natural love is victorious, and faith is defeated. And at the time when after a long struggle, of even years perhaps, he sends Esau after the venison, he shows himself so weak that it is his natural love and desire that have the better of him. But after all, this is not the end of the story. And the result is, under the power and guidance of God, however strongly you may repudiate the fraud on the part of Rebekah and Jacob—the result is that Isaac's faith conquers, and that he blesses Jacob and blesses him willingly.

That also in the case of Isaac faith had the victory, and the patriarch blessed his sons as he did willingly and consciously by faith, is perhaps the most difficult point to prove. Yet if we study the history as it is recorded in Genesis 27 and 28, it soon becomes evident that this is nevertheless the case. To understand this final victory on the part of Isaac, we must follow this development in Isaac's spiritual life. First of all, he blesses Jacob instead of Esau, unwillingly at first, but strongly in doubt as to the identity of the person he blesses. Second, he does not revoke the blessing when the fraud is discovered, but believingly he abides by God's will. Third, he confirms the blessing consciously and willingly when Jacob is on the point of leaving for Padan-aram.

As to the first, we would say that it is really an inconceivability that the fraud of Rebekah and Jacob could have been successful if Isaac had been firmly resolved to bless Esau. We notice all through the history of this incident how strong the doubt of the old father is with regard to the identity of the person who stands before him. First, he is suspicious because the venison came so soon; and this suspicion is by no means removed by the pious answer of his son. For this very piety of the answer rather strengthens the suspicion on the part of Isaac. Hence, he calls him to himself, that he may feel whether it is Jacob or Esau. Having satisfied himself that the hands are rough and hairy like those of his firstborn, he nevertheless maintains that the voice is Jacob's voice. And even after he has eaten, he calls him once more to kiss him, in order evidently that he might smell his clothes.

In short, it is at least very clear that Isaac was not at all convinced that the man who was standing before him was Esau, but that he had a rather strong suspicion that it was Jacob. How then must it be explained that he blessed him nevertheless? We know but one answer: Isaac's faith had told him all the time that it was wrong to bless Esau, and that the blessing should go to Jacob. He was not firmly determined. And now Jacob after all appears before him, he blesses him in spite of the fact that he is strongly in doubt as to the identity of the person. If Isaac had no faith at all, he could have easily waited to discover whether also Esau would return. But his faith was still fighting. His faith still troubled him, even after he had sent Esau after the venison. And this fighting faith was after all the reason that he blessed Jacob.

But yet this would not prove the complete victory of his faith. And therefore, we must not forget to add that when the fraud was discovered for a certainty, when the real Esau returns, Isaac does not repent, nor revoke the blessing, but rather confirms the same. In Hebrews 12, we find that Isaac was not sorry of what he had done. We would expect that because of his strong love for Esau he would have repented when he saw that strong son before him weeping and bewailing his sad condition. We read, however, that Esau found no place of repentance (v. 7), which can mean but one thing, that there was no repentance in the heart of Isaac after once he had blessed Jacob.

And that is also the impression we receive from the narrative itself. When Esau returns, also the natural love that is in Isaac's heart begins to stir and to work. For we read that the old man trembled (Gen. 27:33). But nevertheless, he does not repent. On the contrary, he repeats the blessing, first by saying that Jacob shall indeed be blessed. Isaac is firmly convinced that there was no mistake about it all, but that indeed Jacob was the heir of the blessing according to God's decree. And this he could know only by faith. Second, he inserts in the so-called blessing that he bestows on Esau the well-known words: "Thou...shalt serve thy brother" (v. 40). That was taken, in fact, from the very words God had spoken to Rebekah, his wife: "The elder shall serve the younger" (Gen. 25:23). Hence, Isaac now spoke by faith, and by faith in the word of God alone. After the deed had once been performed, there was no repentance on the part of Isaac, but rather the firm conviction of truth that thus it had to be according to the will of God. Faith now had made him one with God's will, and therefore he had practically gained the victory.

You might object, perhaps, that nevertheless he did not as such perform the act of blessing by faith, but rather by lucky mistake. But do not forget that Isaac actually blessed his son Jacob over again when he is on the point of leaving for Padan-aram. Consciously he had already given the inferior blessing to Esau by faith. In that same faith he now also wishes to give the main blessing to Jacob consciously. And therefore, before he leaves, Isaac calls him and says: "God Almighty bless thee, and make thee fruitful, and multiply thee, that thou mayest be a multitude of people; and give thee the blessing of Abraham, to thee, and to thy seed with thee; that thou mayest inherit the land wherein thou art a stranger, which God gave unto Abraham" (Gen. 28:3-4). Here you have the complete victory, and at the same time the complete realization of the words of our text: "By faith Isaac blessed Jacob and Esau concerning things to come." Here it is that we see Isaac fully victorious over his natural love and inclinations, fully victorious over his weakness of character, consciously expressing the main covenantal blessing upon the head of Jacob. Faith also in Isaac's case was the perfect victory.

Thus it is always. Faith must often conquer our weaknesses and our natural inclinations. In the case of Isaac it was his natural love of Esau that was in his way to obey God. In our case it is often the love of natural things, the love of the world and of pleasure, that prevents us from gaining the victory of faith. But if we have the principle of faith in our hearts, faith must conquer, and faith will surely conquer. That would not be the case if faith was our own work. But faith is the gift and work of God in our hearts. Through faith God reveals his strength in our weakness.

And therefore, the glory is always his. It was his. It was his work that gave Isaac strength to conquer, that gave him power to close his heart to the piercing and heartrending cries of Esau, that gave him finally strength consciously to repeat the blessing upon the head of Jacob. Thus it is also with us. In the strength of our God, through faith, we must not only conquer, but we surely shall conquer—conquer sin, conquer our natural and sinful desires, conquer the world, conquer in the name of our God. And the victory will be ours!

# Chapter 19

# JACOB
# DYING IN THE FAITH

By faith Jacob, when he was a dying, blessed both the sons of Joseph; and worshipped, leaning upon the top of his staff.
—*Hebrews 11:21*

The righteous shall live by faith. Such is the teaching of all Scripture; and this is also the main emphasis of the chapter we are now discussing. The righteous must live by and from the principle of faith. And faith as it is presented throughout in Hebrews 11 is the evidence of things unseen and the substance of things hoped for. We may indeed say that the Christian is as his faith is. His righteousness, his hope, his love, and his entire life are entirely in harmony with his faith. If his faith is clear and strong, he is also assured that he is righteous before God. Then his hope is also firm and unshaken, and constantly he looks for the things that are above, not for the things on the earth. If his faith is strong and assured, then his love of God and of the brethren is also strong and ardent. And then, too, his entire life and walk are indeed to the glory of God. Faith therefore, we may say, is the root of the entire life of the Christian. It is its beginning and source.

It is therefore entirely proper for the Christian to live in the assurance of faith. Many people of God seem to deny this. They seem to speak about the assurance of faith as if that might be the great aim of the Christian but as if nevertheless it were hardly attainable in this present life. In fact, there are Christians, or so-called Christians, who not only live in continual doubt, but who speak as if doubt were the only proper attitude of the child of God. They seem to think that it is pious to doubt. Frequently such Christians even would reprove others who live more joyously in the assurance that they are saved by grace.

In reality, however, this doubt and continual uncertainty is deeply sinful. There is nothing pious about it. There is nothing in such an attitude that can be to the glory of God and that can beautify the life of the believer.

Deeply sinful is such an attitude of doubt, first, because it is not only doubt of our own salvation but in its deepest root is doubt of the word of God. Those who assume this attitude will probably deny this. It is not the word of God, so they say, but ourselves and our own salvation that we doubt. Nevertheless this is only apparently so, and doubt in its deepest root is certainly a denial of the word of God. God assures us in his word that there is salvation in the name of Jesus Christ our Savior, and that the righteous shall live by faith. And if we walk about in the world doubting and lamenting and sighing, we are really doubting the word of God himself.

But, second, such an attitude of doubt is also deeply sinful because from such a principle of life it is impossible to walk in the way of the word of God and to live to his glory and to the glory of our Redeemer, who loved us even unto death. It is impossible to reveal the love of God in our lives and to be conscious of the gratitude we owe to God if our faith is not firm and if we live in an attitude of doubt. The Christian must live in that attitude of faith that the Heidelberg Catechism defines in the first Lord's Day, when it teaches us that it is our only comfort in life and death that we are not our own, but belong to our faithful Savior Jesus Christ. It is therefore very important that we discuss the heroes of faith mentioned in Hebrews 11 and notice how they lived and walked and died by faith.

Faith is the victory. This we have already mentioned a few times in connection with the chapter we are now discussing. Faith is the victory in our entire life. It is the power that can make us living witnesses. It is the strength whereby we embrace the promises of God. It is the evidence of things unseen and the substance of things hoped for. Faith is the victory in hours of trial and temptation, so that no matter what betides we keep our trust in the Lord our God. Faith is the victory, as we noticed earlier, also over our natural weaknesses and inclinations. Isaac loved Esau and meant to give him the blessing. But gradually his faith conquered, so that the writer of this epistle to the Hebrews is actually able to say that by faith he blessed both his sons.

Still more, faith is also the victory in the hour of death. In a way we may say that death is not only the last in the life of the Christian, but also its very climax. And the child of God who spends his entire life in the assurance and in the way of faith may also indeed live his dying hours by that same faith. Oh, it is indeed beautiful to see a child of God live and walk by faith in this world. It is beautiful to see him conquer the world by faith. But in a way we may say that it is still more beautiful to see him victorious by the power of our Lord Jesus Christ over the last enemy, which is death. It is to such a beautiful picture of the Christian's faith in the hour of death that we must now call your attention in connection with the words of our text.

Jacob, so the text tells us, "was a dying" when he performed this particular act of faith (Heb. 11:21). He was already in death's dark vale. Death already encompassed him with its strong and implacable arms. This we must emphasize, as the text also does, in order to understand the beauty of this particular act of faith on the part of Jacob. To be sure, there was faith revealed also in his act of worshiping considered all by itself. And faith was expressed, too, in the act of blessing the two sons of Joseph.

Nevertheless, if we would see the beauty of that faith that Jacob revealed here, then we must not forget that the author means to emphasize that Jacob's faith was still beautiful and strong and unwavering when his eyes closed already upon the scene of this present earthly life. This is evidently the chief intention of the author. For he says: "By faith Jacob, when he was a dying." These words do not simply designate the exact time when Jacob revealed this faith. They mean much more. The original word employed in this text reveals the purpose of the author still more clearly. The word really means "to be in the process of passing away, to die off," as the Dutch would have it, *afsterven*. In a word, the author practically says in our text: Jacob, when he was already in the very arms of death, when the shadows of death already began to cast themselves over him, when he already struggled with the last enemy, when he passed through death's dark vale, showed these signs of faith and blessed the two "sons of Joseph and worshiped, leaning upon the top of his staff" (v. 21).

What is death?

There is to man not a more natural enemy than death. Man was not created to die. On the contrary, he was created to obey and live. Man was not created with the desire in his bosom to pass away, to be carried away in the arms of death from this present world and life. He was created with the will to live in his soul. That will, that desire to live, is indestructible. It can never be removed from the heart of man. And because of this strong will to live, man hates death and all that is connected with it. Death is his most bitter enemy. And when death approaches, it creates a hard and bitter struggle. And in that struggle man can never have the victory, except by the grace of our Lord Jesus Christ. For death is powerful and merciless. It coolly selects its victims and snatches them away. Deaf to the cries of loving hearts, death is implacably severe. And when the shadow of death approaches, man realizes his powerlessness. He is very conscious of the fact that over against that enemy he stands unarmed and that nothing can prevail against him.

But there is more.

Death is suffering. Man is born under the power of death, and therefore he suffers and dies all his life. But especially when the end approaches, that suffering of death often becomes very severe. Oh, it is true that death approaches sometimes all of a sudden, like a whirlwind, like a flash of lightning, leaving no time for its victim either to fear or to think about anything, but carrying him away instantly from the very midst of this present life. Nevertheless, death more often approaches slowly and with repeated warnings of its coming. These warnings, these gloomy forebodings of death, consist in all kinds of troubles and suffering and sickness and affliction and weakness and weariness of the body and in the defects of old age. The body having been under the influence of the principle of death for years, it finally begins to reveal signs of that influence. Sickness sets in. Suffering begins. The body grows weak. The eye grows dim. The hand becomes feeble. And finally the last struggle comes, in which the body succumbs to the enemy and is overcome in the hour of death.

Such is the dying process of man, whether he is snatched away in the midst of life by a severe sickness or whether he dies slowly, in goodly old age. The process of death is always accompanied by suffering. And of course, that suffering is not merely of the body but also of the soul. Our physical condition certainly is very intimately related to the life of our soul, and the one often depends on the other. There is no such thing as a suffering of the body only, without any influence and effect upon our soul-life.

But there is still more. Death after all is not merely a natural result of the process of life, as many unbelievers would have it. On the contrary, it is punishment. All have sinned; in fact, all have sinned in our first father, Adam. All have become guilty. And guilt is the liability to punishment. And that punishment is death in all its forms. And that punishment is inflicted upon us by God, who is righteous and holy, and therefore is the expression of the wrath of God upon us. This is the worst feature of death. Man may deny this, but this denial is very vain. He can never root out the testimony of God in his heart that he is a sinner, that he is guilty, that therefore God inflicts the punishment of death upon him in his terrible wrath. And unless he repents in dust and ashes before the face of God and cries out, "God, be merciful to me a sinner" (Luke 18:13), his temporal death will pass into eternal desolation in hell. This is the terrible significance of death.

In that hour Jacob was when he blessed the sons of Joseph, worshiping and leaning upon the top of his staff. To be sure, he also experienced the suffering that accompanies the hour of death. It was an hour of darkness from a natural point of view also for him. He was a-dying, the text tells us. He was in the process of passing away. He was in the midst of the vale of death with all its horrors and sufferings. It is then that he did by faith what our text tells us. He is now an hundred forty-seven years old. And in that gray old man, stooped and bent under the burden of the years, you would not even recognize the Jacob of old. You could not possibly imagine that this old man is the same person as the shrewd youth, who knew how to get the blessing by fraud from his father instead of his older brother Esau.

Oh, Jacob had changed. To be sure, he changed from a natural point of view. His long and troublesome life had not been without impression upon him. The twenty years of service with his greedy uncle in Padan-aram, the fear of meeting his brother, the death of his greatly beloved Rachel, the bereavement of his dearest son Joseph, whom, as he imagined for over a dozen years, the wild beasts had devoured, the famine in Canaan and the forced exile in a strange land, far from the land of promise—all these troubles and vicissitudes had changed Jacob naturally. They had shaped him into a different man. Under the influence of all his experiences the look of the old shrewdness in his eyes had been rather softened into a look of bright and attractive intelligence. Sorrow and grief had plowed their deep and lasting furrows upon his countenance, and the old Jacob in him is scarcely recognizable.

But above all, Jacob had changed spiritually. He used to have an idea that he would have to help God along in the carrying out of his counsel. He could not completely place his trust and faith in the God of his fathers; and he put his confidence rather in an arm of flesh. But all this had been changed. At the Jabbok the Lord had appeared to him, and there he learned that it is of no avail to fight with mere human strength (Gen. 32:24–32). And the Lord himself had taught him very plainly and lastingly that only in faith, in childlike trust, could be his strength. Jacob had become Israel because he had been struggling with God and gained the victory by faith.

And now Israel was a-dying. He is old and feeble. And although he is not blind, as his father was, nevertheless also his eyes had grown dim, so that he could see but little. His strength had practically gone, and most of his time he spent in bed. Now let us ask: What are the thoughts and meditations of the old man as in the dim light of his tent the shadows of death are creeping over him? Is his mind perhaps busy with the experiences of the past, so that he grows weary and gloomy? Does he perhaps bewail his condition in this hour of death? Is he perhaps so in agony of physical suffering that it is impossible for him to fix his eyes on the things eternal? The very opposite is true, as we hope to see next time, the Lord willing. His faith had the victory even in the hour of death. He had his eye on the promise of God, and on that promise he fixed all his hope. With the fathers before him he looked for the city that has foundations, whose builder and maker is God (Heb. 11:10). And he desired the better, that is, the heavenly country.

May we also live in that faith that is the victory even over death. But remember that if you desire to have the light of that heavenly country shine in your eye when the hour of death approaches, then you must also walk in that faith and not love the things of the world and of this present time. We must set our affections continually on the things that are above, not on the things of the earth. Then, and then only, can we be sure, even when the shadows of death creep over us, that with Christ we shall appear in glory everlasting.

# Chapter 20

# JACOB BLESSING JOSEPH'S SONS

By faith Jacob, when he was a dying, blessed both the sons of Joseph; and worshipped, leaning upon the top of his staff.

—*Hebrews 11:21*

We asked and answered the question whether Jacob, when the shadows of death were creeping over his soul, was so overcome by the suffering of death that he had no thought for the things above and the things eternal. And our answer was, *no*. Even then he looked for the city that has foundations, whose builder and maker is God, and he desired with all his heart the heavenly country and the things that are above. That this is true is evident from the words of our text.

Let us look at these words in the light of history (Gen. 48). When Jacob was a-dying, a messenger had been sent to Joseph, who was leading a busy life in the midst of the strange country in which he sojourned. A messenger had been sent informing him that his father was seriously sick and that there was no hope of recovery. The first son of Rachel hurried to the dwelling of his old father and brought his own boys with him. And as they silently entered into the dwelling of the dying Israel, waiting in the door of his tent for the call to draw near, Joseph was undoubtedly wondering what would be the dying words of his father.

Joseph was rich and honored, one of the foremost men of the country—next to Pharaoh the most important personage in Egypt, practically ruling the country. The two boys he brought with him, Manasseh and Ephraim, were at that time about twenty years of age. Their mother was a daughter of the priest of On, an Egyptian woman therefore; and the boys could hardly be distinguished from the real inhabitants of the land. They were princes in the land and were considered to be of both royal and priestly descent. Their position in the land was equaled only by Pharaoh himself. Evidently they did not spend their life among the people of Israel, but lived in the midst of the Egyptian world. For their grandfather did not recognize them at once, although he spied them in the rear of his tent. It is evident that he met them for the first time, for he expressed his joy that he is allowed to meet the children of his beloved son Joseph.

The latter reverently drew near to the bed on which his old father was now dying, bowing deeply as he approached. Then the old patriarch addressed his beloved son. He first spoke to him about the appearance of the Lord to him at Luz. And then he spoke of the land of promise, of the land that God had promised to them, to the fathers, to Abraham and Isaac, and also to Israel. In the midst of a strange land Jacob by faith spoke of Canaan as the land of their people. It is evident, therefore, that in his dying moments he did not think of the past or of the things of the world, but of the city that has foundations. Thereupon he reclaimed the two boys Joseph had brought along with him and expressed his wish that they shall be to him as Reuben and Simeon, that they shall bear the name of Israel. And finally, he tenderly refers to his beloved Rachel, whom he never was able to forget, and speaks to Joseph of her death and burial. What therefore is the meditation of this dying old patriarch? It is in one word chiefly the word, the promise of God. Jacob a-dying remembers the promises and is busy with spiritual and eternal things.

He notices the two boys dimly appearing before his failing eyesight in the rear of his dwelling. He inquires who they are. And upon the information of their father that they are Manasseh and Ephraim, he calls them, rises from the bed, places them between his knees, embraces them and kisses them, and expresses the joy of his soul that he has been permitted by the grace of God not only to meet Joseph again, but even to see his seed.

Then he is about to bless them. Joseph leads the boys to their father and places them in the right position, as he thinks: Manasseh over against the right hand and Ephraim over against the left hand of the old grandfather. But Jacob wittingly crosses his hands; and placing his right hand on the younger of the two boys and the left on the head of the older, he pronounces the blessing upon them. Joseph, thinking that the old patriarch makes a mistake, tries to change the order. But Israel causes him to know that he is fully conscious of what he is doing, and that the older also in this case shall be inferior to the younger. In this way Jacob, a-dying, blessed both the sons of Joseph.

Now our text tells us that this was an act of faith, an act of the faith that is an evidence of things unseen and the substance of things hoped for. Nor is it difficult to see that it was such. First, the act of blessing the two sons of Joseph in a very general sense of the word was an act of faith. There was also in this case a clear conflict between the things visible and invisible. On the one hand was the greatness of the world and the riches and glory of the world; on the other hand was the sure promise of God, of Jehovah, the God of Israel.

The boys had been born and brought up in Egypt. They were practically Egyptians, both by birth and by education. Their father, it is true, was of the Hebrews. But nevertheless he was king. He was one of the foremost persons of the country. And the boys participated in his honor and glory and wealth. Their mother was an Egyptian, of the priestly caste, and therefore of that class of people whose influence was most weighty and whose power was in reality, if not nominally, even greater than that of Pharaoh. It was really the priestly clan, with their power of advice over the king and with their control over education, that had the power in Egypt. And also to that class the boys belonged by birth.

They were therefore great, and they could expect a splendid future. They evidently did not mingle very much with their own people. In fact, if we judge from the scene before them, it seems that they hardly knew their own people, for Jacob seems to meet them here for the first time. They must have lived among the higher Egyptian classes, and they shared in the riches and greatness of their father and mother. In a word, if they were let alone and if they were allowed to continue in the way they now traveled, if they were allowed to mingle with the people of the land and to become, as we would call it now, thoroughly naturalized, they would surely be great according to a worldly standard.

On the other hand, if Jacob would now bless them with the blessing of Israel, it would mean that they would once more become affiliated with the people of God, with the people who were strangers in the land and who had no foot of ground that they could call their own in Egypt. In short, they would have to bid farewell to all that attracted them in the world. The alternative, therefore, was very clear in their case. It was the often-occurring alternative between the world and the people of God.

However, there was also the invisible side. These boys belonged to Israel even though they had become estranged from their own people for a time. They were of the children of Abraham. And therefore, upon them were the promises God had given to the fathers, the promises that they should become a great people, that they should have the land of Canaan for an everlasting possession, and above all the great and beautiful promise that Jehovah would be their God and their redeemer and their shepherd forevermore.

All this was still invisible over against the visible things of the present state of the young men. All this also Jacob possessed only in the form of a promise. Jacob himself had lived in the land of Canaan for a number of years as in a strange land, dwelling in tents. And even at this moment he had no claim to the country whatsoever. On the contrary, for the last seventeen years he had lived in exile, far from the land of promise. And to the eye of reason it certainly could not look very hopeful, and it did not seem as if the promise of Jehovah was ever to be fulfilled. That was the invisible side.

Now what shall Jacob do? What shall the dying Israel choose? Shall he in the last struggle of death not rather lose his courage, not rather lose his faith? And shall he not judge that it is far better for these boys to retain forever what they now possess? Shall it not be better to leave them affiliated with the people of the land in the rich country of Egypt, rather than once more cause them to cast their lot with the people of God, strangers in a strange land, without a country of their own? Just consider the alternatives. On the one hand was certain riches, honor, glory, greatness, a certain future. On the other hand was exile, poverty, affliction, uncertainty, and a promise for the fulfillment of which the fathers had already waited for years. What shall

Israel choose? If he chooses the one, he uses the judgment of human reason: and then he will not bless them with the blessing of the fathers. If he chooses the other, he lives by faith, and then he will bestow the blessing of Abraham upon them and affiliate them once more with the people of God. What shall he do?

Solemnly the patriarch lays hands on the lads, and the deciding words resound in the stillness of the presence of death from his dying lips: "God, before whom my fathers Abraham and Isaac did walk, the God which fed me all my life long unto this day, the Angel which redeemed me from all evil, bless the lads; and let my name be named on them, and the name of my fathers Abraham and Isaac; and let them grow into a multitude in the midst of the earth" (Gen. 48:15–16). It was the blessing of Abraham, the blessing as it could be pronounced only by faith. The dying Israel is still strong and clear in the faith and clings to the promise of God. Even death must step aside for such a faith. All the power of death and all the efforts of Satan are vain at this moment to conquer the strong faith of this patriarch. By faith Jacob, when he was a-dying, blessed the two sons of Joseph.

In the pronouncement of that blessing there are still two more incidents that draw our attention and that prove the clearness of the vision of the grand old Israel in the hour of his death. First, here already he deprives in actual fact Reuben of the blessing of the first-born. According to all rational judgment and according to things visible, the blessing of the birthright would go to Reuben. But first, it may have been revealed to Jacob that Reuben was not to inherit that blessing. But second, he had also shown himself an unworthy son, carnally minded. And therefore, not Reuben was to have the blessing. The blessing was to be divided between Judah and Joseph. To the birthright belonged the blessing of the covenant, the blessing to bring forth the great seed of the woman. Judah was to receive it. To the birthright also belonged the blessing of the double portion. Joseph receives that double portion at this moment. For Jacob claims both his sons as his own, and they shall be to him as Reuben and Simeon, according to his own words.

And second, those crossed hands also reveal very plainly the clearness of the faith of Israel. Manasseh was the firstborn of Joseph.

Upon him the main blessing was to be bestowed therefore. When Joseph brings the boys to his father and places them as he does, the older opposite the right hand of the patriarch and the younger at his left, it is reason, it is the things visible, that are at work. But when Jacob in spite of this position crosses his hands and thus blesses them, it is faith that conquers reason once more. Whatever may be the reason for this change, and however Jacob may have come to know that also in this case the older should be inferior to the younger, we may safely draw the conclusion that in this case again it was the faith of Jacob that revealed itself. For he does this not by mistake, but wittingly.

Clear and strong the faith of Jacob is in these moments, and in the vale of death, with the shadow of death already darkening over his countenance, his faith still remains vivid and clear. And in the entire transaction he reveals that faith has the victory even to the end. Jacob dies by faith. His spiritual vision remains clear while the natural vision grows dim. And in the darkness of death he clings to the promise of his God.

Beautiful also is the scene that the last part of our text calls to our mind: "And worshipped, leaning upon the top of his staff" (Heb. 11:21). This refers to the history recorded in Genesis 47:29–31,

29. And the time drew nigh that Israel must die: and he called his son Joseph, and said unto him, If now I have found grace in thy sight, put, I pray thee, thy hand under my thigh, and deal kindly and truly with me; bury me not, I pray thee, in Egypt:
30. But I will lie with my fathers, and thou shalt carry me out of Egypt, and bury me in their buryingplace. And he said, I will do as thou hast said.
31. And he said, Swear unto me. And he sware unto him. And Israel bowed himself upon the bed's head.

It is to these last words that the author of Hebrews refers when he says: "Jacob...dying... worshipped, leaning upon the top of his staff."

The main idea of this is very plain. There in the dim light of his dwelling lies the grand old patriarch; and he is dying. The darkness of death overshadows him. His worn-out body can stand it but a little longer. And that old patriarch, in the presence of his son only, with the powerful hand of faith pushes away the tremendous foe of death, in order to rise and bow and worship. In the hour of death he struggles, he battles with the power of death, and has the victory. From his dying lips what do you hear? A groan of agony? A sigh of misery? An outcry of pain and anguish? An expression of fear? Nothing of the kind! This child of God lifts himself under the oppressing hand of the power of death, bows, and says: "O my God, my shepherd and my redeemer, who hast fed me all my life long, thanks be to thee. Thanks, praise, and glory be unto thy name. God my God, I extol thee!" Such is undoubtedly the meaning.

The text tells us that Israel was worshiping. Worship is not exactly the same as prayer. Worship does not mean to ask for something. It means to extol and glorify. It means that the one who is so worshiping is impressed with the greatness and glory of God. To worship is the highest religious expression of faith. When a man worships, God has reached his highest purpose with him and in him. The sinner will not worship, will not acknowledge the greatness and the sovereignty of God. And the highest purpose of salvation is that man may again acknowledge both.

Jacob worships the God of the covenant. He worships in connection with the thought of God's promises. That is plain from the context. Just a moment ago he has spoken to Joseph about the promised land. Just a moment ago he has made his son to swear that he will bury his bones not in Egypt, but in Canaan. And in doing so he has expressed his firm faith in the promises of God. And with the thought of these promises in mind, he realizes his smallness. In the thought of them he feels that this is all too much for him, and that he is unworthy of such abundance of grace.

And realizing the contrast between these great tokens of grace and mercy, on the one hand, and the insignificance and the unworthiness of his person, on the other hand, his faith reaches the climax of its power. He cannot lie down anymore. The heavy hand of death oppresses him. The heavy hand of death keeps him down. But death must go for a moment. And in the power of that strong and clear faith, the old, dying patriarch rises from his bed and bows down. And while his son and his grandsons reverently stand and witness, and while death steps aside, filled with awe for such a revelation of faith, the old man says: "My God, my God, my covenant God, glory and praise be to thee for thy grace and thy mercy, which thou hast bestowed upon me, a sinner!"

Indeed, faith is the victory, the victory also in the hour of death. To be sure, that would not be the case if faith were our own work. Jacob was surely by nature not a man of faith. God had made an Israel out of Jacob by his wonderful grace and power. Faith is the work of God. And as such faith is surely the victory, and the only victory also in the hour of death. Without faith it is impossible to truly live. Without faith it is also impossible truly to die.

Have we that faith? Shall we reveal it in the hour of death when all falls away and when the shadows darken? Once more I ask: Have we the faith to live and to walk by faith? If so, then we shall surely also have the faith to die. May the God of all grace, the God of our salvation, grant unto you and to me that faith.

# Chapter 21

# JOSEPH'S FAITH
# IN THE WORD OF GOD

By faith Joseph, when he died, made mention of the departing
of the children of Israel; and gave commandment concerning
his bones.

—*Hebrews 11:22*

There is a Dutch rhyme that runs as follows: *Wie van niet komt tot iet /
Is tot ander man's verdriet.* This literally translated is: one who comes
from nothing to something, is to the grief of others.[1]

There is a good deal of truth in this saying, even though it is by
no means always true and though there are undoubtedly exceptions
to this rule, even as to many other rules. Nevertheless, one often
observes how actually a person who rises from the lowest level of society to greatness, who climbs from poverty to wealth or from practical
oblivion to honor and public respect, is in grave danger of losing his
balance, so that he likes to forget the low level from whence he arose
and to become a nuisance and offense to others who used to associate
with him. This is true from a natural point of view. A little riches will
often change a person and induce him to seek the company of those
who have money and to separate himself from the people who used
to be his friends and companions. History is crowded with examples
that show us how a man, once having ascended the ladder of worldly
honor and greatness, reveals his pride and conceit and his aversion to
associating with those whom he used to know so well.

---

1 It seems that the most common version of this Dutch rhyme is: *Wie van niet komt
tot iet / Is het allemans verdriet*, which can be translated as: whoever comes from
nothing to something, is a grief to everyone. (My gratitude to Brian Huizinga for
this information and for the translation.)

Far more deplorable, however, it is when the truth of this rhyme is applied to the spiritual sphere. To the church and to the truth of the word of God material advancement is often the occasion, if not the cause, of religious decline and of lukewarmness, if not indifference, to the truth that one has once embraced and confessed. Oh, we know, of course, that faith and salvation is the work of God and that all depends only on his grace. Nevertheless, we may also remember what the Lord said to his disciples in connection with the coming to him of the rich young ruler: "Verily I say unto you, That a rich man shall hardly enter into the kingdom of heaven. And again I say unto you, It is easier for a camel to go through the eye of a needle, than for a rich man to enter into the kingdom of God" (Matt. 19:23–24).

In our text, however, we have a very happy illustration of a child of God who also rose from poverty and even from the shame and oblivion of prison to power and greatness, and who nevertheless by the grace of God in the midst of it all remembered and kept the faith of the fathers and certainly was not ashamed of the people of God who at the time dwelt in the midst of a strange land.

As you undoubtedly know, our text in Hebrews 11 refers to the passage that is recorded in the very last part of the book of Genesis, chapter 50:24–26,

24. And Joseph said unto his brethren, I die: and God will surely visit you, and bring you out of this land unto the land which he sware to Abraham, to Isaac, and to Jacob.
25. And Joseph took an oath of the children of Israel, saying, God will surely visit you, and ye shall carry up my bones from hence.
26. So Joseph died, being an hundred and ten years old: and they embalmed him, and he was put in a coffin in Egypt.

Thus according to our text, "by faith Joseph, when he died, made mention of the departing of the children of Israel; and gave commandment concerning his bones." This, therefore, this was an act of faith, of the faith that is the substance of things hoped for and the evidence of things not seen. This faith on the part of Joseph was revealed in two instances: first, in the fact that he made mention of the departing of

Israel out of Egypt, and second, in the command that his bones should be carried out of the country to Canaan, to be buried there with the fathers and with his people. These two instances, of course, are closely related to one another—we might say even as cause and effect are related. For if Joseph had not believed, and firmly believed, that his people would depart out of Egypt, that ultimately Canaan would be given them as an everlasting possession, according to the promise of God, he certainly would not have given orders that his bones be carried thither but rather would have preferred a princely funeral with the people among whom he dwelt and among whom he rose to glory and power.

Once more we must remember that the author of the epistle to the Hebrews in this chapter speaks of faith as the substance of things hoped for and as the evidence of things unseen. As such, faith clings to the word and promises of God. Without the word of God faith has no basis and no contents. Without the word and promises of God faith cannot be the substance of things hoped for, nor the evidence of things unseen. Without that word of God faith has absolutely nothing and is pure foolishness. Of course, to reason faith is always foolish. Reason cannot possibly understand how the world of unseen things can be real to faith.

Hence, we should never appeal to reason in order to support faith. This, in fact, has often been attempted and is still frequently tried. Many children of God still attempt to fight the battle of faith with reason supporting it. If faith becomes weak, or dark and wavering, they often try to brace up their faith and attempt to prove by reason the things that faith confesses. This, however, is a fundamental mistake. Faith can receive no support or strength from reason whatsoever. To be sure, faith is not unreasonable or irrational; but nevertheless the reason of the Christian must be based on and guided by his faith. Never can any so-called rational proof be of benefit to faith. Faith only has the word of God. Apart from this it has absolutely nothing. To express it very concretely, faith declares immediately and unconditionally and without the support of reason: "The things that are unseen and for which I hope are real to me because God has revealed them to me in his word." God declares that they are real, and this is entirely sufficient for faith.

When we understand and consider this, it is not difficult for us to understand why by the wisdom of God the Christian in this world lives and must live entirely by faith. He probably could have manifested to us the glory of the heavenly country. But such is not his will. He wants us to believe and not to see. He wants to have us trust completely in his own word of promise. Unbelief consists exactly in this, that it will not and cannot trust the word of God and rejects it.

Such was the very nature of sin as it revealed itself in paradise. Man doubted and finally disbelieved the word of God, accepted and acted upon the word of the devil. God had said to man: "The day that thou eatest of this tree thou shalt surely die" (see Gen. 2:17). But Satan, who always contradicts God and who is for that very reason the father of the lie, said to man: "The day that thou eatest of this tree thou shalt not surely die, but be like God" (see Gen. 3:4–5). And man acted upon the word of Satan instead of upon the word of his God, and hence became a slave to the lie.

Now if man is to be saved, he must be led back to believe in the word of God instead of in the word of Satan. He must believe not because he sees that it is true by his reason, but simply because the Almighty has spoken. It must become sufficient for him to know that God has spoken. He must simply believe the word of God, whether he can see it or not. That word of God must be true for him simply because the everlastingly faithful one has spoken it. Hence, God does not want us to live in the realm of sight but of faith. He does not show us as yet the things that are visible, but he simply reveals to us his word. And faith is the power that clings to that word of God, relying entirely upon it. It says: "The things invisible are real to me because God has said that they are, and God is truth." Hence, faith must have that word of God for its basis. It cannot do without that word. Where the word of God does not exist, and where the word of God is not known, faith is impossible.

Hence, it is still the policy of the devil to sow doubt in the heart of the child of God about God's word. Satan can cause the believer often to doubt many things. But the root of the matter is always that they are doubts in the word of God. He can perhaps tell us that we are not children of God, that God would never accept such low and mean sinners as we are. He can come and try to assure us that we have now sinned so often and that we have prayed for forgiveness of sins so repeatedly, but that we sin again and again, so that finally God puts no trust in us anymore and will not listen to our prayers for the forgiveness of sins anymore. He can probably come and assure us that all these things unseen in which we believe are after all not real, but only the imagination of our own mind. Nevertheless, in all these cases the devil attempts to sow doubt in our hearts concerning the word of God, and nothing else.

And for that reason we can fight him only with the sword of the word, and we must follow the example of Christ, who always said to Satan: "It is written" (Matt. 4:1–10). Even if Satan approaches us again, whether directly or through the world, and tells us: "You are all right, and there is nothing the matter with your state; but the trouble is that you still believe in that old storybook, the Bible. That Bible, you say, is the word of God. But that is all nonsense, and an invention of some priests and philosophers, nothing but an old fable that is altogether out of harmony with the enlightened age in which we live"—even then we must cling to the word of God, and with the prayer of the disciples on our lips, "Lord, increase our faith" (Luke 17:5), we must tell Satan and all the world: "The Bible is the word of God. It is the revelation of the God of our salvation in Jesus Christ. In it I believe despite all the temptations and intrigues." If we lose our faith in the word of God, all is gone and there is nothing to appeal to anymore. For it is in the very nature of faith, which is an evidence of things unseen and the substance of things hoped for, that it clings to the word and the promises of God.

Such was the faith of Joseph that he mentioned in the words of our text. This he reveals very plainly, for he makes mention of the departure of the children of Israel out of Egypt. And that departure had been promised by the word of God. To that promise Joseph clung in spite of all things that appeared to be contrary. Oh, it was now years ago that he, and also the rest of the children of Israel, had left the land of promise and had come to the land that was to become their house of bondage. Children of the third generation already had been born unto the original immigrants. They were settled in the country.

Nor had the circumstances that had driven them out of the country of Canaan been very favorable: for nothing less than a terrible and general famine had brought them to the land of Egypt.

And now after many years, after Jacob and undoubtedly many others had already died, also Joseph is approaching the end of his life. And he calls his people unto himself and tells them: "God will surely visit you" (Gen. 50:24). Mark you well, Joseph does not say: "If the Lord shall hear your prayers and visit you and bring you out of this country to the land he promised, then remember my bones and bury them with my people." That probably would have sounded very pious in the ears of many today. But in reality that would have been sinful and would have revealed little or no faith whatsoever. For it would have manifested no certain trust in the word of God that had once been spoken.

Nor does Joseph tell his brethren: "Remember what God has told you, how he has promised you the land of Canaan. And now it is up to you to realize this promise of God. And therefore, when I die, depart from the country and take possession of the land that was promised by God." That probably would also have sounded very religious and pious in the ears of many today. Oh yes, God will save us; but after all we must do it. God gives us the promise of salvation, but now it is up to us to us to obtain the promise. All this is, however, in reality blasphemy of the name of the Most High. For it makes the sovereign God dependent on man.

Oh no, Joseph says nothing of the kind. He knows very well that he and his people must live by faith, by faith in the word of God, by faith in the promise. And therefore, he is certain of the outcome and says: "[The Lord shall] surely visit you, and bring you out of this land" (v. 24). He was sure of it. He was certain of it only and entirely because the Lord God of the fathers had spoken. God had given the promise. He had spoken the word to Abraham and to Isaac and to Jacob. And this was sufficient. And therefore, the expression of certainty on the part of Joseph, "God shall surely visit you and bring you out of this land," is an expression of faith in the promise of God. Faith is complete trust in the word of God, and therefore it is the evidence of things unseen and the substance of things hoped for.

Still more. Joseph also gave commandment concerning his bones. He wished to be buried not in Egypt but in the land of the promise. It was his desire that he might be buried among his own people and that his bones might not remain behind alone in this strange land. Now why, we ask, is Joseph concerned about his bones and his burial place? Evidently he is thinking about the grave, and he is mindful of what shall become of his body after his soul should have left it. But he is thinking of it all in the light of the promises of God and by faith. Why then is Joseph concerned about the place of his burial? Why does he not want to be buried in the land of Egypt, but in the land of Canaan? My answer is: because Canaan was for him the land of promise, and ultimately that land of promise is nothing less than the new heavens and the new earth. That Joseph wanted to be buried in the land of promise means that he believed in the resurrection of the dead, when in perfect glory he shall inhabit the new heavens and the new earth forevermore.

Hence, he gives commandment concerning his bones. Assured that the people shall not remain in but shall depart out of the country and dwell in the land of promise, the land that was promised to Abraham, Isaac, and Jacob, he gives commandment concerning his burial and takes from them an oath that they shall bury him in the land of the covenant. Such was the faith of Joseph.

Is it also our faith? Do we put our trust not in self, not in our own condition, not in human reason, but only in the word and in the promises of God? Then we, too, have already principally departed from the land of Egypt, from the house of bondage, and dwell in the land of Canaan. Then we, too, can look with Abraham, Isaac, and Jacob for the city that has foundations, whose builder and maker is God. Then we, too, may confidently leave our bones in the grave, looking for the glorious resurrection in the day of our Lord Jesus Christ.

*Chapter 22*

# JOSEPH'S FAITH IN SPITE OF THE THINGS THAT ARE SEEN

By faith Joseph, when he died, made mention of the departing of the children of Israel; and gave commandment concerning his bones.

—*Hebrews 11:22*

E arlier, I emphasized especially that the faith of Joseph was perfect confidence in the word of God and in his promises. This time I must still show that his faith was an evidence of things unseen, and that he believed in spite of all things to the contrary.

In order to understand this we must note the circumstances in which the faith of Joseph was revealed. These circumstances certainly were not favorable as far as the promise of God was concerned, that he would lead the children of Israel out of the house of bondage. Joseph, to be sure, was a great statesman. We may perhaps say that his keen insight clearly told him that before long Israel would have to leave Egypt. It is indeed often possible to construe a picture, sometimes rather definite, of the future from a true understanding of the present, simply because the future is linked to the present as effect to cause. And thus we might also perhaps say that Joseph could easily see that the people of Israel would never become naturalized in the country of Egypt and that the Egyptians would after all not allow a strange people to live among them in possession of part of the country, and that therefore they would either be invited peaceably to leave the country or be driven out into the desert before many years passed.

Now indeed they were still allowed to live in the country, but soon Joseph would be no more. The king who knew Joseph and his merits would have died. The relation of friendship based on gratitude would be broken. And the Egyptians would no longer have patience with a strange shepherd people, who lived a separate life in their own country, and who, besides, multiplied fast and became a peril to their national existence. And so, after all, when Joseph predicted that the children of Israel would surely leave the land, it was but another proof of his wisdom and keen insight as a statesman; and perhaps faith had nothing to do with it.

However, such is the interpretation of unbelief. And, of course, the Christian has but one answer to such an explanation, an answer that is all-sufficient. And that is that our text, as well as the historical record, tells us that Joseph's prediction was given by faith, as based on the promises of God. Nevertheless, it may be and undoubtedly is of benefit to ask the question for a moment: Would the keen insight of Joseph into the future actually assure him that the children of Israel would soon leave the country? Were, in other words, present conditions at the hour of Joseph's death such that he could draw the conclusion from the standpoint of reason that they would soon depart? Our answer must be: not at all! Present conditions must already in Joseph's time have pointed in an altogether different direction.

Oh, we readily grant that Joseph was a great statesman and that he was endowed with natural gifts and that he had a keen insight into historical conditions. The fact that he rose to honor and greatness and that he could interpret the dreams of Pharaoh, however, was not because of any power of his own, but because of the grace of God and his revelation. But we, too, believe that Joseph was a great statesman, and that as such he could certainly form a conception of the future in the light of the present. But the great question is: Was this conception that his reason could possibly form of the future in harmony with the sentence expressed in the words of our text, namely, that the children of Israel would surely be brought out of the land and conducted into the land of promise? Far from it!

If we consider for a moment the subsequent history of the immediate future, we will come to the conclusion that it was exactly the opposite that was foreshadowed by the present conditions. What happened in that immediate future? This, that the people of the land, and especially Pharaoh, began to look with anxiety and fear at the development and fast multiplication of the people of Israel in the country. And, afraid that this strange people might become a real peril in the land, they began to oppress them. They caused them to perform hard labor. They began a process of systematic extermination, and thus tried to root them out and to wipe them out of existence (Ex. 1).

And when finally the demand comes from Jehovah to let the people go, is Pharaoh ready to grant the request, so that we may say that Israel left Egypt according to a very natural course of events, which Joseph could easily foresee? On the contrary, Pharaoh refused, and refused very stubbornly. It was only by the mighty hand of Jehovah and by the miracle of his power that they finally were led out of the land (Ex. 7–11).

The latter Joseph could not possibly foresee by reason. The natural course of events was opposed to it. According to the natural course of events, in the immediate future Israel was oppressed. They were enslaved. The attempt was made to exterminate them. And certainly they would never leave the house of bondage. And if Joseph had foreseen anything at all by the power of his reason, if he had any insight into the immediate future at all, if he had known at all the conditions of Egypt and the character of the people of the country, he must have known that his own people occupied a rather dangerous position in the land at that time. He must have been able to see that the horizon looked very dark, that it appeared as if the children of Israel had no opportunity whatever to leave the land, and that they shall be oppressed and exterminated. That must have been the conclusion of his reason at this time.

It seems to us as if the last words of Joseph, which he spake according to the words of our text, were not merely meant as an expression of his faith and not merely an indication of his anxiety for his bones, but that they above all meant to be a comfort and strength to the children of Israel, an exhortation not to lose their faith now that he is about to leave them. Does it not seem as if we hear him say already: "I see dark clouds gathering at the horizon. It seems to me that when I shall be gone away from you, oppression and affliction await you. But be of good cheer. The Lord shall keep you and safely guide you amid all the oppression of your enemies. And he shall visit you and lead you surely to the land of promise. And as a sign of my certain faith you can keep my bones, and bury them not here, but take them with you to the land of promise."

Considered in this light, we have again the sharp contrast between things visible and invisible. According to the judgment of reason, things looked dark to Joseph at this time. According to reason, he did not and could not see a possibility that the children of Israel should ever be delivered out of the land of Egypt. But on the other side was the promise of God. And that promise, that faith in the word, caused him to cling to the invisible things and caused him to say assuredly: "The Lord shall surely visit you." Faith is the evidence of things unseen.

We must still consider the fact that Joseph reveals this faith at the very end of his life. Joseph, when he died, performed this act of faith, according to our text. This expression here does not have the same emphasis as it had in the previous verse, where it spoke of Jacob a-dying (Heb. 11:21). There it referred to the very process of dying and to the very struggle of death. When Jacob was already struggling with death, he revealed his faith. For a moment by faith he overcame the power of death even to worship. In our present text it simply means that Joseph expressed this faith at the end of his life. When Joseph approached the hour that he was to leave this present life, after he had almost finished his life's course, he still revealed this faith. It means therefore that Joseph to the very end of his life's span kept the true faith, the faith of the fathers. And therefore, it was not thus, that Joseph only in the hour of his death thought of the promise, while all the rest of his life he revealed himself as indifferent.

It certainly was not thus, that the fear of death caused him to think of God and the promise given to the fathers. In other words, we have here no example of so-called deathbed conversions. I do not deny that they are sometimes possible, although not very frequently. Sometimes God reveals his grace rather suddenly in the hour of death, as he did, for instance, to the murderer on the cross. Nevertheless, they are exceptions. Never may we build our hope on this moment of death. And it is surely a godless and wicked way to hope and look for such deathbed conversions while in our entire life we reveal ourselves as unbelievers and walk in the way of the world. Such an attitude proceeds from the desire to serve God as little as possible and in the meantime to enjoy the world. This is absolutely wrong and wicked.

We are called upon by faith in Jesus Christ our Lord to serve and to love the Lord our God with all our heart, with all our mind, with all our soul, and with all our strength. Such is our calling. And such was undoubtedly the case with Joseph. He walks in the fear of the Lord not merely in the hour of death, but up to the very hour of his departure from the earth. And when he is about to depart, he still reveals the faith of the fathers.

This is all the more beautiful if we remember the life of Joseph. At the moment when he expressed these words, he had been away from the land of promise for ninety-three years. As a mere boy of seventeen he had been taken away from his home. To be sure, his father must have told him often of the promises given to Abraham and Isaac and to himself. And Joseph would understand and listen and believe. Yet they never had possessed the land at all. It was all a matter of faith. Already for years the people of Israel had waited for the fulfillment, but they had never seen it. Nor did it seem as if they would ever gain possession of the country that was promised them.

When the boy was seventeen, he had been shamefully treated, become an outcast and a slave. His brethren, the people of God, had sold him as a slave into Egypt. Since that time he had lived a long time in a community where he never heard of the promise of God. But among those strange people he had finally risen to greatness and wealth and power. The people of God, his own brethren, had treated him shamefully; but here, in the midst of the people who did not know Jehovah and who had nothing to do with the rich promises of God, here he had been treated with respect and honor, and had become great in the land.

Shall Joseph now not forget the religion of his fathers and the promises of his God? Shall not Joseph, now he is great among a people who differ religiously and spiritually from his fathers, not forget Jehovah? Shall he not be ashamed to confess him? Shall he not blush at once more associating himself with his own people and at affiliating himself and his posterity with a crowd of wanderers, who have no home, no possession, no land, except by promise? Oh no, Joseph remains faithful. And when his dying lips bid farewell to his brethren, it is only to speak once more of the promise, to speak once more of that other country, and to express his desire that he also, like his father Jacob, be buried there. Joseph by faith, when he died, spoke of the promise of God and of his desire to be buried in the land of promise.

All his life, therefore, Joseph had walked by faith, even in the most adverse circumstances. And because all his life he walked in that faith, therefore in the end of his life he can still cling to the promises of God and look for the city that has foundations, whose builder and maker is God.

Can it also be said of us that all our life we are walking in the way of the truth, that we embrace and adhere to the faith of the fathers so that on our deathbeds we may still speak of the promises of God and look forward to the glorious resurrection? I am afraid. Our Reformed fathers came to the wilds of Michigan, more than one hundred years ago, not only to improve their material conditions but also in search of better conditions from a spiritual viewpoint, in order that they might serve their God according to the dictates of the word of God. That word they loved and of the truth of the Reformed faith they were deeply convinced.

And in the virgin woods of Michigan they mingled their psalms of praise with the stroke of the axe. With all their weakness, they were men of strong faith. They laid the foundation for our material welfare; they also laid the foundation for our Reformed church life, in order that their children and children's children might walk in their footsteps and embrace the faith for which they struggled.

Are we doing this?

Once more, I say: I am afraid.

When I consider much of the religious indifference and consider that many walk not only in the world but also according to the standards of the world, that many do not even understand the definite tenets of the Reformed faith that our fathers loved and embraced, then indeed I have reason to ask, with doubt in my mind: Can it be said that we shall be faithful to the principles of the truth that our fathers embraced?

Of course, I know that it all depends upon the sovereign grace of God and that therefore we have nothing to fear. Nevertheless, I would admonish you diligently to study the faith of our fathers and hide it in your hearts. Love the truth in all its implications. Do not be afraid of the reproach of the world. Then, and then only, we will be able to walk in the faith of Joseph and, with him, look for the city that has foundations, whose builder and maker is God.

*Chapter 23*

# THE FAITH
# OF THE SMALL

By faith Moses, when he was born, was hid three months of his
parents, because they saw he was a proper child; and they were
not afraid of the king's commandment.

*—Hebrews 11:23*

There are among the children of God who shall once be glorified
in everlasting perfection giants of faith, but also little ones, whose
faith is not revealed in mighty deeds. Of the former there are many
illustrations in Scripture, also in Hebrews 11. An example of the former we may find in Daniel, the prophet in exile (Dan. 6). The princes
of the land were jealous of Daniel, jealous of the power and honor and
greatness this Jewish prophet enjoyed in the land of Babylon, and jealous also of the favor he received of King Darius. Hence, they plotted
against him, and they conceived of a plan that would seem to seal his
doom. They entered into the palace of the king with a petition that no
one shall within the first forty days ask anything of anybody, or even
of any god, except of the king himself. The petition was granted them,
and the decree was that he who shall ask anything, except of the king
himself, shall be cast into the den of lions.

Daniel hears of the decree and understands its significance and its
purpose. He knows that the decree is directed against him. He understands, too, of course, that his enemies will spy and watch his every
move from now on until the end of the appointed time. And if he
dares to kneel down, as he is wont, with his face toward Jerusalem, he
knows that his fate is sealed. For he is also aware of the fact that any
law of the Persians and Medes cannot be repealed. What shall he do?
Shall he obey? Shall he refrain from his daily prayer in order to escape

the lions' den? Is it not true that safety bids him not to kneel down and pray publicly to the God of heaven and earth? Never does the thought even enter the mind of the prophet. What? Shall he deny the name of the God of Israel just because his enemies are making a plot against his life?

Nevertheless, would it not be a simple matter of wisdom at least to refrain from kneeling down in front of the open window, where all could see him? Would not even God demand of him that he retreat into the closet and there perform his religious worship in secret for the time being? In fact, would it not be tempting the Lord if he would still proceed and in the sight of the enemies kneel down to pray? But Daniel knows better. He knows that his enemies have always seen him pray before the open window. And if now he should withdraw into privacy, he would still deny the God of his people because he is afraid of the results. This Daniel could never do.

Hence, by faith he kneels down as he is wont, not in secret but in public. He worships the God of Israel while the enemies are watching him. We might say: he kneels down on the very edge of the lions' den and prays to the God of the covenant with his face toward the holy city. Daniel is a giant, a prince of faith. And in the face of death he challenges his enemies by faith to make him unfaithful to the God of his people.[1]

The same may be said of the three friends of the prophet (Dan. 3). The mighty king of Babylon makes a great image and issues the command that at the sign of the musical instruments all peoples and nations shall fall down and worship his image. And he threatens all possible violators that they shall be cast into a fiery furnace. The moment comes, and without fear the three friends of Daniel remain standing and refuse to bow down to the image of Nebuchadnezzar. Fearlessly they choose the fire rather than the denial of the name of their God. And without fear, by faith, they enter into the fiery furnace. These are marvels of faith, princes and giants.

Nevertheless, there are also others. Scripture, for instance, also speaks of the faithful Obadiah, who secretly hid the prophets of

---

1  Hoeksema perhaps means something like this: in the face of death, by faith Daniel challenges his enemies to try to make him unfaithful to the God of his people.

Jehovah although he trembled with fear before the wicked king Ahab (1 Kings 18:4). Scripture also speaks of the seven thousand who did not bow down before Baal even though they could not be found in the land because evidently they hid themselves and feared the king (19:18). And thus also, Scripture speaks in the words of our text of the parents of Moses, of whom perhaps no one would have thought as examples of faith (Heb. 11:23). And the text tells us that their hiding of Moses in spite of the king's commandment was an act of faith, as an evidence of things unseen and the substance of things hoped for. To this act of faith we wish to call your attention for a few moments.

In order to appreciate at all that it was an act of faith that was revealed in the hiding of Moses, it is necessary that for a moment we recall the exact circumstances under which this act was performed. Amram and Jochebed, the father and mother of Moses, were Israelites, of the tribe of Levi. They were therefore strangers in a strange land. For as we know, at this time the children of Israel still dwelt in Egypt, the country whither they had turned on account of the famine in Canaan. They had never returned to the promised land. They were strangers in Egypt in every respect. They did not become naturalized, but they lived a rather isolated existence in the country. And their contact with the inhabitants of Egypt was not sufficient to cause them to lose their separate traits as a nation. Strangers they were in a natural sense, for they spoke their own language and had entirely different customs.

But strangers they were also and especially in the spiritual, religious sense of the word. They served a different God than the inhabitants of the land. In this respect there was not the slightest contact between these and the people of Israel. Egypt had its idols, but Israel served and loved its covenant God. They were the covenantal people, and they knew it. They had not yet forgotten that they were the people to whom a promise was given, the promise of the land of Canaan, and that after all they lived in a foreign country as long as they were not delivered from the house of bondage. They still lived in the hope and the faith that the promise given to the fathers would be realized and that they would be heirs of the beautiful land of Canaan as an everlasting possession.

Hence, Israel lived in hope. To be sure, this could probably not be said of every individual who lived in this strange country at this time. There must have been those who had already turned to the gods of Egypt, forsaking the God of their fathers. There were undoubtedly many who had forgotten all about the promise of God and about the God of the covenant. Nevertheless, the people as such, the true Israel, had not lost their identity. The remnant according to the election of grace still believed in Jehovah and hoped in his word. Among them were evidently the parents of Moses, Amram and Jochebed.

But there is more. The times and conditions in Egypt had changed noticeably after Joseph's death. No doubt, as we saw in a previous chapter, Joseph had already seen dark clouds gathering at the horizon when he spoke of the land of promise and bade them to take his bones with them when they were delivered from the house of bondage. Now these dark clouds have indeed gathered over the heads of Israel, and the entire sky of history is dark and overcast.

A king was reigning in Egypt who "knew not Joseph" (Ex. 1:8). He evidently was not acquainted with him and with his relation to these strangers in the land. He knew nothing of what Joseph had been in the land of Egypt in years gone by. Besides, we also know that the people of Israel had increased mightily, so that by this time they were a very numerous people, filling all the land. And this fast multiplication of the people of Israel in the country became more and more a cause of anxiety and fear and jealousy to the king and his counselors.

The result was that a time of persecution ensued. Of course, it was not the fast increase of the people of God that was the real cause of this persecution. Behind it all was Satan, who meant to extinguish the promised seed. Scripture suggests so beautifully that the real cause of the persecution was that the king knew not Joseph. You know, as long as the people of God are a real benefit and profit to the world, the world will be rather tolerant and make room for them. Thus it was in Egypt. Joseph, humanly speaking, had been the savior of the country. For had he not interpreted the well-known dreams of the king, the king and his counsellors would never have known of the seven years of famine that were to come. And had he not made the wise and necessary provisions, they would never have been able to pass through those seven years of famine as they did. Joseph therefore had been of great profit and benefit to the land of Egypt. The result had been that they had crowned him with greatness and honor. Hence, when he had asked for a place also for his own people, they had been but too glad and ready to make room also for them.

Now, however, all this had changed. The years of famine had passed, and they had also been forgotten. As long as the king lived who had raised Joseph to his place of honor, all had been well. But that king had died, and now another king was on the throne of Egypt, who knew nothing of Joseph. Hence, the people of Israel were no more of any advantage to the Egyptians. What was the use of leaving those strangers in the land and of giving them a place without deriving any benefit from them?

Besides, they multiplied mightily and evidently became a strong people. Who knows? Perhaps they would before long surpass the Egyptians in number. Or perhaps in time of war they would ally themselves with the enemy.

The result is that a terrible time of persecution arrives for the children of Israel in the land of Egypt. To be sure, the Lord also employs this persecution as a means to cause the children of Israel to cry unto Jehovah their God and to make them long for the promised deliverance. Nevertheless, for the time being it was an awful oppression and a severe persecution to which they were subjected. At first the wicked king intends to reach two purposes, namely, to derive the benefit of their labor and to prevent the multiplication of the people in the land. He wants to build two cities, and they will have to bake and supply the necessary brick. This attempt, however, is in vain. The people grow in spite of oppression and in spite of the fact that every day their hard task is waiting for them and that they can expect bitter and severe punishment if the work is not finished in due time. In spite of it all they grow in number (Ex. 1:9–12).

Then the godless and wicked king conceives of another plan. Secretly he enjoins the midwives that they shall kill the Hebrew boys as soon as they are born. It stands to reason that if this plan succeeds, the people will lose their identity and their separate existence. But also this wicked plan failed, because of the midwives, of whom we read that they feared the Lord (v. 17). They refused to carry out the plan of the king. Also this plan, therefore, was a failure. But the king, inspired by the devil, is fully determined that the people of Israel shall either be assimilated or exterminated. He now therefore resorts to open and public persecution and issues the command that all the baby boys shall be thrown in the river and be drowned as soon as they are born (v. 22).

Such was the character of the time. It was a time of severe oppression for the people of God. It looked very dark. And under such conditions Moses was born. We can imagine that many a time Amram and Jochebed must have talked together before the boy was born about the terrible times in which they lived. And perhaps they expressed the wish that their expected child might be a girl. And many a time their hearts must have been filled with anxiety and fear as they talked about the command of the king and their future attitude toward it if their child should be a boy. Who would not be anxious in such times as these? Are not the hearts of godly parents often anxious for the future of the children God gives them even in our own times?

Surely, from a spiritual and religious point of view the world looks dark. To them it seems as if the times that must precede immediately the coming of the Lord are not far off. And therefore, naturally many a parent undoubtedly looks with anxiety to the future of his children. Thus it was in a far more definite way with the parents of Moses. They knew that the command of the king was there, and that if the child were a boy, they would have to stab their own heart by throwing the child into the river. What shall they do now that Moses is born? The text has it that they do not obey, but by faith they hide the boy, seeing he was fair and "a proper child" (Heb. 11:23).

Such is faith. In spite of all things to the contrary, in spite of the things that are seen, in spite of terrible persecution, in spite of the fact that Satan is bent upon the destruction of the church and the extermination of the people of God, faith, by the grace of God, always looks forward to the final deliverance and to the victory of Christ Jesus our Lord. For it is an evidence of things unseen and the substance of things hoped for. Let us then, strengthened by the word of God and by the grace of the God of our salvation, be faithful even unto death, that no one take our crown.

*Chapter 24*

# FAITH IN ACTION

By faith Moses, when he was born, was hid three months of his parents, because they saw he was a proper child; and they were not afraid of the king's commandment.

—Hebrews 11:23

We read in our text that this hiding of Moses was an act of faith on the part of the parents and that, as they were hiding the child, they feared not the commandment of the king. Surely, we realize at once that this faith was not like the faith of Daniel. For they did not flatly refuse to obey the king and to throw the babe into the river. They did not openly protest. Yet, on the other hand, we should not forget that in this case it was practically the only thing they could do. If they did not hide the child, the king would surely come and take him away from them and perform the infamous act for them if they refused to obey. To hide the child was to save him.

And therefore, although there is undoubtedly an element of fear in this manifestation of faith, yet we must never forget that the hiding itself was an attempt to save the child in spite of the commandment of the king, and that it was as such an act of faith. By hiding the child, they were at the same time hiding their own violation of the king's commandment. And yet by hiding the child they also revealed that they did not fear the command of the king. This faith was an evidence of things unseen and the substance of things hoped for. That is the point of view from which the author discusses faith in this chapter, and this we must bear in mind also in the present case. And so we come again to ask the question: How is faith, as an evidence of things unseen and as the substance of things hoped for, revealed in this concealment of Moses on the part of the parents?

From the point of view of reason it becomes very evident that it was impossible to hide the child with a view to saving him from destruction. In fact, it was an act of folly. The parents might just as well have made up their mind that sooner or later they would be detected and severely punished and that the boy would be thrown into the river. First, this must have seemed impossible because we may easily surmise that the king had his spies stealing about the dwellings of the people of Israel and ever on the alert to detect a violation of the commandment of the king. We need not imagine that the king just issued an order, without seeing to it that the command was actually carried out. His very determination to exterminate the people of Israel proves the contrary.

This was the third means employed to reach his end. First, as we saw, he thought that the mere oppression of slavery and hard labor might be sufficient to destroy the people. But this had evidently proved a failure. Then he had made an attempt to have the Hebrew babes killed at birth secretly with the aid of the midwives. But also this had failed, because the midwives feared the Lord. But in spite of these two failures the king had not abandoned the purpose to exterminate the people but conceived of a different and far more effective plan to reach the realization of his purpose.

But what would it help if he merely gave the command and did not see to it that the order was also actually carried out? He might easily surmise that the people would violate that command as much as possible and that it demanded a close espionage in order to have the order fulfilled. And therefore, the king must have had his officials, his spies, who would stealthily move around among the people of Israel and keep watch very closely. According to reason, the parents must have drawn the conclusion that they had been discovered before the boy was even born and that the king's spies knew very well that a child was born in the home of Amram and Jochebed. If they had judged according to reason, they might have known that it was folly to conceal the child and that by doing so they were in danger of their very life every day, as long as the commandment of the king was not carried out.

Besides, we can easily imagine that there was jealousy among their own people. And that also would be a factor with which they would have to reckon. The picture we receive of the people of the covenant at any time of the history is not any too bright and attractive. But especially of the time of which we now speak it actually looks repugnant. They were not a brave people who revolted at the very idea of being oppressed and held in slavery; but they allowed themselves to be oppressed and persecuted in the land. They really did not live by faith. We read that they were not only oppressed hard by their overseers and bosses, but that they also fought one another. And when someone comes to take their side and to deliver them, they threaten the very next day that they shall reveal him to their enemies (Ex. 2:13–14). When Moses returns from the desert, commissioned by Jehovah to deliver the people, they lose courage and blame their deliverer as soon as they realize that their deliverance is not effected at once (5:21).

Surely, there was cowardice and jealousy among the people themselves. Amram and Jochebed might easily surmise that some kind neighbor who had obeyed the command of the king with respect to his own children would have the sad courage to reveal to the enemy that in their home also was concealed a baby boy. Only one had to conceive this jealousy in his heart, and the thing was done. Also from this point of view, therefore, it looked folly to conceive of the possibility to hide the child and to save him permanently.

And after all, was the fact not bound to be discovered sooner or later? How could they expect that they would be able to save the child from destruction? The child would grow up, and not always would they be able to keep him in the house. He would have to reveal himself sooner or later. His very age would betray that he had been born after the command of the king had been issued. And would his death, as well as the death of the parents, be certain after all? Would it not be far sadder to see the child snatched away through the cruel command of the king after he had grown up than to cast him into the river or to deliver him to the enemies to do it for them while he was a mere babe, scarcely in the world and hardly able to realize any suffering?

This was the visible side, the side of reason. That was the side of the flesh. According to the dictates of reason, it was the height of folly to imagine that there was any possibility to evade the king's command and to save the child. They could expect certain discovery. They could expect that the child would have to be surrendered sooner or later and that they themselves would be severely punished by the cruel hand of the king. That was the side that could be seen. And nothing else was visible.

On the other hand, there was the invisible side, with which faith was concerned. Over against the command of the king stood, first, the law of God. Surely, the command of the king was quite clear and positive. But the will of God in this instance could not be very dubious either. They were called not only to kill their own child and to commit heinous murder, but they were called besides to commit murder upon a child of the covenant, upon a child who had received the sign and seal that he was a child of Jehovah. The command of the king and the law of God stood directly over against each other.

Still more, believing parents must also have been able to see that this command of the king was nothing but a plan of the devil to frustrate the counsel of Jehovah with respect to his covenantal people. They had the promises, and they knew them. These promises had been given to the fathers. And to Abraham it had been revealed, besides, that this oppression in Egypt had to come before the promises could be realized. The Lord had said: "I will make you a great people, and I will give you the land of promise." But was not this in direct opposition to what was happening in the land of Egypt, in the house of bondage, at the time of Amram and Jochebed? Was not this very plainly a shrewd plan of the devil to frustrate the plan of God? Was not the command of the king in flat contradiction with the promise of God? Oh, surely, it had been a long time since the promise was given. And at the present it did not look as if the promise was ever to be fulfilled.

But Jacob had testified of it on his deathbed, and Joseph before he died had also mentioned their departure and had expressed his faith that the Lord would surely visit them and would lead them to the promised land. His very bones were still in their midst as a silent witness of this. And the faithful Israelite still believed in those promises of God. The believing sons of Jacob looked forward every day to the time that the Lord would visit his people and bring them out of the house of bondage into the promised land. Any day it might come. Any day the Lord might turn the oppression of Israel and deliver them. But how then could the Israelites, living by that faith, cast the children of the covenant, in direct violation of God and his promises, into the river? How could they murder the heirs of the promise, the children of God?

Surely, all this was invisible. They did not see the deliverance as yet. They did not see that the Lord would fulfill his promises. On the contrary, it seemed as if the promise could never be realized. It seemed as if there were no covenant God in heaven. It seemed as if the covenant God himself had forgotten and had abandoned his people. It seemed as if they might as well give up all hope of deliverance and as if they might just as well surrender their children to the stream of the Nile. But by faith they nevertheless clung to their God. By faith all these things were still real to them. By faith they still hoped. And living by faith, it simply was impossible to obey the king. By faith also Amram and Jochebed, although they could not see the possibility of saving the child, trusted that God would crown their efforts and help them in hiding the child.

The text tells us that they hid the child by faith (Heb. 11:23). Faith, therefore, was the motive. No, it was not the parental love that caused them to do it. To be sure, parental love is very strong. And a mother will save her child from the very claws of the lion and endanger her own life to save her darling. But in this case parental love was not sufficient. They hid the child by faith. This shows the terrible condition and awful fear in which the people of Israel were held at this time. The author plainly indicates that if they had had nothing but parental love, they would not have been induced to hide the child. Parental love would rather have cast the child into the river than to wait until the time that the boy had grown older. If therefore there had been a possibility from a natural point of view to save the child, parental love would have been sufficient. But such there was not. It was merely a question between killing the child in his earliest infancy and sure death afterward. And then the choice was not difficult.

But what parental love could not do, that faith did. Faith was the motive. By faith they clung to the word of God. By faith they obeyed him rather than the king. By faith they clung to the promise and believed that God was powerful to save the child and to protect him against the wrath of Pharaoh. That faith it was that made them also sufficiently fearless of the king's commandment to hide the child and to make the attempt to save him.

But there is still more. Our text tells us that the child was a proper child. Really it reads that the child was very fair and beautiful. The same we read in the historical record of Exodus (2:2) and also in the account of Stephen in the book of Acts (7:20). All these passages call attention to the fact that Moses was a fair and beautiful child. And our text calls special attention to the fact that by faith they hid the child because they saw that the child was fair. This can mean but one thing, namely, that the parents did not come to the definite conclusion to save the child until after he was born and they saw that he was a very beautiful child. The beauty of the child was not the motive. The motive certainly was faith, as an evidence of things unseen.

But nevertheless, we may say that the fairness of the child was the occasion to arouse and strengthen that faith so as to bring it into action. Our actions are determined, first, by motives from within. But second, they are also guided by circumstances and occasions from without. The motive in this case was not the fairness of the child, but faith. But that faith had to be strengthened and roused into action. It was weak. It could hardly come to manifestation. And now God uses the fairness of Moses to persuade that faith of the parents to hide the boy. There are giants of faith, but also children. There are also little lambs in the flock of Jesus. And also for them he cares and sometimes uses special means to rouse their faith to action.

We must not misunderstand this. It certainly does not mean that Amram and Jochebed saved Moses' life and hid him because the baby was so beautiful. That certainly cannot be true. It would presuppose that parents love their children more when they are fair and beautiful than when they are homely and defective. And that certainly is not true. But we must undoubtedly understand that this beauty of Moses as a baby was a sign of God. Moses was called in the future unto a very special task in the kingdom. And it is not impossible that the parents, looking upon that baby, already hoped that he would be the one who would deliver Israel from the house of bondage.

God endows the child with such special beauty and remarkable fairness that he is divinely marked. And therefore, the parents also notice that this child is a special child. This divine mark on Moses saves him now, and it also saves him afterward, when the daughter of Pharoah is attracted by it. Hence, the beauty of the child strengthened the faith of the parents, so that they put complete trust in the Lord their God. And in spite of seeming impossibilities, they now believe that God will protect them against the wrath of the king.

A beautiful illustration this is of the fact that God not only remembers the great and the strong and brave among his children, but also the small and the weak, the fearing and trembling lambs of his flock. Little the parents of Moses would have imagined that their little and trembling faith would be put up before the children of God of all ages as an example, and that they would have a place among the heroes of faith in this chapter of Hebrews. And yet there was need also of such little heroes as these. If we would read only of the giants of faith, of Enoch and Noah and Moses and Daniel, we might probably imagine that there was no place for the mere common soldier in the army of the Lord. But such is not the case. It is not only the great and the strong, but also the small and the weak among the children of God who live by faith. Also the little, the common faith, God does not despise and break down. But also in it he recognizes his own work and cares for it, builds it up. And in due time he causes it to come to manifestation to his glory, to our salvation, and to the ingathering of the church.

# Chapter 25

# MOSES' CHOICE WHEN HE BECAME OF AGE

24. By faith Moses, when he was come to years, refused to be called the son of Pharaoh's daughter;
25. Choosing rather to suffer affliction with the people of God, than to enjoy the pleasures of sin for a season;
26. Esteeming the reproach of Christ greater riches than the treasures in Egypt: for he had respect unto the recompence of the reward.

*—Hebrews 11:24-26*

The text speaks of the choice of Moses. Scripture often speaks of a choice, of a choice of man in general, of a choice of the people who belong to the church in the world, and particularly of the choice of the elect, the choice of the true people of God. God chooses, and he chooses his people unto everlasting life. But also man chooses: he either chooses the way of sin, or by the grace of God he chooses the way of life.

And the covenantal people in general—I mean all who are considered and called the covenantal people in the church and in the world, both in the old and in the new dispensation—are placed very definitely before this choice time and again. Just think of the blessing and the curse, which are placed before the children of Israel after they have just entered into the land of Canaan—announced to them from Mounts Ebal and Gerizim.[1] Or again, just recall the choice before which Joshua places the people after this humble and faithful leader

---

1  Hoeksema is probably referring to Deuteronomy 11:29 and 27:12.

of God's people has become old: "Choose you this day whom ye will serve." And remember also the beautiful choice this general himself expressed in the well-known words: "As for me and my house, we will serve the LORD" (Josh. 24:15).

A choice is nothing foreign to Scripture, therefore; and also the covenantal people in the world must always make a definite choice. They must always make a conscious choice between the dictates of their old nature and their regenerated heart. It is the choice between the kingdom of God and the pleasures of the world, the choice between Satan and Christ. And this choice can be made only by faith, which God implants in the hearts of his people. From a natural point of view all the advantages are with the world and its pleasures of sin, in comparison with Christ and his kingdom. But faith is the evidence of things unseen. And therefore, never from a natural point of view can the choice ever be made, but only through the power of faith. It is of such a choice that my text speaks.

The text tells us of the choice that Moses made. And as to the object and contents of that choice, the text tells us negatively, first of all, what Moses did not choose but consciously rejected. Moses "refused to be called the son of Pharaoh's daughter" (Heb. 11:24). But second, the text also informs us what the man of God actually did choose. He chose rather to share ill treatment with the people of God (v. 25). And if you ask the question, how Moses came to this (from a natural point of view) strange choice, the text informs us how Moses finally came to this conclusion, namely: he accounted that the reproach of Christ was greater riches than the treasures of Egypt (v. 26). Such was the choice of Moses, the man of God.

We readily understand, of course, that a real choice is possible only for God's rational, moral creatures. For a choice implies, first, an act of the intellect, an act of reason. It presupposes that there are two or more objects that must be judged according to their relative importance and value, that must be compared, therefore, and to one of which preference must be shown. It also implies an act of the will. The will follows up this act of the reason of man and reveals that it desires and wants the object to which the intellect has given preference. Hence, it is therefore an act that can only be expected of a

creature that possesses intellect and will, a rational and moral creature. A tree cannot choose. An animal cannot really choose, although
an animal can give and show preference in a limited way, instinctively,
to one object above another. An animal cannot make a conscious and
rational choice.

But man can and must choose. He must choose very often in his
life with respect to natural things. Many a time he confronts two or
more objects or possibilities between which a choice is to be made.
But above all, in the spiritual sphere, in the highest sense with relation
to his God, man must choose. He always must and does make consciously a willing choice for or against his God. Or, if you please, he
must and does choose for or against sin and for or against Christ and
his kingdom. Thus it was with the choice of Moses. Our text tells us
that he made a very definite and conscious choice. He chose for the
people of God and against Egypt and its treasures. And this choice, the
text tells us, the man of God made when he was grown up.

The latter fact, namely, that Moses made this choice when he was
grown up, stands to reason. A choice does not merely require a conscious and rational subject, but it also demands a certain stage in the
development of that rational creature, a stage of development more
or less advanced, according as the objects between which the choice
must be made are of greater or lesser importance. Of the babe who lies
in the cradle you cannot expect a choice. Such a babe may very well
be a child of God. It may very well have the life of regeneration in its
little heart. And when it is taken away in infancy, it may very well go
to glory and be saved forever.

But it cannot make a conscious and definite choice, although also
that child is no doubt a rational, moral creature, as well as a grown-up
person. That child has as yet no conscious knowledge of the objects
between which the choice must be made. It knows as yet nothing of
God and his covenant. Nor does it know anything about the pleasures
of sin. Although undoubtedly it has sin, both original and, very soon,
also actual, it has no conscious knowledge of it. On the other hand, it
knows nothing of Christ, of the Savior, and of his work of salvation.
It knows nothing of the people of God, and it is not conscious of the
pleasures of the world.

A child is not in the conscious state that is presupposed to make a choice. It is not in such an intellectual and moral condition that it can make a definite and conscious choice. In almost every respect the choice is made for that child. The parents choose for him. The parents determine where that child shall live, in what kind of environment he shall move about, how he shall be dressed, what he shall eat, where he shall go to school. The parents choose as long as the children are not as yet able to choose and to determine for themselves.

This is even true of the religious life of the child. The parents choose already in infancy to what church that child shall belong, when and where he shall be baptized, and in what doctrine he shall be instructed. Even later the parents decide where and when we shall go to church and catechism and Sunday school. All this is not the object of our own choice as long as we are not of age. And would to God that in our age, too, the parents would just choose a little more strictly, and at the same time a little longer, what is to become of their children, and especially in what church they shall grow up and in what doctrine they shall be instructed.

The time comes that this cannot be undone anymore. The state of development arrives when in all these respects we will have to make a conscious choice ourselves also in regard to religious matters and to spiritual things. In other words, we come to years of discretion. For Moses that time arrived, so our text tells us, when he was grown up. And from history we learn that this was at the age of forty. This does not mean, of course, that he did not come to years of discretion before this time, nor that he did not make a conscious choice before the age of forty. But at the same time, he came to a definite conclusion and revealed his choice.

A strange history this man of God had during these forty years. When he was a babe, his parents had hid him, as we have seen in connection with our former chapters, for three months for fear that the child might be discovered and killed. But when the parents could no longer hide him, they had set him afloat on the river, his sister keeping watch. Pharaoh's daughter had been attracted by the remarkable beauty of the boy and had adopted him for her own child.

Yet for a time, because the babe was still too small, he was returned into the house of his parents, thanks to the cleverness of Moses' sister

(Ex. 2:7–10). There, in the home of Amram and Jochebed, God-fearing people, he had enjoyed his first education. How long this lasted history does not inform us. But surely, judging him in the light of his subsequent history, we may certainly surmise that he was there long enough to become somewhat acquainted with the history of his own people and with the knowledge of the God of his fathers. How otherwise could he have made the choice of which the text speaks at this stage?

Nevertheless, he had finally been claimed by the daughter of the king. And there, at the court, he had been placed in different surroundings. From the humble dwelling in Goshen he was moved to the rich and glittering court of Pharaoh. There at the court he had enjoyed all the facilities a person could possibly think of at the time. There he had been educated by the priestly caste. There he had become versed in all the wisdom of the Egyptians. There he had become accustomed to seeing people treating him with the utmost respect and honor. There, in a word, he had become great. And now Moses was forty years of age. And our text tells us that he had grown up.

It may perhaps surprise us that Moses made his choice so late in life. Why, thus we are inclined to ask, did he not come to this choice sooner? Were not the people of Israel in terrible oppression and suffering all this time? Were not, perhaps, his parents, who most likely were still living at the time, anxiously waiting to see this boy cast in his lot with the people of God? Is it not somewhat late to make a definite choice in respect to God and the things concerning his people at the age of forty? No doubt for us that certainly would be the case. Our young people certainly must not draw the conclusion from the words of our text that they can wait with making their definite choice and with making confession of faith till late in life.

However, we must not forget, first, that Moses' case circumstances were somewhat different. First of all, it is but meet to bear in mind that the entire lifetime of Moses was one hundred twenty years, so that relatively speaking, in terms of our own time, he was about twenty-five years of age when he made his choice. Second, we should not forget that it must have been quite a few years before Moses was actually versed in all the knowledge of the Egyptians.

When we say in our day that a person is grown up, it very often conveys so very little meaning. It simply means to imply that he or she to whom the term is applied has reached a certain physical development. But for the rest it seems to mean very little. But in the case of Moses this was altogether different. It certainly seems to mean that he first of all had a Jewish education, so that at least he was made acquainted with his own people and with the God of Israel. Second, it also means that now he was thoroughly trained in all the knowledge of Egypt, which even at that early date was already quite advanced. Moses had grown up. He really had become a man, not only legally entitled to choose but intellectually able to judge between the objects of his choice.

But finally, and this is more important, we should also remember that Moses, although he came to the final step and to the final conclusion when he was forty years of age, certainly cannot be imagined as having not thought about the choice at all before this. This would seem psychologically and spiritually impossible. There must have been a long and bitter struggle and conflict in his mind and heart. And even after he had reached the conclusion to cast his lot with the people of God and to refuse to be called the son of Pharoah's daughter, he must have contemplated on the best way of realizing that choice. As the objects of his choice gradually became clearer to his mind, he must have thought about the choice before which he was placed very frequently.

And it was no doubt at the same time under God's overruling providence that he did not make the choice before. For in God's wisdom the Egyptian education was no doubt a preparation for the task Moses was called to perform in the future. All these elements and facts taken together, it seems rather natural that Moses took the definite step not before, but just when he was fully grown up and when he was forty years of age.

The object of Moses' choice we wish to discuss later. However, I wish to close with the reminder that we, you and I, must and always do make the same choice as Moses did in the words of our text. He refused to be called the son of Pharaoh's daughter, which means that he decided to cast his lot with the people of God, although they were maltreated and oppressed. So we are called to do the same thing and to make the same choice, not only once but constantly. We cannot belong to the people of God and to the world at the same time. That is impossible.

Moses made the choice of suffering affliction with the people of God instead of enjoying the pleasures of the world for a season. We must and always do make the same choice before the face of God. It is either-or. Never can we choose both. Moses chose the reproach of Christ rather than all the treasures of Egypt. We must and always do make the same choice. Again, it is either-or. It is impossible to choose both, for the two stand in absolutely antithetical relation to one another. Then, too, we may be comforted. For if by faith we make that choice, then we also may look forward to the great recompence of reward in the day of our Lord Jesus Christ.

May God grant us to be faithful in the midst of an evil world.

## Chapter 26

# THE OBJECT AND MOTIVE
# OF MOSES' CHOICE

24. By faith Moses, when he was come to years, refused to be called the son of Pharaoh's daughter;
25. Choosing rather to suffer affliction with the people of God, than to enjoy the pleasures of sin for a season;
26. Esteeming the reproach of Christ greater riches than the treasures in Egypt: for he had respect unto the recompence of the reward.

*—Hebrews 11:24–26*

In the last chapter I discussed especially the choice of Moses and of the fact that he made that choice when he became of age. Now I will ask the question: What particularly did Moses choose, and in distinction from what did he choose? And second, also the question: What was the motive of that choice of Moses?

As to the object of his choice, we have already remarked that the text describes this object from a threefold aspect. First, it mentions the fact that Moses refused to be called a son of Pharaoh's daughter, which, of course, implies that he insisted on his Jewish identity and was immovable in his request to be called the son of Amram and Jochebed. It was principally a question of his identity. He belonged to the people of God. He was born a covenantal child. But he had been taken away from the humble environments of his youth and placed in the rich surroundings of the palace of Pharaoh.

The question was how Moses would reveal himself now that he had the choice between the two. He could do both. He could easily allow himself to be called the son of Pharaoh's daughter, and then manifest himself as a prince in the land. For the daughter of Pharaoh had not only granted him that right, but also had taken pains to have him educated as such. All Egypt would acknowledge him as one of their own not only, but especially as a prince in the land, if only he chose to be such. On the other hand, he had the power to deny this and to refuse that name. For after all, he was an Israelite. He was a covenantal child. He belonged to the people of God. And his very features no doubt revealed it, that he did not belong to the people of the country.

How would Moses reveal himself? That was the question. That was the question that decided all other questions. If he insisted upon being called the son of Amram and Jochebed, he sided with his people and cast his lot with the people of Israel, the people of God. Then he would also decide to share their ill treatment and their reproach and oppression. If, however, he denied his descent and allowed himself to be called the son of Pharaoh's daughter, he could have the treasures of Egypt and the pleasures of sin. All depended on his own free choice and manifestation, just as it is today with the covenantal people of God, particularly now with the young people as they come to years of discretion.

They also have to make the same choice. As they come into contact with the world, they have the power and the freedom to be called the children of the world, for the world is glad to receive them in their midst, is glad to see them deny their church connections, is glad to see them deny their covenantal relation to their covenant God. On the other hand, they also have the right to refuse to be called the children of the world and to insist on being called the children of the covenant even in the midst of the world. In the one case, they deny their people and they deny their God and enjoy all the pleasures of sin and receive the treasures of the world. On the other hand, if they cast their lot with the people of God, they must expect that they will have to bear the reproach of Christ. It all depends upon your choice, upon your manifestation in the world. It all depends upon your own confession. This refusing to be called the son of Pharaoh's daughter was for Moses a confession of faith. For if he had not done so, he would have denied his covenantal relationship and separated himself from the people of God. This was the fundamental choice of Moses.

The other two aspects that are mentioned in the words of our text of the objects between which the choice had to be made are really explanations and specifications of the same thing. For it all depended upon the name that Moses adopted. If he was called the son of Pharaoh's daughter, he could enjoy the pleasures of sin. The latter is really a very striking expression. It evidently implies that sin is the mother of pleasure in this world, that sin gives birth to and yields pleasure.

Of course, you understand that this is only true in the world and in this dispensation of sin. When once we shall have reached perfection, sin shall not be able to yield any pleasure for us anymore. Then the power of sin shall have been broken completely. The new life of Christ shall then be perfected. Then we shall never rejoice in sin anymore, but in the keeping of the covenant of our God and in his everlasting and perfect fellowship. But in this dispensation and in the present world with our sinful nature, sin is often pleasing to us, it seems. At any rate, the natural man finds pleasure in nothing else but sin.

When the text speaks of the pleasures of sin, we do not necessarily have to think of all kinds of gross and vile sins and dissipation. This is not necessarily the case. On the contrary, whenever we choose against the kingdom of our God, against the Christ, and against his people, and for the world and Satan, we sin. And this sin will often yield pleasure for a season. Oh, it may be that simply for a little money or for a little honor, or for some other selfish reason, we fail to confess our God. And in that case we enjoy our money and enjoy our honor of the world, enjoy the pleasures of sin, and escape the ill treatment of God's people. It is the pleasure of sin we enjoy in that case. The same may be said of Moses' choice. We do not imagine that Moses, even if he had never chosen for the people of God, would necessarily have led a life of vile sin and dissipation. He would have been great. He would have enjoyed honor, and he would have seen Egypt bow down before him as a prince.

And in enjoying this pleasure he would have sinned. Honor and greatness and riches are not in themselves sinful, but they become sinful if they are accompanied by a denial of our covenant God. And over against this enjoying of the pleasures of sin for a season was the other alternative, namely, that of reproach and ill treatment with the people of God. We know the condition of the people at this time, and we need not elaborate upon it. The people were poor, despised slaves in the land. They were hated with a bitter hatred by the Egyptians. And they were terribly oppressed. To choose for them meant to choose for their condition and to share in their shame and reproach. Thus were the two alternatives: prince or slave, honor or revilement, freedom or oppression. And this was all implied already in the choice between the name of Pharaoh's daughter or the name of Amram and Jochebed.

Finally the text still mentions another aspect, namely, that of the choice between the treasures of Egypt and the reproach of Christ. The treasures of Egypt is only another name for the pleasures of sin, the one denoting the thing from the point of view of its enjoyment, and the other from the aspect of its riches. Moses could have access to all the treasures of Egypt, material as well as spiritual, if he wanted to. But if he did not want to, the only alternative was to choose the reproach of Christ.

There is a beautiful idea and a store of comfort in this expression. It means evidently that the ill treatment of the people of God and the reproach of Christ are here presented as being identical. Christ and his people are one. And because they are one, he being the head of the body, his sufferings are theirs, so that through his sufferings he atones for their sin. But their sufferings are also his, so that when they are ill-treated, he also suffers reproach. Touch the people of God, and you touch Christ Jesus, and he shall surely avenge them in the day of judgment. And Moses, being thus placed before the choice between the ill treatment with the people of God and the treasures of Egypt, was really confronting the choice between the false glory of the world and of the devil and the reproach of Christ.

Thus were the objects confronting the choice of Moses. A choice between them was peremptory. The objects were mutually exclusive. He could never retain both. He could not retain his Israelitish identity and nevertheless enjoy the pleasures of Egypt. He could not choose for the people of God and at the same time enjoy the treasures and pleasures of sin. But Moses made the right choice. He refused to be called the son of Pharaoh's daughter. He preferred the ill treatment of the people of God and the reproach of Christ.

We ask: Why? What was the motive of this choice? From a natural point of view, any worldly, sound mind would probably judge that Moses was a fool. Already we have stated that a choice is based on the comparison and that it implies, first of all, an act of the mind, of intellect, of the reason. And therefore, from what a man chooses you are allowed to draw a fair inference with respect to his intellectual acumen.

The comparison in this case was indeed very clear-cut and sharp: a glorious son of Pharaoh, with all the world honoring him, or a despised Israelite, with all the world hating and oppressing him. Full and free pleasure, a life of ease and splendor; or ill treatment under the hands of the Egyptians. All the treasure of Egypt, or the reproach of Christ. Certainly, from a natural point of view it is not difficult to make a choice. And when nevertheless Moses chooses the ill treatment and the reproach of Christ and rejects the honor and pleasure of Egypt, any natural mind would certainly draw the conclusion that there is something wrong in Moses' judgment. He was, in other words, a fool.

Nor does the text allow us to think that this choice was made in a moment of thoughtlessness. It was not thus, that accidentally he went to see his brethren and that when he saw the Egyptian maltreat one of the Israelites, his blood began to boil, his judgment failed, and thoughtlessly he killed him in his rage. That certainly was not the case (Ex. 2:11–12). Moses was not sorry for what he had done as he began to think about it. For the text tells us that Moses did some *accounting* before he made the choice. He sat down and deliberated. He compared both sides carefully. He weighed them in the balance. He used business methods, so to speak. And after he had compared both sides carefully, the name and all that was connected with it, the honor and riches and greatness and treasures and pleasures of Egypt, on the one hand, and the ill treatment and reproach of Christ, on the other, he consciously and deliberately chose the latter and refused the former. And therefore, we ask the question: How is this conclusion to be explained? The answer is also given in the words of our text: by faith.

Faith in this chapter, as we know, is spoken of as the evidence of things unseen and the substance of things hoped for. As such, faith is a power that also influences the mind and the reason, so that in the light of faith we see things that the natural mind cannot perceive. Hence faith naturally affects a person's choice. It changes his judgment of things. He puts an altogether different valuation on things that are placed before him, a valuation that one who does not possess the faith cannot possibly understand. And therefore, it causes him also to draw a different conclusion than the conclusion of the world. He makes a different choice.

Thus it was also with Moses. As he weighs the two sides in the balance and carefully compares them—the name of Pharaoh's daughter, the riches and treasures and pleasures of Egypt, on the one hand, and the ill treatment and reproach of Christ, on the other—something else appeared before his mind that was worth considering but that the Egyptians of the time could not see, nor any natural mind of today can possibly perceive. It was "the recompence of the reward" (Heb. 11:26). And that recompense he saw.

He was brought up a covenantal child. And in his heart the covenant God had implanted the faith that is an evidence of things unseen. And that faith came to consciousness as he grew up. And as it came to consciousness, he embraced the covenantal promises given to Abraham, Isaac, and Jacob. They were for him true and real, and they changed the aspect of the people he chose altogether. They were the people of God. They were possessors, heirs, of rich and abundant promises. They would become a great people even though at present they were slaves in the house of bondage. And above all, Jehovah, the God of heaven and earth, was their God. Surely, perhaps these things were not so clear to Moses as they would become later. But nevertheless, according to the words of our text, he saw in these blessings of the covenant, given to the people of God, a recompence of reward so great and so glorious that all the treasures and pleasures of Egypt could not weigh up against it.

And as by faith he saw this recompence and looked to it, the choice could no more be difficult. By faith he chose, and by faith he made a good choice, consciously and deliberately. This, then, is the lesson we may derive from this portion of Scripture. We must also make the same choice. And sooner or later, as soon as we arrive at years of discretion, we do make the choice. It is the choice between the world and the kingdom of the devil, the choice between Christ and Satan, the choice between our covenant God and the pleasures of sin. That choice we must make once. That choice we must make repeatedly. That choice we will be called upon to make our entire life.

From a natural point of view all advantages are with the side of Satan and sin, and all the disadvantages are with the kingdom of God in our Savior Jesus Christ. On the one hand, pleasures and greatness of the world; on the other, reproach and ill treatment. For surely, the words of the Savior are true as long as the world stands: "In the world ye shall have tribulation" (John 16:33). And we are called to self-denial and cross-bearing after our Savior. But also today the recompence of the reward is there, which can be seen only by faith, as an evidence of things unseen. For the world passes away, and the lust thereof; but he who does the will of God abides forever (1 John 2:17). Everlasting life and glory is the recompence of reward. And therefore, choose! Choose deliberately and consciously! Choose with some accounting! If you choose from the viewpoint of faith, the outcome cannot be dubious!

*Chapter 27*

# MOSES
# FORSAKING EGYPT

By faith he forsook Egypt, not fearing the wrath of the king: for
he endured, as seeing him who is invisible.

—*Hebrews 11:27*

Conscious choice leads to conscious and definite action. This is
true in the world and from a natural point of view. But it is also
true spiritually and in the kingdom and covenant of God. All the covenantal people—and I mean now all the people who are in the church,
whether only outwardly or spiritually—confront the choice between
Christ and Satan, between the service of God and the pleasures of
sin for a season. Always the challenge confronts them, as long as this
present dispensation lasts: "Choose you this day whom ye will serve"
(Josh. 24:15). This choice is simply inevitable. From a purely carnal
and natural point of view all the advantages are on the side of Satan
and the world. On that side are the pleasures and the treasures of sin.
On that side are possible greatness and honor and all that looks desirable to the natural eye, while on the other hand there is the reproach
of Christ, the reproach that is connected with and flows principally
from the cross.

All the natural eye disdains and hates from a natural point of
view—suffering and affliction, the ill treatment, the scorn of the
world—sooner or later is yours if you choose for Christ and his people. Oh, you may probably compromise for a while and appear to be
able to choose and enjoy both Christ and the pleasures of sin. And
even the church itself—as, in fact, it often does—may attempt such
a compromise between the truth and the lie, between Christ and
Belial. Nevertheless, such a compromise will ultimately appear to be

quite impossible, and you and the church must make a very definite choice.

There is but one motive and one power that can make that choice in the right direction and that can cause us to cast our lot with Christ and the people of God and to forsake the world and all it offers. And that power and motive is the God-given power of faith—faith as an evidence of things unseen and the substance of things hoped for. For by that faith we look at and evaluate all things in a different light, and we begin to have an eye for the recompence of the reward that shall be given to the faithful people of God at the coming of the day of our Lord Jesus Christ.

Such a choice Moses made when he had become of age. On the one hand, he refused to be called the son of Pharaoh's daughter, which implied that he rejected the honor of the world and the pleasures of sin for a season. And instead he chose for the people of God and for the reproach of Christ. He was fully conscious of the choice he made, for he had become of age. As a child and probably as a youth, he had enjoyed the instruction in the fear of the Lord. And on the other hand, he was also instructed in all the wisdom of the Egyptians and was acquainted with the honor and riches and pleasures of the palace of the king. He therefore could make a very conscious choice. And he chose the reproach of Christ, which he considered far greater riches than all the pleasures of sin and all the treasure of Egypt.

But as I remarked at the beginning of our chapter, conscious choice also leads to conscious and definite action. One who chooses must take a definite stand. To express our preference for one thing in sharp distinction from another, and then to nevertheless take the latter and follow it up in our life and walk is even from a natural point of view dishonesty and folly. But in a far higher sense of the word this is true in the spiritual sphere. To choose for Christ, for the truth of God, and for the things of his kingdom means to take a stand for Christ in our entire life, to confess him and to walk according to his precepts. It implies also to stand for and with his people in the midst of the world. To choose for Christ and to confess that we belong to him, while at the same time we enjoy the pleasures of sin and the treasures of the world, is nothing less than sheer hypocrisy.

And therefore, conscious choice in the spiritual sense of the word must necessarily lead to conscious and definite action. Thus it was in the case of Moses. He chose against the treasures and pleasures of Egypt, refused to be called the son of Pharaoh's daughter, and instead he preferred the reproach of Christ. And he manifested that choice, first of all, in the fact that he forsook Egypt, according to the words of our text.

We read in the words of our text: "By faith he forsook Egypt, not fearing the wrath of the king" (Heb. 11:27). The question arises, to what historical event in the life of Moses does the text refer? This question would not be necessary if Moses had left Egypt only once. But, as we well know, this is not the case. He left Egypt, first of all, after he had killed the Egyptian and after the thing had become known even to the king. In the historical record of the second chapter of the book of Exodus we read that Moses went to visit his brethren. And when he saw that one of the Egyptian overseers smote one of his brethren, he slew him and hid him in the sand. But when on the second day he visited his brethren again, he saw two of them quarreling with each other. And when he came between them, he discovered, first, that the fact of his killing the Egyptian had become public, and second, the far more grievous fact that he could not depend upon his own people, whose lot he had chosen to share. They evidently threatened to report him to the king. In this connection we read in the book of Exodus that Moses feared and fled the country (2:11–15).

The second time that Moses forsook Egypt is still better known, for it was connected with the exodus of the entire nation out of the house of bondage. Many commentators prefer to think of the latter departure of Moses out of Egypt in connection with the words of our text. The reason for this preference is clear, and it must be admitted that on the face of it, it is also weighty. They claim that the text could not refer to the first flight of Moses from the country of Egypt for the simple reason that the historical record of that first departure contradicts all that is said in the words of our text. In the historical record we read that Moses fled. But in the words of our text it is simply stated that he forsook Egypt by faith. There, that is, in the historical record, we read that Moses feared the king, that the king intended to kill him because he had slain the Egyptian (v. 15), and hence, that departure or flight was fear inspired. On the other hand, in the words of our text we read that Moses forsook Egypt by faith, not fearing the wrath of the king.

And because of this apparent contradiction with the first departure of Moses out of Egypt, they prefer to think of his forsaking the country together with the children of Israel. Then indeed his faith shone forth bright and strong and without any fear whatsoever. In spite of the fact that the king hated to see the people go, Moses persevered, or as our text tells us, he endured, and led the people out of the house of bondage, forsaking Egypt forever.

It may be admitted that this is indeed a weighty reason to prefer the second departure instead of the first. Yet it seems to us that we must differ from these interpreters and, with other interpreters, rather think of the departure of Moses immediately after his killing of the Egyptian, which had become known to the king. If it be claimed that the words of our text do not harmonize with the first flight of Moses, their harmony with the second departure, at the age of eighty, is still less apparent. Notice, first, that the writer of the epistle to the Hebrews treats a few incidents in the life of Moses from a chronological point of view, and that, too, in the exact order of the time in which they took place. First he mentions how Moses was hid by his parents, then how he made the true and right choice when he was grown up, next how he followed up that choice by forsaking Egypt, how he celebrated the Passover in that terrible night when all the firstborn of the land were slain, and finally, how they crossed the Red Sea (Heb. 11:23–29). It is evident that the strictly chronological order is followed in this passage. Now, if the words of our text refer to the second departure of Moses, the Passover is represented as following after the deliverance of the people from Egypt, which, of course, is incorrect. But in this chronological account the first flight of Moses exactly fits in with all the rest.

Then too, second, the words "he forsook Egypt" can hardly be applied to the fact of the deliverance of the people of Israel. These words very evidently refer to an event in the personal life of Moses, and an event that pertained strictly to himself alone. The exodus, however, pertains not to Moses but to all the people of Israel, while the particular function of Moses in this deliverance was that he led out the people and that he acted as their deliverer. Third, we must also remember that at the time of the departure of Moses together with the children of Israel there was strictly speaking no need of fear on the part of Moses. For the terrible night just preceding the exodus had made both the king and the people anxious, more than willing, to let the people go. It is true that the king soon changed his mind, but that was after the children of Israel had already departed.

For all these reasons, we cannot think that the writer in the words of our text refers to the exodus of the people, but rather maintain that the reference is to that first departure of the man of God, after he had killed the Egyptian. Then indeed Moses had reason to fear the wrath of the king, for the king was very wroth. That event was something that referred not to all the people of Israel, but to Moses only. And as we said, that even fits in with the chronological order of the entire passage.

Nevertheless, we must explain the contradiction, or rather the apparent contradiction, between the words of our text and the historical record. In the latter, as we have already said, we plainly read that Moses feared the king, and that it was because of this fear that he fled to save his life. But in the words of our text we read exactly the opposite: Moses did not fear the wrath of the king, and he forsook Egypt not because of that fear, but by faith. Yet it seems to us that these apparently contradictory accounts can very well be harmonized, so that it may indeed safely be maintained that Moses fled in the fear of the wrath of the king, and at the same time without fear of that wrath and by faith.

Let me attempt to make this clear by an illustration. Let us suppose that we live in a time of persecution for the faith of Jesus Christ, as was frequently true at the time of the Reformation and as will undoubtedly be the case once more at the time of the end, when antichrist shall have power over all things for a while. Suppose that at that time someone is captured and taken to prison and that the enemy of the church of Jesus Christ tries to persuade him to deny his faith. But that Christian refuses and maintains that Christ is Lord. Suppose that because of his faithfulness he is finally condemned to death and sits the last night in his prison cell with the prospect of being burnt alive at the stake on the morrow. Think you that this man, although he lives by faith, nevertheless does not fear his death at the stake? Do you imagine that although this man puts his complete trust in the Lord and is willing to be faithful even unto death, he anticipates without any sense of fear the moment that his body shall be surrendered to the cruel flames of the stake? He lives by faith and is willing to be faithful unto death. Nevertheless, he fears the cruel suffering that is to come on the morrow.

But now to complete the figure, suppose that in the night preceding the day of his execution this martyr finds an opportunity to escape from his prison and to flee from his enemies. Can it not then be said of this martyr that he fled both in faith and for fear of the stake? He certainly escaped in faith, for he was faithful to the end in confessing his Lord before his enemies, even when his life was threatened. He might have escaped both the cell and the stake in a far simpler way, by denouncing the name of his Savior and by returning to the world and the service of antichrist. But this he refused. And because he refused by faith, he is compelled, when the opportunity arises, to make his escape by flight. Hence, we may say that such a man fled, fearing the death of the stake; and yet he fled by faith, because he was faithful to the very end.

Thus it was with Moses. By faith he had made his choice. He had refused to be called the son of Pharaoh's daughter. And now he acts upon this choice. He visits his brethren and openly chooses for the people of God. This act, however, brings him into trouble and causes him to incur the wrath of the king. The king wants to kill him. And therefore, he flees. From a human point of view, it is but natural that this fear and danger of his life inspires Moses to flee and to leave Egypt. On the other hand, we should never forget that this flight was a forsaking of Egypt by faith. For we should never forget that it was the following up of his choice, which he had made by faith, that caused him the present trouble. Except for his faith, he might still be the son of Pharaoh's daughter, enjoying the favor of the king and all the treasures and pleasures of Egypt.

Therefore, it was not the fear, but his faith, that compelled him to forsake Egypt. It was his faith that had killed the Egyptian, defending his brethren. And therefore, that faith had not feared the wrath of the king. Besides, could not Moses have returned to the favor of the king, confessing his guilt and promising to be the son of Pharaoh's daughter henceforth, and thus escaping the wrath of the king? But he does not even think of it. On the contrary, he pursues the course he has once taken. He does not choose the palace of the king again. And in spite of the fact that his choice so soon caused him trouble and fear, he had nevertheless remained steadfast unto the end. By faith he had chosen. And by that same faith he also flees alone into the desert, forsaking all.

Thus it is with us today, as well as all through the time of this dispensation, even unto the end. Oh yes, we may fear, even as Moses feared the wrath of the king and fled. We may fear to lose our jobs and position for the sake of Christ when we refuse to join worldly organizations. We may fear affliction and tribulation when presently antichrist shall reign in power, so that we can neither buy nor sell unless we worship the beast. Nevertheless, the faith that God has instilled into our hearts so overcomes that fear that in the midst of fear and tribulation we remain faithful unto the end, forsaking the world, confessing our Lord Jesus Christ, and looking forward to the recompence of the reward, the city that has foundations, whose builder and maker is God.

*Chapter 28*

# ENDURING AS
# SEEING THE INVISIBLE

By faith he forsook Egypt, not fearing the wrath of the king: for
he endured, as seeing him who is invisible.

*—Hebrews 11:27*

In the last chapter we emphasized especially the fact that Moses,
although he feared the wrath of the king when he fled after he killed
the Egyptian, nevertheless forsook Egypt by faith. That this was indeed
an act of true faith as the substance of things hoped for and as the evidence of things unseen will become all the more evident if we for a
moment, first of all, consider the circumstances under which Moses
forsook Egypt. Let us attempt to picture to ourselves those circumstances. First of all, we ought to conceive somewhat of the spiritual
condition of Moses when he thus fled from the house of bondage. We
can ascertain this spiritual condition somewhat from the context, as
well as from the natural course of events. And then I would say that at
the time Moses' faith was not only strong; but he was also in what we
might call a lofty state of mind. He was somewhat optimistic. I would
almost say that he was in the clouds.

He was in far different spirits than he was at the time when God
called him forty years later to return to Egypt and to deliver God's
people from the house of bondage. Then indeed he was very small,
and he had all kinds of excuses why God should not send him to
deliver Israel. Now, however, when he visited the brethren in the land
of Egypt, he immediately acted as their defender. And when the Egyptian smote one of his brethren, he killed him and hid him in the sand;
and he forsook Egypt, not fearing the wrath of the king. Indeed we
may say that Moses was in high spirits at the time. Probably we may

say that this is but natural. He had just made the choice by faith for the people of God and had refused to be called the son of Pharaoh's daughter.

And perhaps we may say that there is no happier moment in the life of the child of God than that in which he consciously and definitely chooses for his God in Christ, and against the world and all its treasures and pleasures. At that time we are often in the period of our first love. It may appear to us as if we have already fought our battle to the end. The fact that we have made our choice and that we have done so consciously has instilled a sweet peace and joy into our soul, so that all things look bright. We know that God loves us as he has revealed himself in our Lord Jesus Christ. We know, too, that we love our Savior and that it is our highest joy to serve our God and to love him with all our heart and mind and soul and strength. It appears rather easy for us in that period of our first love, when we have made our definite choice to serve the Lord our God and to fight the world and reject the pleasures of sin.

It is a time of strong faith but also of a faith that is not yet tested. It is a time of strong courage to fight the battle but also a time when grievous disappointments are apt to follow. For although we live by faith, we still live in our sinful nature and in the midst of a sinful people and in the midst of a sinful world. It may be a time of great expectations but also a time that is apt to be followed by severe disappointments, when clouds of darkness shall overcast our spiritual life.

This was evidently the condition of Moses at the time. He was in the period of that first love and of that strong faith that had not yet been tried. He had made his choice for the people of God and against Egypt. For a long time it had probably been a struggle for him, and he had carefully considered the pros and cons. No doubt he had done some accounting as he weighed and compared the two sides of the question. But finally faith had the victory: he had refused to be called the son of Pharaoh's daughter and had rejected the treasures and pleasures of Egypt, and he had chosen for the people of God. At the same time with that choice peace and joy had entered his heart, the peace and joy that always follow upon making the right spiritual choice, the choice for the Lord and against the world. And in that period of his first love he undoubtedly had great expectations and strong courage.

That this was actually Moses' spiritual condition is evident from the words preceding our text, as well as from the historical record. In the preceding we read that Moses deemed the reproach of Christ far greater riches than all the treasures of Egypt (Heb. 11:26). Besides, we read that he looked for the recompence of the reward. All this means, of course, that by faith he had embraced the promises of God, the promises of the covenant as given to the fathers. By that faith, therefore, he learned to regard that reviled and oppressed people of God as a great and glorious people, heirs of the promises and of the recompence of the reward. By faith he looked for the realization of those promises. Oh, what a joy after all, and what a privilege, in the eyes of faith it is to belong to the despised people! These people were the objects of God's love, and they were the heirs of a rich inheritance. These people were not always to be oppressed and reviled. On the contrary, they were to be delivered and to possess the land promised to them by Jehovah their God.

We can easily surmise that Moses at the time was rather impatient to see these promises fulfilled. All this is evident from the record in Exodus 2. He visited his brethren, and he killed the Egyptian. And again, on the second day he is upon the scene, ready to do the same thing if occasion calls him to do so. It is evident that something of the deliverer's spirit is already upon him. And most naturally, in his newborn enthusiasm, he would expect that the people for whom he had chosen were of one heart and mind with him and with one another. Did they not all have the same faith as he? Did they not all hope for the same recompence of the reward? Did they not all look for the realization of the same promises of God? Also this is but natural. Moses at the time could not conceive of the fact that the people of God who were in bondage in Egypt and sorely enslaved could fail to share the same expectation and the same hope of the realization of the promises.

Alas, this ardent faith would be sadly disappointed. Acting upon his choice, he goes and visits his brethren. And in the well-known manner he openly embraces their cause and kills the enemy who ill-treats one of the people of God. In so doing he publicly and openly renounces his relation to the daughter of Pharaoh and bids farewell to Egypt, expecting no doubt that in these suffering people of God he will find sympathy and love. And what now does he find? Does he see the people rise as one man when they see and hear how this man Moses takes their side and dares to kill the enemy?

Alas, the spiteful and threatening remark of one of his own brethren on the second day shows him that the situation is quite different. First, he finds out that even the people of God, of whom he had expected something better, that even they, in their mutual woes and oppressions, in their common burdens and sufferings, are not of one accord, but quarrel and fight among one another. How this must have grieved the man of God. But the situation is still worse. He notices that those same people are even ready to turn against him and to betray him to the king—him who had meant to be their deliverer and who so unselfishly had embraced their cause. What a sad and bitter disappointment!

Oh, Moses had to discover that not all were Israel who were of Israel, that together with the elect there were also the reprobates, that together with the spiritual Israel there were also the carnal element. The same, of course, is true of the church today. And also today that carnal element is a grief and disappointment to the child of God, especially in the days of his first love. Thus, then, it was at the time when Moses forsook Egypt.

There was no doubt at this time a strong contrast between what he had expected and what he actually experienced. Oh, he still had respect unto the recompence of the reward. He still lived by faith and still hoped for the promises of God and their realization. But now it became gradually evident that that reward was still slow in being realized. He had had great hopes of the people of God for whom he had chosen and whom he knew by actual contact; and instead he finds contention and enmity even among them. He had no doubt expected that as he had chosen them, so they would also stand by him. And behold how they also rejected him and mocked at his attempt to deliver them from the house of bondage! The people of his choice had rejected him plainly and had greatly disappointed him. All seems to be lost, all of a sudden.

Surely, from a human point of view it would have been small

wonder had Moses repented of his choice and had he acknowledged his wrong to the king, leaving the people who were not at all worthy of his support and of his deliverance in their trouble and oppression and taking sides with the oppressors. But Moses does not do so. On the contrary, he still adheres to his choice. To Egypt he will not return. And being in danger of his life, he rather seeks the solitude of the desert than beg the pardon and favor of Pharaoh. For Moses did not act from mere natural motives, but from faith, from faith as an evidence of things unseen and the substance of things hoped for. And therefore, we read in the end of our text: "For he endured, as seeing him who is invisible" (Heb. 11:27).

Here Moses even in all his disappointment reaches undoubtedly the summit of his faith. At first he had chosen the people of God. By faith he had refused to be called the son of Pharaoh's daughter, had chosen rather to suffer ill treatment with God's people in the house of bondage. He had bidden farewell to the treasures and pleasures of Egypt, in order to choose the reproach and ill treatment of Christ. He had done so in the faith that the recompence of the reward was for him too. But in that choice he had evidently depended more or less upon the people of God themselves, who were visible. With them he had connected the promises of the covenant of God. With them he expected no doubt to receive the recompence of the reward. And therefore, we read that in his choice he chose for the people of God rather than for Egypt. And his reproach and ill treatment he also had connected with that same people.

He undoubtedly expected bitter results from this choice from a natural point of view. He expected sufferings and tribulations, and he would gladly share them with the people of God. Nevertheless, also this ill treatment he did not have to suffer alone, but he expected to suffer reproach and shame together with the people of God. In all this he was more or less dependent upon the people whom he could see.

But now even those people had failed him. They left him alone. Now he is evidently called to suffer the reproach of Christ even apart from the people of God of whom he supposed that they would suffer the same reproach with him. Nay, what is even worse, he was called upon to bear the reproach of the people of God all by himself and all alone. On that people he could no more depend. But in spite of all this his faith stood firm. He endured, the text tells us, in spite of all things to the contrary. And now his faith clung consciously to God, and to him alone. He endured as seeing him who is invisible.

Indeed, faith is the evidence of things unseen. And as such it reveals itself most clearly and most strongly in its clinging to the invisible God. God is unseen. He is invisible. Yet faith clings to him. Oh, do not take this in the sense in which sometimes the unbeliever also maintains that there is a God, although he cannot see him. That amounts to precious little. That can afford no strength and no courage and no hope whatsoever. That faith the devils also have, and they tremble. But faith, as an evidence of things unseen, does not merely coldly and historically confess that God exists. But it has communion with the living God of heaven and earth as he has revealed himself in Christ Jesus our Lord.

Christ is the face of the invisible God. And by looking at Christ we see God as seeing the Invisible One. Thus he knows God, he loves God, he has communion with God, knows that God loves him and has loved him from before the foundation of the world as he is revealed in our Lord Jesus Christ. He knows that God is with him, and that no matter what betides God will surely fulfill to him his promises. It is that faith that Moses possessed, according to the words of our text. He endured as if he saw the invisible God, as if he had direct communion with him. To Egypt he had bidden farewell. The people of God had failed to support him, had even rejected him. And now he forsook Egypt, and he did so by faith, not fearing the wrath of the king. It was sufficient for him that by faith he knew that the invisible God was his God for ever and ever, and that he would never forsake or reject him. He knew that that Invisible One was the faithful covenant God, on whom he might rely for time and eternity.

Is it a wonder then that Moses endured? Is it a wonder that he did not return to the king and beg for his favor? He had a covenant with the mightiest of all kings, in comparison with whom the mightiest of the mighty was but a drop of the bucket. Seeing him, therefore, in the consciousness that his eye was upon him, he could not hesitate, he could not deny his former choice. He could only go on. For far better it was to be with the mighty God in the lonely desert than with the king of Egypt at the splendid palace and in the midst of the pleasures of Egypt.

That same faith is also sufficient for us. It is sufficient in all circumstances of life. In fact, we see the invisible God much more clearly in the face of Jesus Christ our Lord as he is revealed in his word than Moses ever could see him. And by that faith, which beholds the invisible in the face of our Lord Jesus Christ, we know that he loves us, and that he has loved us from all eternity, and that he will love us, and that all things that betide in this present time must surely work together for salvation to those who love him. May this faith be with us. May this faith grow in strength also through the preaching of the word. And may by this faith we conquer the world and fight the good fight even unto the end, that no one take our crown.

*Chapter 29*

# MOSES' PREPARATION AS A DELIVERER OF GOD'S PEOPLE

Through faith he kept the passover, and the sprinkling of blood,
lest he that destroyed the firstborn should touch them.

—*Hebrews 11:28*

The apostle Paul writes in his first epistle to the Corinthians that the preaching of the cross is foolishness to those who perish but a power of God to those who are saved (1:18). That truth, expressed by the great apostle to the Gentiles, is indeed characteristic of the contrast between the children of God and the children of the world, between the believers and the unbelievers. It is characteristic of sin and therefore of the sinner to exalt himself in his foolishness over against the wisdom of God and to follow the ways of foolishness. The sinner for that very reason, deeming the wisdom of God foolishness, reveals himself by his opposition to God and by his rejection of the ways of God, also of the way of salvation. The believer, on the other hand, by faith appreciates and loves those ways of God and shows his appreciation by following in those ways, by trusting in and relying upon and glorifying the wisdom of God.

This contrast is not difficult to understand. The sinner is the man whose mind is darkened by sin, whose will is perverse. And therefore, he does not discern spiritual things. He has no power of perceiving the wisdom of God in the realm of grace. He does not have the will to follow the way of God's wisdom. He condemns that way by his darkened understanding. And he refuses to follow that way because of the perverseness of his will. It requires nothing less than the power of the Spirit to make a sinner see and acknowledge and follow the wisdom of God. Hence the sinner, because of his very condition, stubbornly refuses to accept the way of salvation, the way that God in his wisdom has devised, the way of the cross and the way of faith.

On the other hand, the believer, the child of God, is a sinner who has been changed in his inmost heart. God has instilled the power of faith in him. And that power of faith controls his mind and his heart, and therefore he is able to discern the wisdom of God and entirely ready and glad to accept that wisdom and its ways above the foolishness of his own mind and nature. That faith, implanted in his heart by the Holy Spirit of Christ and brought to consciousness by the call of the gospel, has changed him into a new man. That faith is the power within him that controls his very life. It enlightens, under the influence of the word of God, his mind, so that he can discern spiritual things and understand them spiritually. And it inclines his will, so that he will follow in the way of God's wisdom. Hence, it is certainly true that the words of the apostle we have just mentioned characterize the contrast between the sinner and the child of God. To the one the cross of Christ is foolishness; to the other it is the wisdom of God. The one rejects that cross and rejects God's wisdom; the other accepts it and glorifies the wisdom of the Most High.

This truth is amply exemplified in the history of the world. It is shown already in the first paradise. For what else was the first manifestation of the power of sin in that early morning of creation than a rejection of the wisdom of God and an expression of preference for the foolishness of the devil? What else was it than a refusal to follow in the way of God's wisdom and a choice of other ways, of the ways of foolishness? The same is true at the time of Noah. The world was mocking at the wisdom of God, not accepting his word nor inclined to follow in his ways, while Noah by faith was building the ark and thereby accepted the word of God as a revelation of highest truth and wisdom. In the life of Abraham we find the unconditional acceptance of the wisdom of God expressed in his word, the word of God's promise, and the most complete reliance on that wisdom of the Most High, so that by faith he was a sojourner in a strange land, accepting the promises.

Nor was it different at the time of Christ. The wisdom of God, the eternal Word, became revealed in the flesh. And the world knew him not; unbelief did not acknowledge him but rejected him and finally nailed him to the accursed tree. It was only the simple believer who clung to him for salvation. Thus it was also at the time when Paul wrote his epistle to the Corinthians. God's way of salvation was foolishness to the Greek and a stumbling block to the Jew. They could not perceive or accept the wisdom of God revealed in the cross of Jesus Christ. But the same cross was the power and wisdom of God to all who believed.

Nor is it different in our own time. Also now the wisdom of the world rejects the so-called blood theology, rejects God's way of salvation. Also today it is true that what is concealed from the eyes of the world, of the great and of the wise, is accepted as truest wisdom by the simple believer, enlightened by the Spirit. This is also plain from the text in Hebrews 11:28.

I discussed the man Moses as he forsook Egypt by faith, not fearing the wrath of the king. We remember that he made his choice of God's own people and that he had refused the treasures and pleasures of Egypt. He had cast his lot with the oppressed people of God. We remember, too, that he had followed up that choice. Perhaps already with the fire of his future calling burning in his soul, he had publicly taken sides with the people against their oppressors. He had killed the Egyptian and buried him in the sand. He felt that he was to defend that people of God and to deliver them even at that early date. Perhaps he had expected that the people would receive him and gladly follow him as he would deliver them from the hands of their enemies. But in this he had been sadly disappointed. And the people, instead of following him in that same enthusiasm that Moses displayed, were even ready to betray him to their oppressors. They quarreled with one another. And when Moses would have it differently, they even threatened that his life would not be so certain if he mingled with them, his own people.

Upon this he had left Egypt by faith, his departure occasioned, as we saw, by the wrath of the king, but finding its root nonetheless in the faith of Moses. He had bidden farewell to Egypt. And though it be that even his own people would not receive him, never would he return to repent of his choice. And leaving the country, he fled into the wilderness of Midian.

God's ways are higher than our ways, and his thoughts higher than our thoughts (Isa. 55:9). This is plain also from the history of this man Moses. His thoughts were evidently that he should without delay visit his brethren and deliver them from the hands of the Egyptians. And full of zeal, he goes and kills those who are set over his people by the king of Egypt. But God's way was entirely different. First, it would have to become evident that not man, not even Moses, but that Jehovah their God had delivered the people from the house of bondage. Second, the manner of deliverance would be entirely different than Moses at this time could even imagine. It would not be by the power of the sword, but by mighty plagues from heaven. It would not be by striking down this and that enemy of the people, but by going directly to the king to demand that he let the people go. And third, the time had not yet come when Moses imagined that it was already ripe. Forty years still were to elapse before Moses should go again to deliver the people in the name of Jehovah.

And therefore, Moses must leave Egypt. He must go to Midian. There he meets with the daughters of Jethro as they come to the well to water the flock. Bravely and gallantly this man Moses defends the maidens against the impudent shepherds and waters their flock for them, as the shepherds would prevent them. And for a long time he dwells with their father, marries one of his daughters, Zipporah, and keeps the flock for his father-in-law. Day after day Moses now wanders in the desert, with nothing but the wilderness about him and the sky above him and the flock for his companions—alone with the invisible God, to whom he had clung by faith. Then, finally, after forty years he is called by the Almighty from the burning bush to go back to Egypt, to lead the people out of the house of bondage.

And now notice what a change had come over this man of God! Forty years ago he was filled with ardent enthusiasm to deliver the people, and while right in their midst he started to kill the inhabitants of the country. And now he hesitates and would be relieved of the heavy task and responsibility of delivering the people of Israel. Just hear him present his objections! He is now fully aware of his own weakness and inability. In himself there is no strength. Only he does not yet understand that such is exactly the deliverer Jehovah needs:

a man conscious of his own weakness, in order that the glory of God may be revealed in and through his weakness and that it might become apparent that not man but God delivered his people out of the house of bondage.

And hence, his objection. Says he: "Lord, who am I that I should deliver this people?" He is now fully conscious of the difficulty of the task and of the stubbornness of the people. No doubt he remembers that forty years ago they were not at all willing to be delivered. Hence, his objection: "They shall ask, What is the name of him that sent thee?" And: "They will not believe me."[1] He is now fully conscious of his own defects, and even physically he is not the man to deliver this people. He cannot appear before Pharaoh, for he is slow of speech. And after the Lord had met all these difficulties, he begs to be excused and asks that the Lord may send someone else in his stead.

But finally this man, forty years ago so confident of his ability to meet with and overcome all difficulties, now so deeply conscious of his weakness and inability, goes, relying by faith upon God who had sent him. He meets with the elders. He meets with the king. He delivers his message. But the king refuses, hardening his heart, that the power and the glory of God might be revealed. And thereupon, plague upon plague is sent upon the country. Nine plagues have come and gone. And after the ninth plague the king seems further than ever from being inclined to let the people go. And now the Lord announces the most terrible one of all the plagues that had been sent upon the country. All the firstborn of the land shall die. And at midnight, while the people of Israel are eating the Passover and, covered by the blood of the lamb, shall escape the terrible scourge, the destroyer shall pass through the land to leave death and anguish in all the homes of the Egyptians.

Such had been the history of those forty years, up to the time of the words of our text. It had no doubt been a period of preparation. Forty years ago the time was not yet ripe, as Moses had thought it was. Now it was indeed the time, although Moses did not think so when the Lord his God called him from the burning bush. God's ways are

---

1  This is a recounting of the exchange between God and Moses in Exodus 3.

higher than our ways. Long the time may seem to us that God waits before he delivers his people; but he will surely visit them and deliver them exactly at the proper time.

A period of preparation it had been for Egypt. Forty years ago the measure of iniquity had not yet been full; now it was. Surely Egypt had been set, no doubt, to be a manifestation of the power of God. But from a spiritual and ethical point of view the land had to be ripe for the judgment before the Lord would come upon the land with his destruction. The old king and all that generation had died, but the oppression of God's people continued and was more severe than ever. The day of judgment and of accounting was there. The time was ripe for Egypt.

But a period of preparation it had also been for the people of Israel. Surely God delivers his people. But in this deliverance he treats them as rational and moral creatures. He will not drive them out of Egypt as long as they do not sorely feel the need of deliverance and as long as they are not longing and crying for their redemption. Forty years ago they were not ready; but they have learned to cry for deliverance, and their cry has come to Jehovah their God in heaven. Also for the people the time is now ripe. The Lord will surely deliver his people when they cry to him for help.

But finally, a period of preparation it had also been for Moses, who was to deliver them. As we have remarked already, Moses was now a different man. His education had been completed in the desert. The wilds of nature so often must serve to prepare the servants of God. Thus it was with Elijah. Thus it was with John the Baptist. Thus it was even with our Savior. Thus it was also with the mediator of the Old Testament.

First he had received his education in the home of his parents, his covenantal training in general. Then he had been educated at the palace of the king, and Egypt had to be instrumental in the hand of God to prepare this man for his great task from a mere natural and human point of view. For he had become versed in all the knowledge of the Egyptians. Now, finally, in the desert he had finished his education, alone with his God, and he had been spiritually trained to deliver Israel. A different man he was. He had learned to acknowledge his own weakness. His character had both been strengthened since he learned to rely upon Jehovah alone and also tempered. And in that desert the man Moses had become meek, more than any man. Now Moses was fit to be an instrument in the hand of God and nothing more. And now it also could be evident and plainly revealed that it was the covenant God who delivered Israel and not any man.

Thus it is always. There can be no question about the truth that God will surely deliver his church. But the time for that deliverance must become perfectly ripe. The measure of iniquity of the world must become full, as it will become at the time of antichrist that is to come and that probably is to come soon. But also the people of God must cry for that deliverance, must long for the salvation of God, and must understand and acknowledge that not by man, nor even by the preaching of the gospel through man, but by God alone the deliverance and salvation of his church shall be accomplished. Let us then put our trust not in an arm of flesh but in the strong arm of Jehovah our God, who has revealed himself in Jesus Christ our Lord, and who will surely deliver us even unto everlasting perfection in the glory of God's tabernacle with us.

*Chapter 30*

# MOSES KEEPING
# THE PASSOVER BY FAITH

Through faith he kept the passover, and the sprinkling of blood,
lest he that destroyed the firstborn should touch them.
—*Hebrews 11:28*

In the passage that we are discussing at present we read that Moses by
faith kept the Passover and the sprinkling of blood, that the destroyer
of the firstborn might not touch them. In the original we read literally:
"By faith Moses made the passover." And therefore, we evidently must
refer this to the institution of the Passover by Moses upon the divine
injunction. Also the others kept the Passover that night; but that they
kept it was only because Moses by faith had first followed up the word
of his God and instituted it. And the emphasis in this ordaining of the
Passover no doubt falls in this connection on the sprinkling of the
blood. The sprinkling of the blood was part of the Passover and not
something separate from it. In the night of the deliverance of the people of Israel it was put on the doorposts and lintels; and later the blood
of the Passover was poured out at the altar in the central sanctuary.
And therefore, it is especially that sprinkling of blood that our text
means to emphasize and to call before our attention.

We are acquainted with the history of this first Passover, no doubt.
Nine plagues had already passed over the country. The water of Egypt
had been turned into blood. Frogs had covered the country. The dust
of the land had been changed into lice. All kinds of vermin and flies
had been a plague to man and beast. Murrain had killed the cattle.
Boils had broken out on man and beast. Hail and fire had devastated
the land. Locusts had eaten the crop. For three days the people had
groped in darkness day and night. All these plagues had come and

been removed. And in spite of them all, the king had hardened his heart and would not let the people go.

One more plague was to be sent upon the land, a plague so terrible that all Egypt would groan with anguish and sorrow, so that finally they would urge and beg the people to leave. All the firstborn, from the crown prince to the son of the common laborer, of man and of beast, would be struck that night by the destroyer and die. But Israel would not be touched. The Lord made a distinction between Egypt and Israel; and that night it would become plain who were the people of God in the land. In that night Israel would be delivered (Ex. 11). In that night Israel would commence to live as a separate people. In that night Israel would be consecrated as a people unto their God. And for that reason they were to eat the Passover and celebrate their birth as a people of the Lord.

We know how that Passover was celebrated that night. The tenth of the month Abib, later called Nisan, they were to separate a lamb from the flock. The lamb was to be a year old and was to be without blemish. Then, four days later, they were to sacrifice the lamb, but not to part or cut it into pieces, nor break a bone of the animal. The blood they were to put on the doorposts and the lintels of the house with hyssop, and the lamb they were to roast whole and eat it by families, or companies if the family were too small. Eating the Passover, they were to be ready to depart from the land. Their loins were to be girded. Their shoes were to be on their feet. And standing with their staff in hand, they were to finish the lamb, leaving nothing till morning but burning whatever was left. Thus Moses received his instructions through the word of the Lord. Thus he delivered the message to the elders of Israel, and by faith ordained the Passover. Thus the people gave execution to the orders of the elders that came that same night (Ex. 12).

We naturally ask: What was the significance of this Passover in that night of deliverance? In general, we may say that it was a sign to them of their deliverance from the house of bondage and of their consecration as a people to their covenant God. Till now Israel had not been a separate nation, living a separate existence and possessing a separate land of their own. They had been dwelling in Egypt. They had been concealed from the eyes of the world as a people of Jehovah. They had been more or less swallowed up by the country in which they dwelt. God had his people, his own chosen people, in Egypt; but they were not evident to the world. They were not yet delivered. And neither the world nor Egypt did know that Jehovah had a people—at least they did not believe it. But on the contrary, in their low and abject state in the land of oppression they rather gave the lie to the truth that they were the people of God and that he would protect and care for them.

But now they were to be delivered from the house of bondage. From that time on they were to be a separate people of Jehovah in the midst of the world. This deliverance was to be accomplished and accompanied by the destruction of the enemies who had oppressed them so long. Clearly a distinction was to be drawn that night, a distinction between the people of God and the people of Egypt— a distinction, first, because the Lord would pass [over] his people, so that the destroyer would not touch them; and a distinction, second, because they were to be separated from the house of bondage and issue forth from Egypt as a people of God. Egypt was to give birth to the people of God and at the same time suffer the real woes and agonies of that birth.

But why were the Israelites the people of God? And why was this distinction to be shown to them? Was it because Israel was worthy of this distinction? Was it because there did exist such a distinction between Israel and Egypt that the latter was worthy of destruction and the former deserved to be delivered? We know better. Israel was not in itself a people of God. Nor was there anything in them that made them worthy of this glorious distinction. They were by nature as bad as, if not worse than, the Egyptians. And their past history even at this time had clearly shown it.

But they were the people of God because of his own covenant that God had established with them in his everlasting grace. Israel was the chosen people of God. And the distinction of the people found its origin in the free grace of Jehovah. God had chosen them and not Egypt; and therefore they had become the objects of his grace. And this grace was to reveal itself in the bestowal of the covenantal blessings upon

Israel. And they were to inhabit and to possess the land God had sworn to the fathers. Therefore, they were to be delivered.

But this deliverance of an unworthy people could be performed, could be realized, only through blood. In itself Israel was unworthy. In itself Israel had deserved to be destroyed as well as the Egyptians. For also Israel was a sinful people. And therefore, only with the expiation of their sins through blood could they be delivered, so that their deliverance did not contradict the righteousness of the most high God. Of this deliverance through blood, of this expiation of the sin of the people, the Passover was a sign. It was the sign of the blood of the Lamb. It was a sign to the people, as Scripture emphasizes so plainly, of the cross of Christ. It was not a sign to Jehovah. For what need would Jehovah have of signs? Nay, but it was a sign from Jehovah and to his people.

In the night of destruction they were to put the blood on the doorposts and lintels, the blood of the sacrifice. The door is the symbol of the entire house, just as the gate is often used in Scripture to designate the whole city. And therefore, by putting the blood of the sacrifice, the sacrifice of the lamb, on the doorpost, the people expressed that they covered themselves with the blood of the lamb that atoned for their sins. That this is actually the case is plain from the fact that the blood was to be put on the posts of the doors with hyssop, which is always in Scripture a sign of purification and expiation of sins. Hence, once more, the act of putting the blood on the doorposts and lintels was the act of receiving the sign of deliverance, was the act of accepting God's own way of salvation. By this blood alone could Israel be consecrated as a people of God.

If we bear this in mind, it is not difficult to see that Moses ordained the Passover by faith. Surely, also of the people as a whole, though not of every individual, it might undoubtedly be said that they performed an act of faith by following up the orders of the Lord. But Moses received the word of the Lord. Moses acted upon this word. Moses instituted the Passover. And therefore, our text mentions Moses, and not the people as a whole, and says that it revealed the faith of this mediator of the old dispensation in that he ordained the Passover.

Once more faith was an evidence of things unseen, also in this case. From that point of view Hebrews 11 treats faith, and from that point of view we must also regard the faith of Moses. And then it becomes manifest as such in two ways; first, because Moses ordained this sign of deliverance while the people were still in bondage. They were still in Egypt. Nor had the king given any hope that he would actually let the people go. Nine times he had refused; and the last time he had seemed harder than ever. It therefore did not seem very likely from a natural point of view that the people should be delivered that night. And yet the Passover was to be celebrated as a sign of deliverance, a celebration of their freedom and liberation while they were still groaning in prison. They were to be ready to depart; with loins girded, shoes on their feet, staff in hand, they were to eat the Passover.

Hence, it was an act of faith, as an evidence of things unseen, that the Passover as such was ordained by this man Moses. What a folly their celebration would prove to be if on the morrow the people would still remain in the country, without hope of deliverance! But Moses had the word of the Lord. And to faith that is quite sufficient. In that word he saw the deliverance. In that word he saw the people go from the house of bondage in the morning. In that faith he ordained the Passover.

But the text mentions especially the sprinkling of the blood as an element of this Passover (Heb. 11:28). And to this we must therefore pay special attention. This ordaining of the sprinkling of the blood was an act of faith on the part of Moses. And this can be explained in but one way, namely, that to the faith of Moses it was the deliverance of the people through blood. By faith Moses accepted that the people could be delivered only through the expiation of their sins through the grace of God, and that this could be manifested only through the blood of the sacrifice of the lamb.

Nay, not if we take the shallow view that this sign of the blood was a sign to Jehovah. That indeed is the common view. Often this is presented, even in our own midst, without any further explanation. There is no doubt an element of truth in this presentation, in so far, namely, that Jehovah would surely enter with destruction into the homes even of Israel if there were any home not covered with the blood of the lamb. But not because Jehovah needed a sign, for that is not the case. And yet, that is the way it is most frequently presented, so that even the critics love to dwell on the primitive idea that Israel had of its God, thinking evidently that God needed a sign to discover where the Israelites dwelt in that awful night of destruction.

But even from a mere historical point of view this interpretation is the greatest folly. First, as we have mentioned before, Scripture tells us that the sign of the blood was given them as a sign to them, and not as a sign for Jehovah (Ex. 12:13). Not he but they needed that sign. And second, this is not the first time that Jehovah had made a distinction between his own people in Egypt as he inflicted the punishment of the plagues upon the country. More than once the people had been exempt while the rest of the country groaned under the chastening hand of the Lord. Even during the three days of darkness light had been in the dwellings of the children of Israel. And would the people now have the idea that Jehovah needed a sign in order to find where the people of Israel lived or stayed in the night of the Passover? We feel immediately that this was neither a fact, nor was this idea in the mind of Moses or of the people of God in general. And therefore, this false interpretation must be rejected as unworthy even of consideration.

Not to Jehovah but to the people it was a sign. A sign, first, that the destroyer would pass them in that awful night of destruction, so that he would not touch them. And a sign, second, that the Lord would deliver them from the house of bondage that very night. A sign, in a word, that the Lord would make a clear distinction between Egypt and the people of God. And this distinction was based on the blood of expiation in the sacrifice of the lamb.

Thus understood, we clearly see that this institution of the Passover and the sprinkling of the blood was indeed an act of highest faith. It was the acceptation of the sign by faith. It was a confession of faith, of faith that the Lord would pass his people, of faith that the Lord would deliver his people that night, but also of the faith that the deliverance could be done only through the blood of the sacrifice. It implies plainly a confession of sin, a confession that the Lord could not bless Israel except through grace, and that this grace could not be revealed except through blood. No, surely Moses did not understand these things fully at this time; but he understood the meaning in a figure, no doubt. For the rest, it was not necessary for him to understand fully the things that were to come. For him it was enough that he had the word of God. And in obedience to the word of God he accepted God's way of salvation. Faith is an evidence of things unseen. And though Moses did not see the use of it all, he certainly saw the wisdom of God by faith.

From the point of view of reason all this was folly. What? Would a little blood, struck on the doorposts, save them as the angel came to destroy the children of Egypt? Or again, could not God save them without that blood on their doorposts and lintels? Most assuredly he could. But from the point of view of faith it was the highest wisdom. For faith understands that the people of God can be saved only through the sign of the blood, ultimately through the blood of Jesus Christ our Lord. And the outcome of Moses' faith was glorious. The faith was crowned. The Lord passed them with his destruction, and he led them out of the house of bondage to save them and consecrate them as his own people in his everlasting covenant.

And thus it is still. God's way of salvation is still through the sign of the blood, struck on the doorposts and the lintels of our hearts. It is only faith that can do so. To unbelief all this is folly. Abundant proof we have of this in our own time. What? God save us through blood? Thus we hear unbelief object. God should be the originator of such a blood theology? That is folly according to them. Christ is merely our example. And if only we follow him in an ethical, moral way, all will be well. We shall be saved individually and saved as a world. The world will gradually become better. Universal peace shall reign supreme. And all this without the sign of the blood.

But that is not the way of God's salvation. Only then, when we receive by a true faith the sign of the blood and by it confess our own sin and death and at the same time glorify God's grace, shall the destroyer pass and we be saved forever. He who believes on the Son of God has everlasting life; but he who believes not the Son shall not see life: the wrath of God abides on him (John 3:36). That is God's way of salvation.

*Chapter 31*

# PASSING OVER
# THE RED SEA

By faith they passed through the Red sea as by dry land: which the Egyptians assaying to do were drowned.

*—Hebrews 11:29*

You will understand that my text refers to the history of the children of Israel as recorded in Exodus 14. From this I will quote only the following:

21. And Moses stretched out his hand over the sea; and the LORD caused the sea to go back by a strong east wind all that night, and made the sea dry land, and the waters were divided.
22. And the children of Israel went into the midst of the sea upon the dry ground: and the waters were a wall unto them on their right hand, and on their left.
23. And the Egyptians pursued, and went in after them to the midst of the sea, even all Pharaoh's horses, his chariots, and his horsemen.
24. And it came to pass, that in the morning watch the LORD looked unto the host of the Egyptians through the pillar of fire and of the cloud, and troubled the host of the Egyptians,
25. And took off their chariot wheels, that they drave them heavily: so that the Egyptians said, Let us flee from the face of Israel; for the LORD fighteth for them against the Egyptians.
26. And the LORD said unto Moses, Stretch out thine hand over the sea, that the waters may come again upon the Egyptians, upon their chariots, and upon their horsemen.

27. And Moses stretched forth his hand over the sea, and the sea returned to his strength when the morning appeared; and the Egyptians fled against it; and the LORD overthrew the Egyptians in the midst of the sea.

28. And the waters returned, and covered the chariots, and the horsemen, and all the host of Pharaoh that came into the sea after them; there remained not so much as one of them.

29. But the children of Israel walked upon dry land in the midst of the sea; and the waters were a wall unto them on their right hand, and on their left. (Ex. 14:21–29)

Now the author of Hebrews emphasizes that the children of Israel passed over the sea *by faith*. However, it is evident that this was not true of all of them but only of the remnant according to the election of grace. For thus we read in 1 Corinthians 10:1–5,

1. Moreover, brethren, I would not that ye should be ignorant, how that all our fathers were under the cloud, and all passed through the sea;

2. And were all baptized unto Moses in the cloud and in the sea;

3. And did all eat the same spiritual meat;

4. And did all drink the same spiritual drink: for they drank of that spiritual Rock that followed them: and that Rock was Christ.

5. But with many of them God was not well pleased: for they were overthrown in the wilderness.

It had been better for them that they had never left Egypt, or even that they had drowned in the sea together with the Egyptians. These were the reprobate chaff, the ungodly unbelievers among Israel. Nevertheless, the whole of Israel is not characterized by them but is judged rather by the elect remnant. And thus the author of Hebrews can say that it is by faith that they passed through the Red Sea.

The text also strongly reminds us once more of what the apostle writes in 1 Corinthians 1:25, "The foolishness of God is wiser than men; and the weakness of God is stronger than men." For this truth, whatever else it may mean, certainly implies that in the end the wisdom of God shall have the victory, and the wisdom of the world shall be defeated. Not God's wisdom but the wisdom of the world shall in the end stand condemned as foolishness. The wisdom of the world and the wisdom of God shall each travel its own way; and the end, the outcome, the destination, of each way shall prove that the wisdom of the world was foolishness indeed.

Of this truth we have several examples or illustrations in Holy Writ. Enoch sharply condemned this wickedness of the wicked world, and the foolishness of the world must have laughed and mocked at him. But the end was that Enoch was taken away without seeing death. He had the victory, and the world was condemned. When the wisdom of God built the ark in the time of Noah, the wisdom of the world spurned scornfully and refused to heed the warnings of God's wisdom through Noah. But the outcome was that the wisdom of the world miserably perished, and the wisdom of God prevailed. And thus it was no doubt at the time of the apostle Paul in relation to the cross of Christ. That cross claimed through the preaching to be the manifestation of God's wisdom. But to the Greek that cross was foolishness.

And the same is true today. Always the wisdom of God is foolishness to those who perish. Carelessly the world lives along, smiling and rejoicing and making merry. Of sin and of righteousness and of judgment they know not at all. Over against the wisdom of the word of God also the world today places its own wisdom. The word of God informs us that the world as such is virtually in the power of darkness and in the power of the prince of this world, though principally he is already condemned in the cross of Jesus Christ our Lord. That word informs us that toward the end that power of darkness shall grow stronger and that there will be hard and dark days for the church of God in the world. For more and more that world will be forsaking Christ and opposing him openly. Nevertheless, that word also informs us that finally the Lord shall have to come personally to break and destroy the power of darkness and to establish his own kingdom in glory, sending all the enemies of his kingdom to eternal destruction while he receives all his people to everlasting glory.

But the wisdom of the world does not believe this. According to that wisdom, it will be exactly the other way. Gradually the world is improving, advancing on the road of development with tremendous strides. Oh yes, the world will continue to follow in the steps of Christ Jesus, to improve the world as he wants us to do in our own strength and on his own example. Ultimately there will be universal peace. But the wisdom of the world shall also in this case be brought to nought, and destruction shall come upon those who trust in it, while the wisdom of God, however foolish apparently, shall prove to be victorious and prevailing unto and through the end.

This is also the history of Egypt at the time to which our text refers. The power and the wisdom of God, on the one hand, and that of the world as represented in Egypt, on the other hand, had been opposing each other for some time. Ten plagues had already been sent upon Egypt, and one would think that this would be enough to prove to Pharaoh that the wisdom of God was wiser than he, and the weakness of God stronger than he. But he keeps right on hardening his heart, till ultimately the battle between the two is finished. And the words of our text express very definitely that the wisdom of God was victorious, while that of the world perished.

I find in the words of our text in connection with the history recorded in Exodus, first of all, an apparently foolish move.

A long procession it was that set out on the journey to the promised land in the morning after the Lord had sent the last plague, the death of all the firstborn, upon Egypt. I say it was a long procession because the people of Israel had increased mightily in the land of Egypt even though it had been a land of oppression. Approximately two million people all told, women and children included, must have left the land, carrying with them the gold and silver they had demanded from the Egyptians in remuneration of their hard labor, and driving along their cattle and their sheep. Five abreast they marched out of Rameses to go to the land promised them as the land of the covenant. As we watch them march out of the country, we cannot help contemplating how few of these travelers ever reached the promised land, and how many of them never could enter because of their unbelief.

From Rameses the children of Israel took their course in an almost directly easterly direction, though slightly bending toward the north, till they reached the place called Etham. From a natural point of view this course is already somewhat surprising. For it certainly was not the shortest route to the promised land, while we might expect that such a procession as this, with women and children, cattle and sheep, encumbered with a load of baggage, would deem it expedient to choose the shortest route thither. That shortest route was undoubtedly the way of the Philistines, along the coast, in a northeasterly direction from the starting point of the children of Israel.

Still more surprised we are to find that they turn in a southerly direction from Etham on. The word of the Lord comes to them, and he tells them to turn back and encamp before Pihahiroth, between Migdol and the sea. This would mean that they would have to follow the western shore of the sea, or rather, that arm of the Red Sea that is called the Gulf of Suez. On their left they would have the sea; on their right and before them, the mountains and the wilderness. Now whatever may have been the exact location of their crossing point, so much is certain, that from a natural point of view this course seemed utterly foolish. Even if we bear in mind that their immediate destination was not the land of Canaan but the Mount of Horeb, it cannot be maintained that from the point of view of human reason this was the right course.

The mountain lay in the southernmost part of the peninsula formed by the two arms of the Red Sea, the Gulf of Suez and the Gulf of Aqaba. Or, if you please, the mountain was on the eastern side of the sea. It could only be reached by passing around the northernmost point of the sea and following the eastern shore of the gulf. But now the children of Israel are following exactly the opposite shore, which makes it simply impossible for them ever to get out of the land and ever to reach either the Mount of Horeb or the land of Canaan. Never could they expect to cross that sea. And we do not wonder that upon Pharaoh it made the impression that the children of Israel, together with their leader, were a crowd of fools who did not even know the way they had to take in order to reach the place of their destination.

Pharaoh, who no doubt had been watching the Israelites as they passed out of the land from his residence in Zoan, draws the conclusion that they are now miserably entangled in the land and have lost their way. And the sight of their folly, together with his burning wrath because of the hard blow he received in the bygone night, causes him to make up his mind to pursue the children of Israel. The king is quick to perceive the folly of the people of God. And remembering the experiences of the last few weeks, especially of the last night when all the firstborn of the land had been killed by the angel of destruction, he laughs with scorn and bitterness and decides upon their certain destruction. To him it became very evident that they are lost and forsaken. Moses does not even know the way. And the Lord on whom they had trusted evidently does not show them the right way. He has forsaken them.

The king gathers courage to take bitter revenge. He quickly gathers his entire army, his chariots, and his horsemen. And with hardened heart, bitter with the purpose to take revenge upon these people, he sets out to pursue them, either to lead them back to the land of Egypt or to destroy them in the wilderness. Indeed, the condition of the children of Israel would seem desperate enough. As they turn their eyes, they see the army of the Egyptians in the distance. And they immediately realize their precarious condition. On their left is the sea. Before them and on their right is the mountainous wilderness. Behind them is the army of Pharaoh. And little we are surprised that they feared and raised their cries to Moses, who had led them out.

At this moment something occurs that seems to be either a desperate move or a proof of their utter folly. This is not so if we have the idea that without any intervening natural cause the waters were divided and stood in two perpendicular walls on each side of the Israelites. Then, we repeat it, it could not look foolish to the natural eye to pass through and cross the sea in between the walls of water. For in that case it would have been visible enough not merely to the eye of faith, but to anyone, that the Lord was holding these walls of water by his mighty arm.

But that was evidently not the case. Suddenly a strong east wind began to blow and struck a path through the sea, which at this point was both narrow and shallow. This fact is emphasized in Scripture and mentioned even three times, first in Exodus 14:21, where we read: "And Moses stretched out his hand over the sea; and the LORD caused the sea to go back by a strong east wind all that night, and made the sea dry land, and the waters were divided." And this is repeated in the song of Moses that the children of Israel sang after they had passed through the sea (Ex. 15:8, 10).

The miracle was therefore not so much that the sea was divided (for that was caused by the east wind) but that the wind and the path struck through the sea occurred at the same time that Moses lifted up his hand over the water, so that evidently the Lord sent the wind at his command. Nevertheless, the children of Israel must have considered it all as being rather natural. All they saw was that the wind blew upon the surface of the waters and that it struck a path right through the midst of the sea and that part of it was dry land and that the waters were divided.

But again, this made it rather appear foolish, or a desperate move. Was it not foolish to enter into that path through the sea in order to cross it? How long would the east wind last? Might it not stop as suddenly as it arose? And what would become of them if the wind would cease to blow? It is true, the sea was undoubtedly narrow at this point; but it must have been at least some five or six miles across, and there were some two million people to pass over, with their baggage and their cattle and sheep. Besides, even if the wind continued, what help could they expect from this path through the sea, with the Egyptians so close on their heels? Was it not more than probable that. the enemy would cross with them? And how could they expect deliverance from passing on the dry ground through this path struck by the east wind?

And therefore, we repeat: from a natural point of view the entire course of the children of Israel was foolish. Folly it was that they had not chosen the way of the Philistines and that they had become entangled in the land. Folly it was also now to entrust themselves to the treacherous wings of this strong blast that might stop at any time, and to cross the Red Sea through the path on dry land.

But is this not often true with regard to the people of God in the world? Is it not so that also the road that the people of God must travel today is often a way of suffering and tribulation and death? Does it not seem often as if we are traveling on the wrong side of the sea and are entangled in the land, so that it seems as if we can never reach the promised land? Is it not true with respect to the history of the world? Why does not God show plainly that the wisdom of the world is foolishness? Why must it seem so often as if the world possessed the true wisdom and as if the wisdom of God only brings misery and corruption among those who trust in it? Indeed, often it seems as if the foolishness of the world is wisdom indeed, and as if the way of the children of God is the height of folly.

However, do not forget that the words of our text emphasize that it was by faith that the children of Israel crossed the Red Sea. And faith is the evidence of things not seen and the substance of things hoped for. Faith clings to God in Christ Jesus our Lord. And that, no matter how things may appear to the natural eye, is truest wisdom indeed!

*Chapter 32*

# THE WISDOM
# OF FAITH

By faith they passed through the Red sea as by dry land: which
the Egyptians assaying to do were drowned.

—*Hebrews 11:29*

This time I wish to emphasize that, as the text tells us, the power
and motive that lay behind the apparently so desperate and foolish way that the children of Israel pursued was nothing else than faith
as the evidence of things unseen. It was not fear or folly, but faith in
the Almighty God, that caused them to pursue the way in which the
Lord led them. And it was nothing less than faith that was the motive
for them to cross the Red Sea.

In the preceding verse the author spoke in the singular, of Moses
alone. There he told us that by faith he ordained the Passover (Heb.
11:28). Here, however, he speaks about the people of God in general
and tells us that by faith they crossed the Red Sea. Now we know, as
I also remarked in the previous chapter, that this does not refer to all
the children of Israel individually. By no means all in that tremendous crowd were believers. Nay, we may speak still more strongly and
say, as the succeeding history shows very plainly, that most of them
were unbelievers. This is also evident from the text I quoted in the
previous chapter, 1 Corinthians 10:1–5. Oh indeed, they all passed
through the Red Sea. They were all under the cloud. They were all
baptized into Moses in the cloud and in the sea. They even all drank
of the spiritual rock that followed them and ate of the spiritual food.
Yet in spite of it all God was not well pleased with them but struck
them down in the wilderness. They could not enter the land of promise because of their unbelief.

Most of them, therefore, did not have the faith. They simply went along with the people of God. Outwardly they belonged to the people, for they were Abraham's seed, and therefore in the outward sense of the word children of the covenant. But in their hearts they really belonged to Egypt, and they might better have stayed there. They went along, no doubt, for different reasons, from selfish motives, for the beautiful land and the freedom from oppression, for the milk and the honey they might expect in that land. But they had no faith. And thus we find that when they see Pharaoh behind them and the sea on one side, with the wilderness before them and on their right, they begin to cry in their unbelief. Already they rebelled against the Lord. Why did not Moses leave them in Egypt, so they cry. Was it not far better to submit to the oppression in the house of bondage than to die the miserable death here in the wilderness? Oh, to be sure, they went along for carnal reasons. And when they do not see the milk flow and the honey in the comb as soon as they expected, they begin to murmur and rebel.

And thus it is with many today who go along with the people of God in the world for a time. They go along for the milk and honey of the kingdom of God. Oh, that does not always mean that they accompany the people of God for earthly gain. No, but they like to go to heaven instead of going to hell, and that is all their religion. They are afraid of death, and they are afraid of hell. They think that salvation consists exactly in that, that they will go to heaven no matter in what relation they stand to God and his kingdom. When they are called to sacrifice for the cause of the kingdom of God, these people cannot be found. No, in their heart of hearts they really care not for the kingdom of God as such, and still less do they care for the glory of God. What they care for is their own selfish ends, both in this time and for eternity. Thus there are many, no doubt, among the people of God today. And so there were also many among the people of God who crossed the Red Sea.

And yet the author makes no mistake when he tells us that they crossed the sea in faith. For it is not from the point of view of the hypocrites or of the carnal and unbelieving element that the people of God are viewed in Scripture, but only from the aspect of the real believers. Thus it is here. If the unbelievers had gone through the sea alone, they surely would have perished. But now the people of God pass through, although among them are also the unbelievers, the carnal children. And it is of these people of God in general that the author informs us that they passed through the Red Sea by faith.

The unbelieving element soon becomes evident. When they encounter the enemy in the land of Canaan, they refuse to enter. When they notice that danger and sacrifice is connected with the taking possession of the land, they fear and draw back. They reveal themselves as without faith, and they perish miserably in the desert. But now the unbelieving and carnal element are among the people of God as we read of them that they crossed the Red Sea by faith.

Faith is the evidence of things unseen and the substance of things hoped for. This was also true for the children of Israel as they passed through the sea. To be sure, their faith was also far more. It was by faith that they clung to their entire salvation. Faith was the power of their entire life. But it is not of faith in general that the author speaks. And therefore, it is not of faith in general that we are called to think in connection with the words of our text. Faith is looked at as an evidence of things unseen. These people of God, when they set their foot on the path struck by the east wind through the sea, believed that this was the way of their deliverance. They believed that this was the way, and the only way, to the promised land. They believed certainly that they would safely reach the other side and that the waters would remain standing divided till the last one of them had reached the other shore. They believed also that their salvation would be the destruction of the enemy. They believed that if they took this path, they surely would escape the wrath of Pharaoh.

This was a matter of faith. There was no natural ground for this belief. How could they possibly know that the waters would stand till they had passed? How did they know that this path actually led way across the sea, so that they would not be going into a real trap, from which they could not escape? They could not see it. And granted all this even, how could they feel sure that if they crossed safely with all their women and children, with all their luggage and cattle, that the swift army of Egypt could not accomplish the same feat, and much more easily than they? To be sure, it was all invisible. But they had the word of Jehovah their God. That word had delivered them from Egypt. That word had led them on this path, and on no other. That word now told Moses to lift up his staff over the sea. That word had brought the east wind. And that same word of the Lord now told them to take the path struck through the sea.

And on the basis of that word they knew by faith that back of the east wind and back of the divided waters was the power of the Almighty God, their God. It was he who sent the wind. The wind was the blast of his nostrils. It was he who braced the waters. These waters stood at his command. And therefore, it was not to the wind and to the waves that the army of the Israelites entrusted itself. But it was to the power and the grace of God that they committed themselves entirely. By faith they clung to the invisible God. By faith they knew that they were surrounded by their God, that God protected them as they passed through the midst of the waters. And knowing that it was God's power that sent the wind and that upheld the waters, they felt confident that these waters would stand as long as he wanted, that is, as long as the people passed through the sea and until they safely, to the last man, reached the other shore.

And this meant for the people of God two things. First, it meant to them the truth that the love and the grace of God over his people accompanied the strong power of Jehovah, so that the waters would surely stand till they were saved. And second, it meant also for them that the wrath of God would accompany that same power of Jehovah so that his enemies would perish if they ever should attempt to pass through that same path in the sea. This was clearly the faith of Moses and of all the believing children of Israel. For Moses assures them in the well-known words with respect to the Egyptians: "Never shall ye see them again."[1]

And their faith actually proves to be the highest wisdom. What seemed foolishness to the world and to the natural mind, to Egypt, to Pharaoh and all his host, now proves to be the highest wisdom. Folly it seemed to follow this path along the western shore of the Red Sea. For

---

1   A paraphrase of Exodus 14:13.

anyone can see that they would never be able to reach the mountain or the land of Canaan along this road. The sea was an insurmountable obstacle. Yet in actual fact that sea became their salvation. Had they chosen the road of the Philistines, the Egyptians might have pursued them and easily have destroyed this miserable army of Israel. But now they cross the sea, safely reach the other side, and every insurmountable obstacle becomes their salvation and deliverance.

Thus indeed it is often, nay, thus indeed it is always with the children of God. The path they must travel may look foolish to the natural eye, as leading to destruction. But when once we shall have reached the promised land, we shall eternally thank God that he has led us exactly along these ways. For then we shall acknowledge that they were the ways of eternal salvation and of highest wisdom.

The text concludes by saying that the Egyptians assayed to do the same thing as Israel and were drowned (Heb. 11:29). The wisdom of God prevails over the wisdom of the world also in this case. Even as the faith of Israel saved them through this path, so it is also easy to see how it was the unbelief of Pharaoh and Egypt that led them to destruction. They reach the spot where Israel has entered into the seabed. They see the path. And they are very quick to notice the cause. Undoubtedly they see nothing strange in the entire phenomenon. It is easy to explain, for they feel the wind, the strong east wind; and they know that it is the wind that has separated these waters and struck the path through the sea. Are they less brave than the miserable army of the Israelites, so that they would not go through? Can they not pass through the sea far more easily and far more swiftly than this crowd of men and women and children, with their cattle and sheep? Are they not much stronger, and do they not have the advantage in every way?

Surely, from a natural point of view they do. And from a natural point of view it is nothing but wisdom to follow in the path that the Israelites have just taken. For now they will still reach their point and gain their objective. They will overtake the people and destroy them or bring them back into bondage. So it looks to reason. And by reason and worldly wisdom they entered and tried to pass through the sea on dry ground.

But the trouble with the Egyptians was that they did not have the faith and the power to see things invisible, and that therefore they crossed in unbelief. Their unbelief was their destruction. Had they had the same faith as Israel, as an evidence of things unseen, they would never have entered the path. For then they also would have acknowledged that it was not the wind that struck the path, but that behind this wind was the power of the God of Israel, and that in these divided waters they had a sign that he who had sent these terrible plagues upon the country was still protecting his people. Then they would have been able to draw the conclusion that by entering the Red Sea they entrusted themselves to the sea as enemies of the people of God, and that this could but lead to their destruction. Thus they would have reasoned if they had had the power of faith as an evidence of things unseen.

But in their unbelief they entered. In their unbelief they went to encounter deliberately the power of the wrath of God, as enemies of his people. And that same God destroyed them. Behold, the people have reached the opposite shore. And the enemy, discomfited already in the midst of the sea by the God of his people, so that they cannot go on, are still struggling in the midst of the sea. The word of the Lord proceeds out of his mouth. The hand of his servant is raised over the waters. The wind ceases, or changes. And the waters roar wrathfully together to swallow up the wisdom of the world. By faith the people of God were saved through the Red Sea. By unbelief the world perished in that same angry sea.

Once more the foolishness of God is wiser than men, and the weakness of God is stronger than men. This is evident from all history. It is evident from the portion we have just discussed. It is the express word of Scripture. Believe this, and be it your strength and comfort in the midst of the world. The highest revelation of God's wisdom is also the greatest folly to the world. The cross of Christ is the way of salvation for sinners. Believe this, and be saved. Even though the world thinks that we are lost and entangled, even though unbelief mocks at that cross, even though to the natural eye it may seem foolishness to follow the way of blood as a way of salvation, even though on that path you are called to self-denial and self-sacrifice, even though you must on that path forever say farewell to the treasures of Egypt and the pleasures of the world, even though suffering and persecution and scorn and mockery are your lot, never you fear! Believe and follow the path of wisdom, of the wisdom of God!

And that wisdom of God shall prevail. The blood of the cross is your certain salvation and deliverance. And the same sign of the cross, mocked at by unbelief, will be the destruction and the condemnation of the world. Once we shall sing as the children of Israel the song of Moses and of eternal victory, delivered from fear and danger, delivered from Egypt and sin, before the throne of God and of the Lamb, and to the glory of his grace that struck a path through the sea to deliver us from Egypt, the house of bondage of sin, and caused us to enter into everlasting glory in his tabernacle.

*Chapter 33*

# RAHAB THE HARLOT SAVED FROM DESTRUCTION

By faith the harlot Rahab perished not with them that believed
not, when she had received the spies with peace.

—*Hebrews 11:31*

In 1 Corinthians 1:26–31 the apostle Paul describes the work of salvation and the plan of God in regard to the work of salvation as follows:

26. For ye see your calling, brethren, how that not many wise men after the flesh, not many mighty, not many noble, are called:
27. But God hath chosen the foolish things of the world to confound the wise; and God hath chosen the weak things of the world to confound the things which are mighty;
28. And base things of the world, and things which are despised, hath God chosen, yea, and things which are not, to bring to nought things that are:
29. That no flesh should glory in his presence.
30. But of him are ye in Christ Jesus, who of God is made unto us wisdom, and righteousness, and sanctification, and redemption:
31. That, according as it is written, He that glorieth, let him glory in the Lord.

We must remember that the way of salvation is the way not of the wisdom of the world, but of the wisdom of God. And that wisdom of God is foolishness with the world. The way of salvation is the way of the weakness and the foolishness of the cross; and that certainly is not the way of the flesh. The strong according to the flesh certainly have no need of a savior who died on the accursed tree, for that would be a confession of their weakness and their misery. The way of salvation is the confession of guilt and sin before a bloody cross, but the wise and noble according to the flesh would be ashamed to confess their sins and transgressions and to admit that they were worthy of condemnation before a holy God. And thus it is not the strong and the noble and the wise according to the world and according to the flesh who have need of this salvation, who seek for it and cry for it to God. But on the contrary, the foolish, the weak, the base, and the despised after the flesh, they seek the salvation of God, and that, too, because they have become despised and weak in themselves through the grace of the God of our salvation.

But as the apostle points out, there is also a theological reason for this plan of the almighty God. For the purpose of this wonderful plan is that God might be glorified. The saved in Christ are the product of God Almighty, of his power, of his wisdom, of his grace. This power, this wisdom, and this grace must shine forth most gloriously in the people whom he has chosen and whom he has prepared by his grace for the salvation he has wrought, so that there may be no reason whatsoever to glory in self. The Most High must receive all the glory absolutely, that according as it is written, says the apostle Paul in this same section, "he that glorieth, let him glory in the Lord" (1 Cor. 1:31)

This is also evident from the words of our text. Had Israel understood this, they would not have gloried in being the descendants of Abraham, and they would have understood the words of Jesus when he told them that God was powerful to make children of Abraham out of those stones (Matt. 3:9). For at the very threshold of their own history as a nation they found a warning example of how God actually was not dependent on Abraham's seed, but how in his almighty and sovereign grace he had chosen the weak and the foolish and the base things of this world to confound the wise and the strong and the noble. For, according to the words of our text, "by faith the harlot Rahab perished not with them that believed not, when she had received the spies with peace" (Heb. 11:31).

Rahab is one of the few who are mentioned in Scripture as being ingrafted from heathendom into Israel, the people of God. As we all know, God in the old dispensation had his chosen people among the nation of Israel. In that sense we may say that religion was a national affair. Israel was the chosen race, and Jehovah was the God of Israel in distinction from the nations. This does not mean, however, that all the seed of Abraham were also children of God just because they belonged to the descendants of the father of all believers. For the Lord explains this quite differently in the epistle of Paul to the Romans, chapter 9. For there we read:

6. Not as though the word of God hath taken none effect. For they are not all Israel, which are of Israel:
7. Neither, because they are the seed of Abraham, are they all children: but, In Isaac shall thy seed be called.
8. That is, They which are the children of the flesh, these are not the children of God: but the children of the promise are counted for the seed. (vv. 6–8)

Not by any means, therefore, were all saved who bore the name of Israel. But it certainly does mean that God had all his people among Israel, and that he left the nations to walk after the wicked imagination of their own heart and in their sinful ways to certain destruction. Not all Israel were the children of God, but all the children of God were, as a rule, Israelites. Salvation belonged to the Jews. However, also in that old dispensation we have a few examples that clearly point to the universality of the future kingdom, that are a prophecy of the time when the people of God shall no more be identical to members of a certain race or nation, but when God shall have his people out of all nations and tongues and tribes. There are a few examples that must have informed Israel that after all the grace of God was not limited and was not destined to be limited by the boundaries of just one country and just one nation but was ordained to be and to become universal.

A few examples there were that God would save the heathen as well as the seed of Abraham, and that if he chose the seed of Abraham, it was not because of any merit or worth in them but because of his sovereign and free grace. We do not now refer to the enormous number of proselytes who were made by the people of Israel, and especially by the Pharisees in later times, any of whom were made children of hell worse than they themselves, according to the words of Jesus (Matt. 23:15). No, but we have reference to those proselytes who were made by God the Lord, the Lord of the covenant himself, in such a wonderful way.

And then we think especially of Rahab and Ruth, and perhaps also of Tamar, the heathen harlot of Judah. All three were heathen women, and all three were grafted into the divinely chosen race of the old dispensation. And what is still more striking, all three are in the line of the generations that end in the birth of the Savior. For in the genealogical list of Matthew 1 we read: "And Judas begat Phares and Zara of Thamar...And Salmon begat Booz of Rachab; and Booz begat Obed of Ruth; and Obed begat Jesse; and Jesse begat David the king" (vv. 3, 5–6). Only three women are mentioned in the entire list, and these three all are of Gentile origin, ingrafted into the chosen race and family from without.

And so we find that undoubtedly also in the line of the generations of our Lord Jesus Christ Gentiles have been ingrafted, so that, in fact, he remains indeed the son of Joseph and Mary, an Israelite, but also the Son of Man in the more general sense of the word. Of the Jews and for the Jews, first, but not without the other nations, Christ came. God had not forgotten them. Rahab, the Gentile woman, who had been brought up in the land of Canaan, who had served the heathen gods, who had never been accustomed to anything but the heathen religion of the Canaanites, Rahab is saved when her people are destroyed because of their disobedience. A wonderful dispensation this is of the free grace of God. Rahab becomes one of the mothers of our Lord.

Rahab was a heathen woman. And what is more, Rahab, according to the words of our text, was also a harlot. This has been translated, especially by the Hebrews, as *innkeeper*. The rabbinical interpreters translate it thus. It has been alleged that the word that is used the Hebrew original may just as well be rendered *innkeeper*. And the rabbis, in order to save the reputation of the spies, have preferred that translation. The spies, so they claim, would not enter the house of a harlot. And since it is true that the Hebrew word may be rendered in a different way, they prefer this. But this is not the case, however. At

RAHAB THE HARLOT SAVED FROM DESTRUCTION

any rate, the word as we find it in the words of our text, that is, in the Greek, is always translated *harlot* and means nothing else.

And therefore, this meaning we will have to retain. Rahab was a harlot. She was one of the lowest and most despised class of sinners. She was one of those women who would sell their womanly honor for money and who lead men in their cunning snare. For years she had perhaps practiced this devilish occupation, and even in the city of Jericho—not famous for its high state of morality, as we shall see presently—she was known as the harlot in the city, to whom men could turn to find satisfaction for their devilish desires and lusts and to be led to destruction, body and soul.

Rahab was a harlot. She belonged to the rabble, to the most despised of women. She certainly did not belong to the mighty and the noble and the wise and the respectable of the inhabitants. If the Lord would save any of the people of Jericho, no doubt he could find those who were morally not quite as debased as this woman. He undoubtedly would be able to find those who, though they might have belonged to the exceptions, were classed with the respectable and who did not take part in all the immorality of the inhabitants. But he took the despised after the flesh, the ignoble and the base.

We would say that we must bring Rahab first a little nearer to the kingdom, that the way she is now there is no chance for her. First we must elevate her to a somewhat higher level of society before there can be a question of her salvation. First she must learn to see that she can lead a respectable life in her own strength, and then probably there is a chance for her to enter into the kingdom. We would have turned to others in the city, had we looked for one who might be saved, and not to this miserable harlot who lived on the city wall.

But God turns to Rahab, to the harlot, to her who lives on the city wall and who is well-known as the most base of sinners. And Rahab the harlot he saves. Not the noble and the strong after the flesh, but the base things and the weak, that he may put to shame the things that are! Certainly, the way of God's grace is wonderful. It is also full of comfort. The nice and the sweet and the respectable in this world, the lady of high repute, well-known for her loveliness and sweet appearance, well-known for the good works and kindness, well-known for her high standard of morality, that lady may be passed by the grace of the Almighty and may be lost forever because she has no need of the grace of the cross. But the base and the despised and the low and the woman of bad repute, the harlot, whom everybody regards as lost and who is sunk deep in the mire of sin—that woman is the object of God's grace and is saved forever.

Rahab was saved indeed. For our text tells us that she did not perish with those who were disobedient. Of course, in these words we are referred to the inhabitants of Jericho. And that they perished means, first, that their city was taken by Israel and that they were all killed. But this implies that they actually were lost forever. The destruction in the temporal and historical sense of the word of the inhabitants of Jericho was but a type of their destruction in eternal damnation. Little question can there be about this truth if we consider the reason that is given in the words of our text for their destruction, namely, that they were disobedient. Our text mentions the inhabitants of the city as those who were disobedient, in other words as ungodly and wicked people, the measure of whose iniquity was full.

And this was necessary before the children of Israel could enter the land to possess it. The measure of the iniquity of the inhabitants of Canaan, that is, of the original inhabitants, must be made full before the children of Israel could enter the land. God must be justified in the destruction of the wicked because of their wicked deeds. This is also the reason why the Lord cannot come until the wickedness of the world in general is fulfilled to the very end. The establishment of God's kingdom in the land of Canaan was accompanied by the downfall and the destruction of the kingdom of the world in that country. But as such it was merely a type of the establishment of the eternal kingdom in the end of time. God shall establish his eternal kingdom in Christ when the latter shall come back on the clouds of heaven. And also this establishment shall be accompanied by the destruction of the kingdom of Satan and of all who belong to him. And for that reason the measure of the iniquity must first be full, and only then can the Christ come.

So it was with the people of Jericho. They were destroyed not merely because the Lord had a notion to give the land to his own people; but they were destroyed also because of their wickedness, which had become terrible, so terrible that the work of the law of God written in their hearts must have openly condemned them, so that they were without excuse. Repeatedly the children of Israel are told that this is the case. They are warned not to follow in the steps of the nations.

In the eighteenth chapter of Leviticus some of the abominations too horrid to enumerate here are mentioned. And then the Lord concludes: "Defile not ye yourselves in any of these things: for in all these the nations are defiled which I cast out before you: and the land is defiled: therefore I do visit the iniquity thereof upon it, and the land itself vomiteth out her inhabitants" (vv. 24–25). And in Deuteronomy 9:4 that same truth is emphasized, and the Lord says: "For the wickedness of these nations the LORD doth drive them out from before thee." And in the eighteenth chapter of this same book of Moses we find again the warning that the children of Israel shall not walk after the abominations of the nations that are driven out. Some of these abominations are mentioned by name, such as, for instance, that they cause their children "to pass through the fire", the practice of divination, and augury, enchantments, and sorcery (vv. 10–11). And then we read: "Because of these abominations the LORD thy God doth drive them out from before thee" (v. 12).

Sufficient proof this is indeed that they were driven out because of their disobedience and iniquity, which had come to terrible manifestation in the sight of God. It was the wrath of God that destroyed the inhabitants of Jericho. And it was from this destruction that the Lord in his grace saved Rahab the harlot. And even as the destruction of the people was destruction forever, so we may say indeed that the salvation of Rahab was a salvation eternal. Rahab is saved from the destruction of Jericho but is also saved from sin and death by the wonderful grace of God.

*Chapter 34*

# RAHAB THE HARLOT
# SAVED BY FAITH

By faith the harlot Rahab perished not with them that believed
not, when she had received the spies with peace.

*—Hebrews 11:31*

In James 2:25 we find that Rahab was justified, and therefore saved,
by works: "Likewise also was not Rahab the harlot justified by works,
when she had received the messengers, and had sent them out another
way?" Thus, the apostle argues.

Of course, it is not true that there is a contradiction between
James and Paul, so that the one would say that we are justified by
works, and the other that we are saved by faith without the works
of the law (Rom. 3:28). On the contrary, the two supplement each
other. What Paul is always combatting is dead works. And hence,
the central theme of his epistle is really: "Whatsoever is not of faith
is sin" (Rom. 14:23). What James is combatting is a dead faith. And
hence, his main topic is: "Faith, if it have not works, is dead in itself"
(James 2:26). Paul fights the superficial Christianity without faith in
the atoning blood of Christ; James is fighting a dead orthodoxy. And
also the latter is important for many of us, if only rightly understood.
"You have faith?" says James, "Well, that is very nice; and never will
I deny that that is absolutely necessary. You must indeed have faith.
For otherwise I agree with Paul that you can do nothing. But what
I maintain is that this nice talk about your faith does not help you
one bit.

Faith, I say, is a power, a strong power, a power that must reveal
itself. It is not merely a nice belief that there is a God and that God
will take you to heaven. No, it is the power whereby you are connected

with that living God in Christ, and through which you therefore must reveal yourselves in works of faith! I maintain, therefore, that faith which does not reveal itself in works is not faith at all, and that there is no faith where there are no works. You may talk ever so nicely about your faith, my brother," so James means to say to you, "but as long as you do not show this faith in your works, I must have nothing of it. You have no works, and yet you maintain that you have faith? Perhaps so, but with that faith you may very well go to hell. The devils also believe as you do," says the apostle, "And they are in hell: why should you not go there? And therefore, I say that faith must reveal itself in works, and that it is through these works of faith that man finally is justified." And then the apostle goes on and mentions a few examples. He mentions the example of Abraham, who by his faith offered up Isaac. And he mentions also the example of Rahab, who was justified by works when she received the messengers and sent them out another way.

Nor is it difficult to see James' point of view. The fact is simply this, that if Rahab had not done as she did, she would never have been saved.

We know the history. Joshua had sent spies to view the country and to report conditions as they found them in the land. They crossed the Jordan and passed through fertile plains that separate the river from the first city in the land, and approached Jericho. However they may have been led to the place, we know not. But they entered the house of Rahab the harlot on the city wall, with no door, but a window on the side that looked over the plain outside the city. Perhaps Rahab, who had heard of the people of Israel approaching the land, and expecting them every day, had her plans all ready and was on the lookout continually. And seeing these Israelite men stealing around the city, she invited them to stay with her. And especially do we know that God meant to save Rahab, and that therefore it was by his providence that the spies were led into her house. She received these spies in her house, and they slept there. Not long it is, however, that the king remained ignorant of these men staying with Rahab. And he demanded that they be surrendered. She hid the spies on the roof of her house and deceives the messengers of the king, telling them that the messengers, whom she did not know, have already departed from her house and left for their camp. And she saved the spies by caus-ing them to escape through the window outside of the wall and by informing them as to the direction they are to take. The spies follow her advice. They go in a northerly direction, stay in the mountains three days, and then return to their people safe and sound.

These are the works of Rahab. And by these works she was saved, no doubt. Had she not received the spies, had she not hid them, had she not let them down by the cord on condition that she and her father's house might be spared when the city was destroyed, had she not hung the cord out of the window while the city was being encom-passed for seven days, she would have been destroyed with the people of the city, and nothing would have distinguished her from the rest. Now, however, Rahab did hide the spies, did save them, and did hang the cord outside the wall; and she was saved from the destruction that came upon the disobedient. In that sense, therefore, she was saved by works.

However, there is no contradiction between the epistle of James and the words of our text (Heb. 11:31). The text maintains that Rahab the harlot was saved from destruction by faith. Also our text, however, mentions the works that Rahab did when it adds: "Having received the spies with peace." In other words, James simply tells us through what means she was saved and how the works led to her salvation, while, on the other hand, our text calls our attention to the fact that after all this was a salvation through faith, seeing that she could never have performed those works in hiding the spies except by the power of faith. In this entire chapter, the author means to show of what great things faith as an evidence of things unseen and as the substance of things hoped for is able. And so also in the words of our text, he tells us that these works that led to the salvation of Rahab were the works she performed in the faith as an evidence of things unseen and the substance of things hoped for. And that behind all that Rahab does is actually this power of faith is clear from the entire history.

In the first place, let me call your attention to the fact that we may characterize the works of Rahab in a general sense as a separation, a breaking with her own people, and a choice for the people of God. The most beautiful parallel we have of this is the choice of Ruth. As she accompanies Naomi, she goes not merely because of her mother-in-law, but also because she has broken with her own people and has been led to choose the people of God.

And thus it is also here. It was indeed a dangerous, but, from a natural point of view at the same time, a very low act of Rahab to receive the enemies of her country and to betray the city to the spies. In time of war, we would compare Rahab with a traitor. And such acts of treason are never to be approved except under one condition: if our patriotism would demand of us to act contrary to the God of heaven and earth. Treason from a worldly point of view becomes then an act of faith. Thus it was with Rahab. To her, the situation appeared as a choice between her sinful and condemned people against Jehovah, the God of heaven and earth, or for the God of Israel but then against her people. And the latter choice, she plainly makes.

She breaks with her people in faith as an evidence of things unseen. For, mark you well, this break is not made after the city is taken, but before. She cannot see that the children of Israel are actually going to take possession of the city. She cannot see that the children of Israel will be victorious. No, on the contrary, for all she knows, her own people may very well be victorious and the children of Israel be defeated. For the city is strong, and the walls are high, and the people are giants in comparison with the nomadic people that come against them. And the gates will be kept closed, so that not a living soul can either enter or leave the place.

And therefore, at the time when she makes the choice for the people of God and against the people among whom she had lived, she cannot see the advantage of this with the natural eye. The only way she can reason this out is by faith. Only if she believes in the power of Jehovah, only if she believes that this powerful God is on the side of Israel, only if she believes that Jehovah means to give the land to this people and that he is faithful to fulfill the promise—only then can she conclude that the cause of her people is lost and that the people that come against them will surely have the victory when they come against the city of her people. But this faith as an evidence of things unseen also gives her the courage to perform what she does, to brave the danger from the side of the king and his servants, to hide the messengers, to deceive the king's servants, and to save the spies that are sent to spy out the country. By faith, as an evidence of things unseen, Rahab received the spies with peace. By faith, therefore, she was not destroyed with the city.

That this faith is actually her possession, and that she is conscious of it to a large extent, is evident also from her own confession before the spies whom she has received in her house. Said she:

9.  I know that the LORD hath given you the land, and that your terror is fallen upon us, and that all the inhabitants of the land faint because of you.

10. For we have heard how the LORD dried up the water of the Red sea for you, when ye came out of Egypt; and what ye did unto the two kings of the Amorites, that were on the other side Jordan, Sihon and Og, whom ye utterly destroyed.

11. And as soon as we had heard these things, our hearts did melt, neither did there remain any more courage in any man, because of you: for the LORD your God, he is God in heaven above, and in earth beneath. (Josh. 2:9–11)

Such was her confession. Wonderful indeed is this confession of this Gentile woman before these spies. How mysterious are the ways of the Almighty! How free is his grace! There were among the people of Israel, no doubt, any number that had been witnesses of the mighty deeds of Jehovah of which this woman was speaking, and of a good many more just as mighty and wonderful, who nevertheless did not believe, did not have the true faith in the God of their fathers, were in reality not the spiritual Israel, just as it is among the people of God today. Any number there are, from youth up, instructed in the knowledge of the Most High and of Christ Jesus our Lord, whom he has sent, and who in spite of it all turn away from the ways of the covenant. And here is a Gentile woman, who has been brought up in the religion of the Canaanites and who had led a life of sin and dissipation as the harlot on the city wall, and who is educated in the truth by a few stray rumors that had come to her from afar; and nevertheless she makes her firm and beautiful confession. She believes in Jehovah as the God of heaven and earth, and therefore no more in her own gods. She believes that this God of heaven and earth, this Jehovah, has given the promise, the covenant promise of the land of Canaan, to his people, and that he is faithful and powerful to fulfill that promise. And she fosters the hope that she may perhaps escape the destruction of her people and share in the mercy and grace of the God of Israel. Wonderful dispensation of the grace of the almighty God, who had in a mysterious way sanctified these rumors to her heart and saved her by faith!

Truly, by faith, by faith as an evidence of things unseen and the substance of things hoped for, by faith wrought in her heart by the power of the Holy Spirit, by the power of the God of Israel, Rahab perished not with the disobedient. By faith, she received and saved the spies of Israel.

Rahab is an example, full of comfort and consolation, but also full of instruction to the church of God. The foolish and the base and the weak things of the world God has chosen, that he might glorify his own name and confound the mighty and the wise and the noble after the flesh.

Do we have the faith of Rahab? Do we have the faith that God will give his people the fulfillment of the promise of the covenant? And if we do have that faith, shall we also make the choice of Rahab against the enemies of God's people and for the people of God? Shall we reveal that faith in love, in love to God's people, in love to his cause? Shall we reveal that faith in our hope of eternal life, in our confidence in the promise of God? Shall we reveal it in the works of faith in general?

We are justified by faith, to be sure—saved from the destruction of the world, justified by free grace for absolutely nothing, and not by the works of the law. But that faith nevertheless, as James has it, must reveal itself, become manifest as a power in the midst of the world that dares to brave the world, to condemn it, and to choose definitely and openly and always and everywhere for the people of God and for the kingdom of heaven and its righteousness.

### Part Three

# THE RACE THAT IS SET BEFORE US

*Chapter 35*

# RUNNING THE RACE

Wherefore seeing we also are compassed about with so great a cloud of witnesses, let us lay aside every weight, and the sin which doth so easily beset us, and let us run with patience the race that is set before us.

*—Hebrews 12:1*

We now really have come to the end of our discussion of one of the most beautiful chapters of Scripture, the chapter on the so-called heroes of faith. In the chapter we have now finished it is faith as an evidence of things unseen and the substance of things hoped for that demanded our attention. It is true, we have not yet finished the chapter entirely; but a glance at the chapter will convince us that from now on it assumes a somewhat different nature than in the verses we have already discussed. Heretofore the author did not only mention the names of the examples of faith, but also pointed to specific instances in their lives, to particular acts of theirs, by which it became evident that they lived from this faith as an evidence of things unseen.

And thus he mentioned various examples. He referred to the time before the flood; and out of that prediluvian period he mentioned the names of Abel and Enoch and Noah as illustrations of the faith by which the righteous must live. He pointed us to the time of the postdiluvian period and called our attention to particular instances in the lives of Abraham and Sarah, Isaac and Jacob and Joseph, to show us that they also possessed that same faith as an evidence of things unseen and the substance of things hoped for. He called our attention to the time of Moses and the deliverance of Israel from the house of bondage, and referred to Amram and Jochebed, to Moses and Joshua and Rahab, to the crossing of the Red Sea and the capture of the city of Jericho. All these examples he has mentioned. And in all of them he has shown how faith, as an evidence of things unseen and as the substance of things hoped for, gained the victory.

But now he comes, as it were, to himself for a moment. He stops for a while; he realizes that he has mentioned one example after the other and that he has already written a long chapter on the so-called heroes of faith. And as he looks forward, he also is aware of the fact that he has by no means reached the end of the illustrations and that he could perhaps write a large volume if he would continue the way he commenced. The cloud of witnesses rather thickens after he has spoken of Rahab. For the period of the national history of Israel that now follows is crowded with examples of this living faith. There is the period of the judges, the period of the kings, the period of the prophets. What a rich abundance of material to select from! One after the other comes to his mind; they arise before his imagination in rapid succession. And as they come before his consciousness, he also realizes that there is no end to telling what they have done in the power of faith.

And therefore, he changes his method: "And what shall I more say?" so we hear him ask. "For the time would fail me to tell of Gedeon, and of Barak, and of Samson, and of Jephthae; of David also, and Samuel, and of the prophets" (Heb. 11:32). And so he mentions only their names. And in the verses that follow he simply enumerates what they have done and what they have endured and suffered by the power of faith. And then he comes to the final conclusion, which also we wish to take today as the basis of our text: "Wherefore seeing we also are compassed about with so great a cloud of witnesses, let us lay aside every weight, and the sin which doth so easily beset us, and let us run with patience the race that is set before us" (12:1).

The main thought of this exhortation is, as you can tell at a glance: "Let us run with patience the race." To these words the mentioning of the cloud of witnesses and of the laying aside of all that hinders is subordinate. And therefore, the question arises, first of all: What does the author mean by the running of the race? It is clear that he employs figurative language here, language derived from everyday life in the world, in order to impress a spiritual truth upon the minds of the believers. And in this case the phrase "running the race" is derived from the great feasts that were periodically celebrated in the country of Greece at the time when this epistle was written. At various places in the country these festivities would be held. At these feasts, which were celebrated with extraordinary joy and amusements, the games or exercises that were held occupied the chief place on the program. These exercises consisted chiefly of leaping, running, boxing, throwing the javelin, and wrestling.

And it is to one of these exercises at these festivities that the author of this epistle refers when he exhorts the Hebrew Christians to run the race patiently. The race was considered one of the chief exercises at the Grecian games, since swiftness, or fleetness, was deemed one of the greatest virtues that could possibly be developed with a view to bodily perfection. For this race the contestants would prepare themselves assiduously and painstakingly and with indefatigable perseverance. A long time in advance they would be trained willingly. They would confine themselves to a certain diet in order to keep their weight down, and reduce the weight of their body to the desired minimum, remove all hindrances that could be removed, and deny themselves many things that were considered to belong to the legitimate pleasures of life, merely for the honor of winning the race and of receiving the crown of victory.

On the day of the race, they would strip themselves of as many clothes as they could spare and lay aside all that possibly would hinder them in running the race. A great crowd had assembled from all parts of the land to be witnesses of the contest. It was the cheers and shouts of the crowd, but above all the knowledge that at the end of the racetrack there awaited them the crown of glory for him who reached it first, that spurred them on and inspired them to utmost exertion.

On the last day of the games the prize, whatever it might consist of, whether it were a crown of olives or of pine or of other material, was conferred upon the victor with great pomp and solemnity. Amid the cheers and congratulations of a great throng of relatives, friends, and countrymen in general, the crown would be pressed upon his brow. Those nearest to him would lift up the victor on their shoulders, carry him around under a thunderous applause from the crowd, till they would place him in the triumphal chariot and ride him to the city in a continual shower of flowers. In his honor the wall of the city was broken down to give him special entrance. And in many places a subsistence was given him for life, while always he was exempted from taxes. Such is the complete figure the author employs in these words. And he means to say: just as the contestants in such races ran patiently and for the sake of the victory denied themselves many things, so run ye also patiently the race that is set before you.

When now we come to investigate the simple meaning of this phrase, we wish to say, first, that these words have often been wrongly or partly wrongly interpreted in application to the life of the Christian in the most general sense of the word. According to this interpretation, our life is the path we must walk, the racetrack that must be finished to the end. And therefore, the author here refers to our going through this present life in its most general sense. In this life we meet with all kinds of adversity and disappointments, sufferings and evils. The sky does not always look clear and bright, but is often overcast, cloudy, dark, pitch black sometimes. And then we would be inclined perhaps to sit down by the wayside and lose our courage and our patience. And now the author tells us that we must not lose courage in the midst of this suffering and evil of life in a general sense of the word, but that we must patiently go through life and run the race that is set before us to the end, and that, too, with patience.

Now we do not wish to deny that there is meaning in this interpretation and that also this thought is implied in the words of our text, in so far, namely, as the Christian must also bear the general sufferings of this present time by faith, and for that reason patiently. He may not murmur when his God sends him suffering and affliction, for he knows that all things are coming to him from the hand of his heavenly Father and that all things must work together for good to those who love him. He must also in the midst of suffering run a race and glorify his God. In that sense the suffering of this present life is certainly also implied in the words of our text.

And yet we may not for a moment imagine that this would exhaust the meaning of these words, or that this is really the fundamental thought in the mind of the author. And this will be plain if for a moment we adhere to the figure and investigate what ideas are really implied therein. First, we find that the runners of the race in the Grecian games had a certain definite goal to reach, and that to attain to this goal first was the all-overpowering purpose of their actions. They were possessed of a predominating, of an all-overpowering purpose in all that they did. And that great and powerful, that overpowering purpose that dominated their action was the desire to reach the goal first and to be the winner of the crown of glory.

Second, let us notice that for this purpose they exerted themselves to the utmost. They did not trust their good luck and patiently wait till they would receive the crown; but to receive the crown they exerted themselves to the utmost. For a long time they prepared. And as the day for the race arrived, they still exerted themselves to the utmost of their physical power in order to win the prize.

And third, for this all-overpowering and dominating purpose they denied themselves, and all that could be of hindrance to them in the reaching of the goal they would set aside. Only that which was essential to the running of the race would they do and keep. And whatever had nothing to do with their attaining their goal they carefully avoided.

If we apply this for a moment to the spiritual running of the race, we find that also the Christian, first, is possessed of such an all-dominating purpose. That is not true of the man of the world. He may have a purpose in life, may have many purposes in life, in fact. He may have great ideals. He does not, he cannot have one great purpose, one great ideal, that dominates his entire life so strongly that for it he will set aside all things. And this cannot be for the simple reason that his ideal vanishes with the last breath.

But this is not the case with the believer. His ideal, his life's purpose, does not vanish with death, but is rather realized completely when he leaves the earthly house of this tabernacle. His purpose therefore is above, transcends this present life, and reaches far into eternity. His purpose is an eternal and immortal purpose, a purpose that far transcends all that stands related to this present life. And because this is a fact, he is willing, when he is truly inspired by the glory and the power of this purpose, of the goal that must be reached, to lay aside all that is nonessential to the reaching of this great and glorious purpose.

What then is the goal that must be reached? That goal is nothing less than eternal life and the glory of that eternal life in the tabernacle of God. Hence, we do not look at that glory in the morbid sense in which it is often taken, as if the believer merely strove for the place called "heaven" in order to escape the place called "hell." Never does Scripture, never does the Christian thus describe the goal when he is asked for what he really is striving.

If you ask him what is the crown that awaits him after he has successfully run the race, he will say that this crown consists of eternal perfection, perfection in body and soul, and perfection in all creation. He strives for that place where there shall be no more effects of sin, for that state wherein the consciousness of sin shall trouble him no more, for that condition where he shall be freed from sin and where he can forevermore satisfy his thirst to be as God wants him to be and to serve and glorify the Most High in perfection, where sin and guilt, where sorrow and pain, where grief and affliction, where want and persecution shall be no more, but where he shall be in everlasting and perfect communion with his God forever. In a word, the goal of the Christian's running is perfection in every sense. His sin, his imperfection, his rebellion, his defilement is his misery; his bliss will be his being completely delivered and ennobled to serve and glorify his God forever. To attain to this goal the Christian must run the race.

You understand, of course, that the author does not mean to say that by our running of the race we must merit the crown: for this is certainly not true. As far as that is concerned, all has been fulfilled by our Lord Jesus Christ. We receive the crown of life for nothing, of free grace, as all has been merited by our Lord and Savior. Never can we merit even an ounce of gold of this crown of glory. No, that crown and the race thither has been set before us. But it has pleased the Lord to treat us in the gaining of this crown as his own moral, rational children in the midst of the world. Indeed, he might have laid out an easy path that led to the crown of everlasting life, so that we could simply sit down and wait until the angels pressed the crown on our brow. But this is not the case. The Lord has set the race before us, has laid out the path of self-denial and exertion for all his children. That path and the traveling thereof, the running of the race, can never become the ground or the merit of which we receive the crown. But it is the way in which we receive it. He gives us the crown. He gives us the strength and the desire to fight and struggle. But he also lays out the path set before us.

And the race must be run, shall we ever attain to our goal and receive the crown of glory. And therefore, we must, just as the runners in the race at the Grecian games, exert ourselves, struggle, fight the battle of faith, in order to attain to that goal of perfection. "Work out your own salvation with fear and trembling. For it is God which worketh in you both to will and to do of his good pleasure" (Phil. 2:12–13). And finally, even as the runners in the race were so inspired by this all-dominating purpose to win the race that for it they denied all other things if necessary, so also the believer must deny himself whatever might be of hindrance to him in attaining the purpose of his life, the goal set before him. Run the race! Strive for perfection! Glorify God! And be not satisfied before you have realized in yourself the words of your God: "Be holy, for I, the Lord your God, am holy!"[1]

---

1   See Leviticus 19:2, quoted in 1 Peter 1:16.

# Chapter 36

# RUNNING
# WITH PATIENCE

Wherefore seeing we also are compassed about with so great
a cloud of witnesses, let us lay aside every weight, and the sin
which doth so easily beset us, and let us run with patience the
race that is set before us.

*—Hebrews 12:1*

Thus far I called your attention to the meaning of running the race.
I came to the conclusion that to run the race means to live lives
dominated by this tremendous purpose, namely, to reach perfection
and to glorify our God through Jesus Christ our Lord. It surely implies
to reveal ourselves as believers in every sphere of the world, that we
have made our definite choice for Christ and his kingdom and have
said farewell to Satan and his dominion, to reveal in life that we have
chosen for the wisdom of God and forsaken the foolishness of the
world, that we have chosen the reproach of Christ and abandoned
the pleasures of this present time. It means that we confess our Lord
always, everywhere, and that we show ourselves as those who belong
to him with body and soul, for time and eternity. It means that we give
ourselves wholly to him with all that we have and are, that we seek
first the kingdom of God and his righteousness and for that kingdom
sacrifice all, deny ourselves, and strive for its coming with all our powers, and fight against the kingdom of darkness in every walk of life. It
means that we live as believers publicly as well as privately, confessing
the name of our Lord Jesus Christ in word and deed.

Then we shall have a struggle in this present life. For this confession we can never make, and this life we can never lead, without
being persecuted and molested, molested by the enemies of God and

his Christ. There is the archenemy of the kingdom of Christ, Satan, who goes about as a roaring lion in his foaming wrath and raging fury against the kingdom of our Lord. And this archenemy is not at all such a far-off and abstract being as we may probably imagine. He has powerful allies—first, in our own heart, where sin still reigns to a large extent, but second, also in the world that hates Christ and his kingdom. So the Lord has told us.

So the Hebrew Christians experienced it. They had walked faithfully for a while, as we may learn from this epistle. They had bravely sacrificed their possessions, yea, their lives, for the kingdom of Christ. For they lived in a time that the world manifested itself in persecution of the church. Bravely they had borne the brunt of the battle and the violent onslaughts of the enemy. For they kept before them the glorious future. Especially the coming of Christ they expected speedily, when he would destroy his enemies and give the everlasting victory to his people. But behold, Christ tarried. The persecution became more severe. And the result was that they had lost courage, lost their Christian patience, were in danger of falling away.

And so it is today. Oh, in our time the world does not manifest itself in open persecution. But the principle of the world is still the same. We may depend upon it, faithful confession, a faithful Christian life, dominated by the vision of the eternal goal, a life for nothing else than the kingdom everywhere, will also today incur the wrath of that world, will also today, therefore, demand self-denial, will also today require the power of faith as an evidence of things unseen.

And therefore, for us as well as for the Hebrew Christians the exhortation is perfectly proper: run the race with patience! That does not mean that we must have considerable patience with a view to the goal, for this is entirely out of harmony with the meaning of our text. A good many Christians are far too patient with respect to the goal that must be reached. They do not seem to be in a special hurry whatever to reach that goal of perfection. They feel rather at home in this world and hate to leave it. Their desire for Christ and for perfection seems to be very weak. And the result of this sort of patience is exactly that there is little or no struggle for the goal, little or no running of the race.

No, but patience with a view to the sufferings and deprivations for Christ's sake is the meaning of the author. And again, not so that we must consider the suffering of this present time with stoical indifference, not so that we must bear it with sheepish passivity, but so that we keenly feel our suffering and deeply regret our being derided, but nevertheless also joyfully and persistently, without drawing back, bear all these things for the sake of Christ and his kingdom. For that kingdom dominates our life. The love of Christ spurs us on to reach out for the goal of perfection. And as we then meet with persecution and opposition, with the necessity of self-denial and sacrifice, we gladly and with patience of faith sacrifice all for the goal that is set before us. Not now and not here, but in the eternal future and in the new heavens and the new earth we shall be fully compensated for all that we have sacrificed in our running of the race, even as the runners in the Grecian races were doubly rewarded for all their trouble by the crown awarded to the victor.

In this running of the race, the author says further, we must "lay aside every weight" (Heb. 12:1). We realize that this language is still derived from the figure of the games and the races in the country of Greece. The runners in the Grecian races would carry nothing along with them that was not absolutely necessary as they strove for the goal. Long before the festivities they would try to reduce their weight to a proper minimum; and as they ran, they just wore so many clothes as were absolutely indispensable. To win the race they laid aside every weight.

This was not true at the time of the Hebrews to whom the author wrote this epistle. They had not entirely weaned away from the Old Testament ceremonies and the temple service of the old dispensation. They tried to cling to them partly. And in their Christian race they made an attempt to drag along with them all this burden of the law and of the shadows that had nothing to do whatsoever, was absolutely not essential to their reaching of the goal. And all the worse they became since they noticed that the truth of Christianity did not become very popular among their own people, that their people as such, as a nation, were not likely to be won for the cause of the Christian faith in this world. The more they tried to carry along of this burden of the Old Testament ordinances, the more they actually weaned away from the Christian faith and the more they slackened in the running of the Christian race, till it seemed as if they would fall back into Jewry altogether.

But so it is also with us, that is, with the believers, with the Christians, of today. Also we often try to carry a good many things along in our running of the race that are absolutely nonessential to the attaining of the goal and that simply hinder us from reaching the purpose that is set before us. There are some who make a desperate attempt to carry the entire material world along with them and who so cling to the gold of this world that it hinders them in the running of the race and in the making of sacrifices for the kingdom of Christ. There are others who run the race encumbered with all the pleasures of the world. They run the race, but every once in a while you see them depart from the track and swing out into the world to reach out for some of the pleasures of the world. And the pleasures of the world and of sin hinder them in the running of the race. Still others are running the race burdened under a load of worldly honor. The world honors them, and they are making a name. And the result is that the more the world bestows its honor upon them, the more they are bound to cater to its glory, and the more they slacken their pace and fall back in the running of the race.

And so we will find, one and all, that we carry a good many burdens as we run the race, a good many weights that are superfluous, of which we shall one time be sorry that we tried to drag them along with us. And so the author comes to us with the admonition: drop them as quickly as possible, drop them at once, for they have nothing to do with the all-dominating purpose that is set before you and can be of no help to you, but only hinder you in the running of the race.

As a special species of these burdens the author mentions the sin that does so easily beset us. Also that we must lay aside. Of course, we may safely take this as referring to sin in the most general sense of the word, first, to sin as it still has its place in our minds and in our wills, and which so easily offers a connecting link to the pleasures of the world. The running of the race is the struggle for perfection, and it is but natural, we would say, that in this running we lay aside sin. It is the fight against sin. But if we understand nothing more by reading those words, we would fail to catch the specific meaning of the author. For he speaks of "the sin which doth so easily beset us," of the sin that does so easily surround us and entrap us and lead us away from the right track. And now it is true that this is the case of all sin. As long as sin still rules in our sinful nature, it will also remain true that sin in its most general sense will be a power against which we will have to guard. For it surely has a hold upon us, and a mistake we would make if we should imagine that we are liable to one sin and not to others.

But although this is true, it is not true of all sin in the same measure. What I mean is this. First, there is a difference between various sins as to their attraction for different individuals. The one is greedy; the other is pleasure loving; a third is proud and thirsting for honor and glory; a fourth is weak in some other respect. We are all liable to sin. Sin besets us all easily. And therefore, as we said, we must guard to lay aside all sin and to fight against it. But it is also true that we all have our peculiar weak spot and that one sin besets us more easily than others. And it is especially against this personal sin that besets us, that so besets us that it is our personal sin more than other sins—against this we must guard especially. For if we succeed in laying aside this personal sin, we will surely more easily succeed in regard to sin in general.

Second, we may also in this aspect mention the sin of the age. There is what is called a spirit of the age. In one age there is one sin; in another age there is a different sin that seems to be prevailing and that for that reason is easily besetting us, a sin that, as it were, we are breathing in with the atmosphere. So also in our time, as its special sin we might perhaps point to its materialism and love of money and love of pleasure, which, with a view to the church, is called world-ly-mindedness. That is undoubtedly the sin of our own time, the sin that easily attracts us, against which we have to guard in order to lay it aside. Thus laying aside every weight, and the sin that does so easily beset us, let us run the race with patience, denying self, sacrificing all if need be for the kingdom and for our King. Striving for the goal, and dominated by this singleness of purpose, let us run the race.

Of course, you understand that all this can be done only in the power of faith and by the grace of our God in Jesus Christ our Lord. Nothing less will do. Not the example of others can spur us on. Not the picture of the crown in itself will do any good. Not even the example of Christ is here sufficient. Only in the power of faith and by the grace of God can this run be made. It is for that reason that the author has called the attention of the Hebrew Christians to the fact that the righteous shall live by faith only. It is for that reason that he has mentioned all those examples of faith that occur in chapter 11, to show that they all lived by the power of faith.

For this running of the race is not so easy. The road is beset with many difficulties. The fight is hard. And besides, we must give up the visible for the invisible. Many a time we must deny ourselves the treasures and pleasures and the glory and honor of this world as we strive for the goal. And what is this goal? Has this glory ever been seen? Why no, it is absolutely invisible. God and Christ, heaven and perfection, the kingdom of glory that is to be established in the end, the crown after which we are striving, they are all invisible. They all belong to the world of unseen things. Self we deny for Christ, this world for the world to come, the seen for the unseen. So is the race. So we must run.

But this is possible only by faith. For faith is the evidence of things unseen. By faith we know that this world of unseen things, though it may not be perceptible by our natural eye, nevertheless is not a product of the imagination but is actually existing, is very real indeed, and that as we strive for it we do not pursue a phantom but tangible reality, tangible, however, only by faith. And therefore, faith is indispensable. For by faith we keep our eye fixed on the goal set before us. And inspired by the beauty and the glory of the crown, we gladly deny ourselves and sacrifice the world of visible things if necessary for the attainment of the crown.

But although this is true, this faith, where once it exists, may be braced up. The knees of faith sometimes may grow feeble; the eye of faith may sometimes grow dim; the courage of faith, in fact, often grows weak in our running of the race. And then it is an inspiration to see that others have run the same race before us, and that they were not disappointed but actually were victorious by faith. And it is for that reason that the author has referred to all the heroes mentioned in the preceding chapter and that he now mentions their presence as an inspiration to all the runners in the race, when he says: "Seeing we also are compassed about with so great a cloud of witnesses" (Heb. 12:1).

Some have thought that this cloud of witnesses refers to the onlookers in the race. The crowd at the Grecian games would naturally be witness of the running and by their cheers would encourage those running in the race. So also the cloud of witnesses are supposed to look down upon us as we run the race. But this is not the meaning of the text. It rather means that we have the testimony of all the heroes of faith mentioned in chapter 11, the testimony that they fought the battle and ran the race by faith and had the victory. This testimony may encourage us. Looking at their testimony, we may know that there is no reason to be discouraged but that we, too, may run with patience the race that is set before us.

This, then, is our message for you. Run the race with patience, deny yourselves, knowing that in the day of our Lord Jesus Christ we shall surely have the victory in eternal glory.

# Chapter 37

# GOING FORTH TO CHRIST WITHOUT THE CAMP

Let us go forth therefore unto him without the camp, bearing his reproach.

*—Hebrews 13:13*

The context that determines the special significance of this word of our text of the sacred writer is found practically in the entire epistle. The writer is addressing the Hebrew Christians. These Christians were in grave and imminent danger of abandoning the true faith in Christ, in order to cling tenaciously to the shadows and Levitical rites of the old dispensation. On the one hand, they were still under the influence of their former education and life; and that former conception was still strongly impressed upon them by their entire surroundings. They lived in the land of Canaan, and most of them probably in Jerusalem, the holy city, and therefore in the immediate vicinity of the temple. In that temple the Old Testament rites and sacrifices and ceremonies were still daily observed in all their outward beauty and significance.

The Christians from the Hebrews used to take part in them. They used to find their salvation so closely connected with these rites and ceremonies. And we can easily imagine that it was extremely difficult for them to bid farewell to the old-time religion. It was hard for them to understand that by bidding farewell to the shadows they simply received reality in their place. It was difficult for them to believe that there was nothing more contained in that beautiful temple worship than the shadow and type of reality. And therefore, it was extremely difficult for them to wean away entirely from those ceremonies in the temple that were so beloved to them as they were daily performed before their eyes. And therefore, they already were lapsing back into Judaism and abandoning the true faith.

But there was still another factor that entered in to explain their falling away from the faith. If they only had been wholeheartedly in the faith and with all their might had clung to the faith that is in Christ Jesus, there would not have been a weighty factor in this other matter. But now they were already in doubt as to the legitimacy of abandoning entirely the worship of the temple and of the law, the service of the tabernacle. Now the fact of persecution and reproach became indeed a very weighty additional cause for their drawing back into the circle of their one-time brethren. The Christians in Jerusalem were the objects of much reproach and of bitter hatred. They were despised by the powerful Jews and made the object of their contempt. They were persecuted and caused to suffer. And since the Hebrews already were in doubt regarding their own stand, they were too weak to resist the persecution that threatened. And therefore, they were in grave danger indeed.

And the author, realizing this danger, writes this epistle to them in order to explain to them the relation between the Old and the New Testament and lead them in the way of the true faith. Thus he warns them in the entire epistle. They who serve the tabernacle, so he writes, have no right to eat of the altar of Christ (Heb. 13:10). And therefore, a choice must be made between Christ and the Old Testament ceremonial law. The sin offering of the old dispensation had only typical significance, and the real sin offering was brought when Christ "suffered without the gate" and entered into the sanctuary with his own blood (v. 12). Now then, he comes to them in the words of our text that we wish to discuss today with the admonition to go forth unto him outside of the gate, or outside of the camp. And if that manifestation of solidarity with Christ causes suffering and reproach, they must patiently bear also this.

In order to understand the words of our text, we must look upon Christ particularly from the viewpoint of his being the sin offering. In our text the Lord is presented under the symbol of the sin offering, as is plain from the expression that we shall go forth to him outside of the gate. And therefore, we must have this sin offering before our mind in order to understand the text. In the preceding verses the author called the attention of his readers and of the church to a very special sort of sin offering that was brought in the temple of the old dispensation among Israel, the sin offering, namely, that was characterized by its blood being brought into the sanctuary and its flesh being burned outside of the gate (v. 11).

We may notice that there were mainly two kinds of these sin offerings among Israel. First, there were those that made atonement for all, the priests themselves included, or for the priests only. And second, there were those that were made for the people, exclusive of the priests. In the latter case the flesh of the sin offering was eaten by the priests; in the former it was burned outside of the camp. In the one case the blood was sprinkled in the holy place before the face of God; in the other case the blood was merely poured out at the altar of burnt offering that stood in the court. And now it is plain from the text that the writer refers to those sin offerings whose blood was carried within the holy place by the high priest on the great day of atonement and whose flesh was burned without the camp.

Jesus, so he says, is the great sin offering, of which all the sin offerings of the Old Testament were but types and shadows. He has offered himself. He has shed his own lifeblood, and with this blood he has entered into the holy place above, there to appear as our great Mediator and head before the countenance of the Father. And therefore, in his blood there is reconciliation, and we must partake of him. We must no more serve in the tabernacle: for all that service simply pointed to him. But leaving the service of the tabernacle, we must eat of the real and only altar, Jesus Christ, in order that we may be perfectly and forevermore satisfied with the blessings of our salvation. In this light the purpose of our text becomes plain. Therefore, then, says the writer, for the reason that the service of the tabernacle has had an end, for the reason that in Christ we have the reality of which the shadows were found in the tabernacle and temple, let us go forth, let us go away from the service of the law and of the shadows, and let us cling to the reality there is in Christ Jesus our Redeemer.

Special emphasis, no doubt, must be placed on the fact that Jesus suffered without the gate. For the writer finds great significance in this. Jesus actually did suffer just a little way outside of the holy city. According to the best identification of the place, Golgotha must be found just a little way outside of the second wall that was around the city at the time of the Lord's crucifixion. There, two or three minutes' walk aside from the main road that leads to the north, is a small elevation presenting the shape of a human skull, whence perhaps the name "place of a skull" (Matt. 27:33). Near this place are the garden tombs, in one of which Jesus was buried. And therefore, there is much in favor of the assumption that this is actually the place where the bloody tree was erected on which the Lord shed his lifeblood for the sins of his people. Besides, this place is outside of the gate, in accord with the words of our text. And this place, again, is near the city, in harmony with John's indication of the place (John 19:20).

Here, then, we may assume, Jesus was crucified. Here he suffered as no human being ever did suffer nor will suffer even in hell. For what the condemned in hell suffer eternally, without ever being through with the bearing of the wrath of God, Christ suffered at once, in the space of a few hours. The infinity of the wrath of God was poured out over him. Physically he was broken and crushed. After having been exhausted by all the suffering that had already been inflicted on him in the palace of the high priest, by the scourging of the governor, and the thorny crown that was pressed on his brow by the soldiers, he was finally led outside of the gate, stretched and nailed upon the bloody tree, in order there slowly to shed his lifeblood in the most unbearable agony.

Spiritually he had suffered the maltreatment of his people, his own people: their mockery and reproach, their contempt and bitter hatred. He had experienced that his disciples left him in the hour of darkness and that one of them had denied him. And now he hangs there, the object of revilement and reproach by all who are witness, except a few silent disciples who stand afar off. But above all, spiritually he there suffered outside of the gate the terrible reality that even his God had forsaken him, had actually loaded all the sin of his people upon him, in order that then he be forsaken utterly as the object of his wrath, so that it was pressed from his anxious soul: "My God, my God, why hast thou forsaken me?" (Matt. 27:46). Surely, there, outside of the gate, Jesus suffered, and the angry billows of God's wrath roared over his head.

In this suffering, however, outside of the gate the inspired author finds special significance and one more point of resemblance between Jesus and the sin offering that was brought in the days of the old dispensation. The flesh of the sin offering to which he has referred in the preceding verse was "burned without the camp" (Heb. 13:11). So Jesus suffered without the gate.

In order to understand this significance, we must recall the ritual that was connected with the sin offering under Israel. You remember that when the sacrificial animal was brought before the door of the tent of meeting, the elders of the people would lay their hands on the head of the victim, thus symbolizing that they laid all the sin and impurity of the people upon the animal that was to be killed (Lev. 4:15–16). By this act the body of the animal was symbolically sin-laden. Its flesh became the flesh of sin. It was, as it were, saturated with the sin of the people that was an abomination in the sight of God. And therefore, after the animal had been killed, and after the blood of the offering had been carried into the holy place, that sin-laden flesh was carried without the camp; and there it was burned (vv. 16–21). This burning of the sacrificial animal outside of the gate pictured to Israel that their sin, which was symbolically contracted in the body of the beast, was entirely destroyed.

But what we must learn now is the significance of the fact that it was carried outside of the camp and there burned. And then we may first of all express the general idea that this carrying outside of the camp represented the thought that the victim, sin-laden with the transgression of Israel, was conceived a horrible abomination, not fit to remain within the boundaries of the camp. That camp as it was established in the desert whenever the people rested in the wilderness was at the same time the boundary of the kingdom of God. In that camp the people of God dwelt. There was the kingdom. And in that typical kingdom, over which God ruled as the great and only Sovereign, yea, in the midst of which God dwelled, sin was an abomination, a horrible reproach, that could not be tolerated. And when that sin of the people, that could not be tolerated in the camp of Israel, was, as it were, contracted in the flesh of the sin offering, that body was to be carried outside of the gate. And therefore, in this carrying of the victim's body outside of the camp the people expressed their horrible contempt for all that abominable thing in which their sin was gathered. It is this idea of abomination that prevailed in this act and that is evidently brought to the forefront by the writer of this epistle.

Now I wish to emphasize that Jesus is our sin offering, that he bore all our sins and all our iniquities on his mighty shoulders, and that therefore they are all removed forever. He, the Son of God in the flesh, suffered outside of the gate as the sin offering for his own people. And therefore, we may believe, in spite of all our sins and all our transgressions that we still experience, that Jesus has atoned and satisfied forever, and that our sins are no more. And believing, let us go forth to him, outside of the gate, and let us bear his reproach, the reproach that the world heaped upon him when they led him outside of the gate, and that the world still heaps upon him when they reproach him, but now in his people. He is glorified, but his people are still in the world. And we, as his people, must bear his reproach and suffer with him, that we may be also glorified together.

For we must remember that these two, namely, that Jesus suffered as a sacrifice for our sins and that he suffered outside of the gate, can never be separated. They belong together. Hence, another Jesus than the one who suffered outside of the gate and there brought his atoning sacrifice, there is none. And that Jesus is always an abomination to the natural man and must always suffer the reproach of the world.

Oh, the world may and does change the picture of the real Jesus into an imaginary one, that of a good man and a worthy example for us to follow. In that case he is no abomination, for then it is denied that he suffered outside of the gate as a sin offering. Then we do not have to bear his reproach, but then, at the same time, we lose him who saves us from our sins. And therefore, there are only two alternatives: either you believe in a Jesus who is not an abomination and a reproach to the world and who did not die for your sins; or you embrace him as your redeemer from sin and death and as the one who is always a reproach to the world. Let us, therefore, go to him outside of the gate, bearing his reproach.

# Chapter 38

# BEARING
# HIS REPROACH

Let us go forth therefore unto him without the camp, bearing his reproach.

*—Hebrews 13:13*

I especially discussed the sin offering that was sacrificed by the priest, and the bodies of which were burned outside of the camp, or outside of the gate. Now the writer means to say that Jesus also suffered outside of the gate. First, he finds, no doubt, in this fact an additional proof that with the suffering of Jesus all our sins were absolutely removed. Our sins and our transgressions were, as it were, contracted in him. God had made him sin. And when he had made him sin, he crushed him and killed him and broke his flesh. That flesh of sin, therefore, was forevermore destroyed on Golgotha. As such he is our great sin offering. As such he is our altar. And approaching him by faith, we partake of all the blessings of salvation that are found on this altar.

But in our text the author finds still another idea, namely, in this fact, that Jesus suffered and still is an abomination to the world. He suffered outside of the gate. And that gate was the gate of the holy city. And that holy city was symbolic, centrally, of the kingdom of God. And in that leading of Jesus outside of the gate and there crushing him, the Jews expressed their contempt of him, expressed their conviction that he was not worthy of even being killed within the holy city. They hated him. He claimed to be the Messiah, but how different a Messiah he was than they expected. They did not believe that Jesus is the Christ. They wanted a national glory. They wanted reestablishment of the throne of David through the power of this national Messiah whom they expected. But this Messiah had stubbornly refused to cater to their purely national pride, had consistently refused to receive an earthly crown, and had spoken of an entirely different kingdom than they had fancied.

Hence, they had gradually come to hate him with all the bitterness of their Jewish heart. To them he was an impostor, a deceiver, an abomination in the midst of Israel. He was a liar, a false prophet. A horrible thing, indeed, it was. And they had given vent to their feelings. They had clearly expressed their abomination of him in their attitude over against him. They had reviled him. They had buffeted him. They had spit upon him. They had demanded, finally, that he should be led outside of the gate to be crucified. In a word, even as the animal that contracted typically the sin of the people in the old dispensation was an abomination to the people, and therefore led outside of the gate, so Jesus was also an abomination to his people, in the midst of whom he dwelt. And he was cast out. He was a castaway. As a horrible thing and as an abomination, despised by all, he suffered outside of the gate of the holy city.

Now, then, the writer in the words of our text comes with the admonition that we also must go forth to him outside of the gate. No doubt this applies, first, to the Hebrew Christians to whom the author is writing. As we have already remarked, they had not entirely separated from their former connection, from the service of the temple, from the Old Testament rites and ceremonies. On the contrary, the persuasion that these rites and ceremonies were absolutely necessary for their salvation gradually gained hold upon them, so that they already had left off frequenting the assembly of the brethren.

To this was added, as we have remarked in our introduction, the danger of persecution. Jesus had not only been a reproach and an abomination to the Jews as long as he suffered outside of the gate; but he still was such an abomination to them. His very name was disgusting to them. They could not bear the memory of his name. And therefore, they persecuted those who mentioned and confessed the name of Jesus. Hence, the Hebrew Christians, half-hearted as they were in their faith, were in danger of entirely relapsing into the service of the tabernacle.

That is why the author in this passage draws the contrast so sharply. He tells them that if they serve the tabernacle, they have not the right to eat of the altar Jesus Christ (Heb. 13:10). Naturally not! To those who served the tabernacle, to those who still clung to the shadows, Jesus was not the reality of all these things. But he was an impostor, and therefore an abomination. If therefore they took their company among those who served the tabernacle, they preferred the company of those among whom Jesus was regarded as an abomination and an impostor. It was exactly because the Jews did not recognize that Jesus was the fulfillment of their typical temple service that he was a reproach and abomination to them and that they hated him so bitterly.

And therefore, the contrast is plain. Either they must choose the service of the tabernacle, or they must choose the Christ. There was no compromise possible. The one excluded the other. If they chose the service of the shadows, he who claimed to be their complete fulfillment was surely an abomination to them. If, however, they recognized Jesus, they must admit that the service of the tabernacle and of the law has an end.

And so he comes with the admonition to them, first of all: "Go forth, outside of the gate. There is Jesus. Leave the service of the tabernacle. Leave the company of your former surroundings. Leave the company of those who consider Jesus an abomination and who do not believe in him. And go to Jesus, the Savior of your soul." Separation of the old ties and assumption of the new relation is what the writer here holds before them, and that not only privately, but publicly. If it were possible, of course, that with their hearts they believed in Jesus and well understood that the service of the tabernacle had been fulfilled in him, while for fear of the Jews and for fear of persecution and reproach they nevertheless took part in the service of the tabernacle, they might do so. But this may not be: they must go forth outside of the gate.

The picture that the writer really draws before their mind is that of Jesus still suffering on the hill of Golgotha. There he is surrounded by the enemies. These enemies cling to the tabernacle and temple and find in Jesus nothing but an abomination. They wag their heads. They mock at him. They find pleasure in his suffering. And now the writer means to say: "Go forth, outside of the gate, in the midst of those enemies, and claim Jesus publicly. Tell these enemies that this Jesus, whom you crucify, is your Savior and Redeemer and King. Tell them that you are through with the service of the temple and that he is the fulfillment of it all. Tell them, in a word, that you believe that you belong to him whom they cause to suffer." Outside of the gate is the abomination of the hostile Jews. Thither they must go to embrace Jesus.

But this is not all. Also for us this word holds good today. We must surely go forth to Jesus on Mount Golgotha. First, no doubt, we must do so in the privacy of our personal faith. Jesus is the sin offering for our transgressions. God caused all the sins of his people to come together upon him and then punished him for our transgressions. And therefore, if we are to have reconciliation and redemption in the full sense of the word, we must eat of that altar, and of that altar only. There is no salvation outside of the cross of Golgotha. There is no God who is our Father in heaven, there is no kingdom in which we shall be saved, except through the blood of the Redeemer. Not in Bethlehem alone, not in a man of Galilee, but in the sufferer on the accursed tree we find our all for the privacy of our personal faith. And whatever men may chatter today about the beautiful picture of Bethlehem and the noble teacher of Galilee is nonsense, and worse than idle talk, as long as it is not rooted in this procedure of the private faith to the place of skulls, outside of the gate, to embrace the blood-dripping tree of crucifixion.

But this is not all. And this surely is not the main idea of the text. The idea of the text is that we must publicly own, that we must openly appropriate, Jesus, and that, too, as the sufferer on Golgotha, or if you please, as the abomination in the sight of the world. The contrast is indeed a little different in form today than it was among the Christians from the Hebrews to whom the writer addresses this epistle. But essentially it is still the same. The Jews of that day believed in the service of the tabernacle and temple, in the observances of the law and of their own ceremonies. And they imagined that these were of value in themselves. Not the bloody tree, but their own observance of the law and rites would be pleasing to God.

The same is true of the world today. It is frightfully alarming how Christianity—let me say, how the world—develops in this very direction. There is a good deal of talk about the lovely Jesus, about the man of Galilee who preached the gospel of the kingdom and taught us to love. There is a good deal of talk about the establishment of the kingdom for man and by man, a kingdom in which peace and righteousness shall dwell. But there is no talk about the bloody tree and the blood of atonement and vicarious suffering of Jesus who is the Christ. It is a service of the tabernacle of self-righteousness and of the exaltation of man. To the Jews of that day Jesus was for that very reason an abomination. And they led him outside of the gate to express their horror for that Jesus, the impostor.

But the world of today does the same thing. If Jesus would be on earth today, and if he would again preach that same truth and again agitate against the self-righteousness of the hypocritical Pharisees and chief priests and claim that we must eat his flesh and drink his blood, the world would literally lead him outside of the gate and crucify him again. In other words, if Jesus would again emphasize the fact of the wickedness and sinfulness of the world, and of its absolute helplessness, and of the only possible cure in the vicarious blood he shed on the accursed tree, the world would call him an abomination as well as in the days of the Jews. Now the admonition comes to us as well as to the Christians of that day: "Go forth openly, publicly, from the tabernacle of the world that calls Jesus an abomination. Go forth outside of the gate, that is, to the place that is characteristic of Jesus' reproach, and claim him, confess him, acknowledge him as your Redeemer and as your King."

Go forth unto him, the abomination of the world. That means surely to confess him in the midst of God's people, cast in your lot with them, choose the company of the people of Christ and in their midst confess his name, confess him before the church. It is an admonition, surely, to all of us that we go forth to him outside of the gate and confess him in the midst of the people of God. It surely implies that we shall reveal our solidarity with Christ at all times. We cannot serve the tabernacle that calls Jesus a reproach and eat of the altar Christ.

And it is well that we emphasize this fact. There is a growing and deepening spirit of worldly-mindedness revealing itself and accompanied by a manifestation of a lack of spiritual life that is truly alarming in our day. Anything and everything the Christian in our day can do, except confess his Lord and live to the honor of his name in the midst of the world. He can take in all the pleasures of the world, laugh and joke with the world; but as soon as it comes to the test of the confession of Jesus, a truly alarming silence is often the only phenomenon. It is well once again to ring the message that otherwise would seem so simple and clear: you cannot serve the tabernacle and eat of our altar; you cannot serve God and mammon; you cannot be in favor of Christ and of the devil; you cannot go to heaven and after all hanker after hell. That is truly impossible.

Go forth, therefore, outside of the gate to him who is called an abomination! It means that this accursed one, this offering for our sin, shall have the central place in our entire life, in our thinking and our willing, in our word and in our walk. In every sphere of life, always and everywhere, shall we confess him. Always and everywhere shall we be a separate people in exactly this respect. We shall acknowledge him as our King in society and in the state. We shall acknowledge him as our King in home and school, as well as in the church. Always and everywhere we shall first go outside of the gate, that we may walk about in garments dipped in and sprinkled with the blood of the accursed. Go out, therefore, unto him outside of the gate.

The result is plain. First, there is the positive result that we have already mentioned, namely, that we have a right to eat of the only altar, Jesus Christ, the result that we have the forgiveness of sin, that we have redemption and sanctification, that we are children of God and have eternal life. For all these blessings are in Jesus Christ our Savior. We shall appropriate Christ more and more. And surely, these are blessings that cannot be had anywhere else and that cannot be compared with anything else. The knowledge that we are reconciled to God and that we have peace with him in the blood of Jesus is a knowledge that passes all understanding, that is more precious than life itself.

Nevertheless, there is also a negative result. And that negative result consists in this, that we, as the writer expresses it, bear his reproach

(Heb. 13:13). That is, we share his name and also his shame. The same opinion the world expresses of Jesus it will express of those who are one with him. Naturally, it cannot be any different. The servant is not greater than his master. If you are found in continual company with thieves and robbers, you will be judged with them. If you are found in comradeship with the world in practically every sphere of life, the world will own you as its own. If you are always manifesting the stamp of the devil's property, the devil will think you belong to him. And thus it is with our relation to Christ. Go outside of the gate, where the enemies are, and claim Christ Jesus, and you will receive the same reputation Christ had in their estimation.

That this reproach was and still is present is very evident. He is an outcast, an abomination, a horror, a contempt. That same reputation will naturally descend from the cross outside of the gate upon you. You stand in the shade of the accursed tree and confess that suffering Lord. Thus the Christians among the Hebrews experienced it. If they went forth outside of the gate, renouncing the old law and rites and taking their company among the saints of Christ Jesus, they would have to endure the reproach of Christ and be persecuted. But no less is this true today. That the world is so tolerant and that the Christian moves so easily in the midst of the world is not because the world has changed, but because the Christian is so miserably lax and lukewarm.

And therefore, let us bear this in mind. There are but two alternatives. We must remain in the tabernacle of the world and escape the reproach of Jesus, or we must go forth unto him outside of the gate and bear his reproach. But nay, there is no choice. The Christian who through the omnipotent and irresistible power of the grace of his God has learned to go out to Jesus and claim him as his Lord and Master must confess him. He may sometimes be unfaithful and weak, small in faith. The principle of his life nevertheless remains. And therefore, he must claim him, and that always. And it is also inevitable that the world will hate that Christian as it hated the Christ, and that he shall be called upon to bear his reproach, the reproach of his Lord, even as his Lord bore the reproach of the cross personally.

We are one plant with him in very fact. We are one with him in faith and hope and love. We are one through our spiritual implanting into him. We are one with him in the manifestation of himself in the midst of the world. We are identical with him also in his reproach. And therefore, because our faith is often weak and wavering, let us hear the words of our text:

*Let us go forth therefore unto him without the camp,*
*bearing his reproach.*

# SCRIPTURE INDEX

# SCRIPTURE INDEX

# SCRIPTURE INDEX

# FROM THE SAME AUTHOR

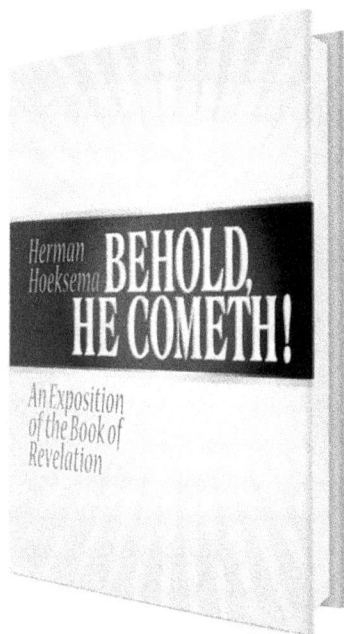

"The treatment of the text is definitely Reformed in character in that it always ascribes all the glory to God and traces his way in history...I warmly recommend the book." —William Hendriksen, in *The Banner*, September 5, 1969, 24

"Rev. Hoeksema preached through the book of Revelation twice in his ministry, once soon after World War I and the second time during World War II, the latter time to very large crowds of hearers. The series of messages in this volume—fifty-three in number—thoroughly expounds the comforting truth in this last book of the Bible...A student of the Book of Revelation can hardly do better than this!...By all means get a copy of it." —*The Outlook*, Volume 52, No. 6 (June 2002)

"May this superb work goad us to long, pray and work for the second coming of our Saviour, when the cosmic conflict shall end, when Christ shall yield up the kingdom to his Father, and God shall be all and in all" —*Peace and Truth*, 2001:4

# Righteous by Faith Alone

A Devotional Commentary on Romans

## Herman Hoeksema

Edited by David J. Engelsma

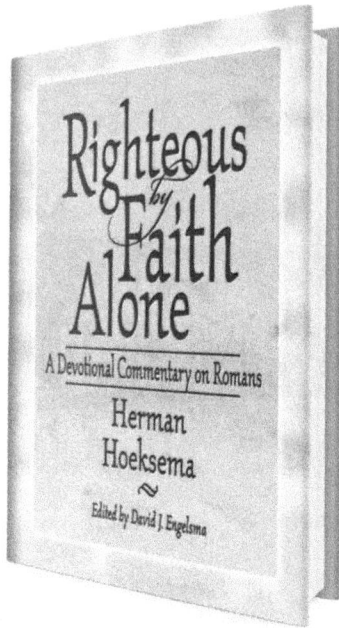

"If you want to know why the likes of Prof. Cornelius Van Til would make his way to hear Hoeksema preach, then you should get this book...I cannot recommend it highly enough." —*English Churchman*

"Handling the deepest doctrines with a sure and sanctified hand, afraid of no difficulties, Hoeksema had also the common touch in making his exposition easy, lucid, and very readable indeed...Those who invest in a copy will, I believe, come to treasure it as a choice blessing from the Lord." —*British Church Newspaper*

"There is nothing dryly theological in this exposition. The messages are from a heart to hearts. It is stirring reading because it follows the author closely—alive with Scriptural application...The personal benefits from this exposition are a fine gold. Procure it!" —*New Focus*

"This book is thoroughly recommended. I have read it every day at the close of my own devotions for the past eight months, with great benefit and thankfulness to God." —*Evangelical Times*

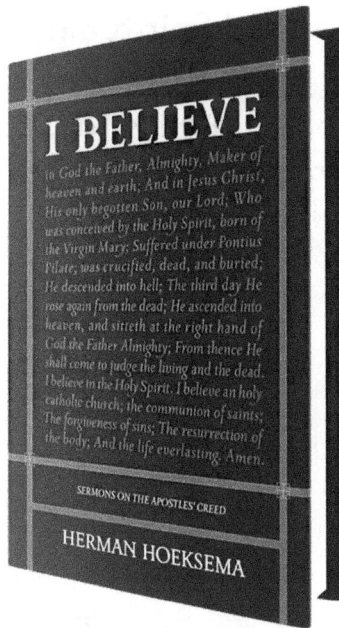

I BELIEVE

in God the Father, Almighty, Maker of heaven and earth; And in Jesus Christ, His only begotten Son, our Lord; Who was conceived by the Holy Spirit, born of the Virgin Mary; Suffered under Pontius Pilate, was crucified, dead, and buried; He descended into hell; The third day He rose again from the dead; He ascended into heaven, and sitteth at the right hand of God the Father Almighty; From thence He shall come to judge the living and the dead. I believe in the Holy Spirit. I believe an holy catholic church; the communion of saints; The forgiveness of sins; The resurrection of the body; And the life everlasting. Amen.

SERMONS ON THE APOSTLES' CREED

HERMAN HOEKSEMA

"Believers can easily fall into the practice of treating the Creed as only a simple statement, a statement which we do not think about too deeply...This fine volume on the Apostles' Creed, replete with many Scripture references, will cause our faith and understanding of biblical truth to grow." —Rev. Jerome Julien, emeritus minister in the United Reformed Churches in North America

"As elsewhere in Hoeksema's writings and sermons, here is exegetical-doctrine preaching and teaching at its best for godliness and Christ-centered living for all believers and battlers for the crown rights of Jesus and the glory of God." —Rev. Mitchell Dick, pastor of Sovereign Grace URC (Comstock Park, MI)

# Reformed Spirituality set:
## *Peace for the Troubled Heart,*
## *Communion with God,*
## *All Glory to the Only Good God*

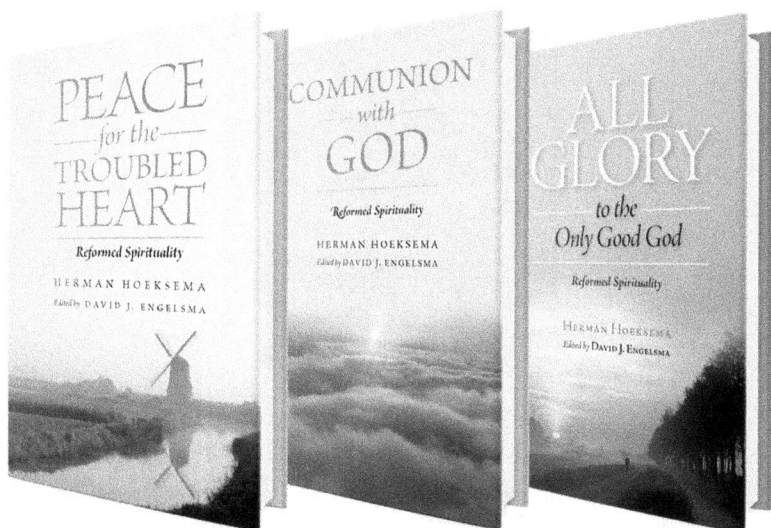

These poetic, experiential, and sound meditations are for every believer who desires to be edified and encouraged along the Christian pilgrimage with all its trials and triumphs. Though deep, Hoeksema's writing is clear and the chapters are short, which makes these books ideal devotional material.

# REFORMED
## FREE PUBLISHING
### ASSOCIATION

## Our Mission

To glorify God by making accessible to the broadest possible audience material that testifies to the truth of Scripture as understood and developed in the Reformed tradition.

Reformed Free Publishing Association
1894 Georgetown Center Drive, Jenison, MI 49428-7137
Website: rfpa.org

www.ingramcontent.com/pod-product-compliance
Lightning Source LLC
Chambersburg PA
CBHW060315100426

42812CB00003B/784